Reading in the Middle School

SECOND EDITION

Gerald G. Duffy
Michigan State University
Editor

ɪɹa
International Reading Association
Newark, Delaware 19714

The International Reading Association attempts, through its publications, to provide a forum for a wide spectrum of opinions on reading. This policy permits divergent viewpoints without assuming the endorsement of the Association.

Copyright 1990 by the
International Reading Association, Inc.

Library of Congress Cataloging in Publication Data

Reading in the middle school / Gerald G. Duffy, editor. – 2nd ed.

    p.   cm.
Includes bibliographical references.
  1. Reading (Secondary) 2. Middle schools – United States.
I. Duffy, Gerald G. II. International Reading Association.
LB1632.R37 1990 90-34028
428.4'071' 2–dc20 CIP
ISBN 0-87207-121-9

Second Printing, May 1991

Graphic design: Boni Nash
Typesetting: Wendy Mazur
Staff Editors: Karen Goldsmith, Romayne McElhaney, John Micklos

Photo Credits:
Mary Loewenstein-Anderson, pg. 230; Robert Bennett, pgs. 216, 227;
Laima Druskis, pgs. 7, 19, 45, 52, 102, 121, 160; Robert Finken, pgs. 13, 83, 91.

CONTENTS

PART TWO

Curriculum and Instruction in Reading

❧ **5** ❧

Content Knowledge in Reading: Creating a New Framework

Charles W. Peters

❧ **6** ❧

Cognitive and Metacognitive Goals in Reading and Writing

Beth Ann Herrmann

❧ **7** ❧

Affective Goals in Reading and Writing

Donna E. Alvermann, K. Denise Muth

❧ **8** ❧

Instructional Planning and Teaching in Reading and Writing

Mark W. Conley

❧ **9** ❧

Assessing Reading and Writing

Sheila W. Valencia, William McGinley, P. David Pearson

PART THREE

Implementing Reading Programs

PART FOUR

Reading in the New Decade

❧ 15 ❧

Where to from Here?

Patricia L. Anders, Gerald G. Duffy

—————— 225 ——————

FOREWORD

Our typical educational pursuit is characterized by a search for the answer, the solution, the perfect program. And, characteristically, our best efforts are followed by dissatisfaction: we can always do it better. We have learned that answers, solutions, the best we can do—these are no more than momentary perceptions. Tomorrow brings different answers, different solutions, better bests. What we envision today is unlikely to be what exists tomorrow. We imagine and strive, but who could have imagined our present family structures, the social issues affecting how and what we teach, and the needs and motivations of today's middle school students? Consequently, planning and innovation must occur without a preconceived picture of what will be when the new program is in place. And once the program is in place, a new picture emerges and, again, we are dissatisfied.

So what does all this have to do with the second edition of **Reading in the Middle School?** Hopefully, it puts it in a historical perspective. This book is neither a beginning nor a solution; it is a necessary stage somewhere in between. At this time, the hopes, biases, perceptions, and prescriptions expressed by the authors are the best they can be. But they will have to move over for others that will come along. For, like other educational enterprises, the middle school reading program must be a dynamic phenomenon.

While it is true that reading programs must change with changing societal and student needs, it is also true that nothing comes to pass without the passage of time. So program developers are caught between the need for change and the need for time to let change work, a discomfiting situation. Several chapter authors in this book express their disappointment with the gap between past recommendations for middle school reading and actual classroom practices. They are understandably disappointed in how slowly schools change. Piet Hein, a Danish poet and aphorist, expresses the factor of time cleverly:

T.T.T.

Put up in a place
Where it's easy to see
The cryptic admonishment
T.T.T.
When you feel
How depressingly slowly you climb
It's well to remember that
Things Take Time

The first reality for all who work to improve reading education for middle school students is that those who speak today are unlikely to have the last word. Who knows what's around the corner: a middle school with no structured classes, no tests, no report cards, no books (at least not as we know them now), no teachers? To what grand and currently unthinkable programs will middle schools evolve?

The second reality is that new programs can be planned faster than they can be implemented and tested. Things take time.

This book is an important contribution to the evolution of middle school reading programs. It will not be the last word, and it will take time to put it in place and test the recommendations of the authors who have looked at what was, what is, and what might be. They have turned some corners. What they have written for this book is thoughtful and timely. In a historical sense, they stand between the past and the future—a necessary position if the future is to be better than the past.

Richard J. Smith
University of Wisconsin–Madison

PREFACE

The middle school concept is simultaneously compelling in its rationale and frustrating in our failure to achieve its potential. What middle school reading instruction **should be** is one thing; all too often it is something less. This book helps teachers, reading consultants, and administrators bring instructional practice closer to the ideal.

The book's major purpose is to reaffirm the unique and integral roles reading and literacy play in middle school curriculum and instruction. Additionally, the book emphasizes (1) the research-based rationale for what we teach in reading and how we teach it; (2) an integration of reading with writing; (3) an acknowledgment that middle school reading instruction occurs within a context that imposes constraints which, in turn, shape the nature of middle school reading curriculum and instruction; (4) the importance of gradual, contextually bound change relative to the conditions imposed by both policy and environment; and (5) a strategy of creating effective instructional improvement through collaboration among practitioners, teacher educators, and theorists.

The book is divided into four parts. Part 1 includes four chapters that provide a frame of reference for middle school reading. The five chapters in Part 2 focus on middle school reading curriculum and instruction. Part 3 consists of five chapters in which reading educators and/or practitioners describe a particular perspective on how effective reading programs are implemented in specific school settings. Part 4 consists of a single chapter that foreshadows what to expect in middle school reading during the 1990s.

It is our hope that this book will be of practical assistance to practitioners seeking to achieve the potential of the middle school concept, particularly as it relates to literacy development.

GGD

ACKNOWLEDGMENTS

This book could not have been compiled without the assistance of many people.

First, the conceptual frame for the book results from the collaborative efforts of Patricia Anders, Donna Alvermann, Mark Conley, and Laura Roehler. Second, the individual authors provided substantive chapters in a timely fashion. Third, Christine Harvey provided extraordinary editorial assistance that was essential to the success of the book.

Additionally, the authors of Chapter 2 wish to acknowledge the contributions of E. Ellen Thornburg and to note that the chapter was based on work done by the late Hershel D. Thornburg. Richard Allington, author of Chapter 3, wishes to acknowledge the assistance of Nora Boxer, Anne McGill-Franzen, and Kathy Broikou.

GGD

CONTRIBUTORS

Richard L. Allington
State University of New York
Albany, New York

Donna E. Alvermann
University of Georgia
Athens, Georgia

Patricia L. Anders
University of Arizona
Tucson, Arizona

Mark W.F. Condon
University of Louisville
Louisville, Kentucky

Mark W. Conley
Michigan State University
East Lansing, Michigan

Gerald G. Duffy
Michigan State University
East Lansing, Michigan

Kathryn U. Foley
Lansing School District
Lansing, Michigan

Peggy Glider
University of Arizona
Tucson, Arizona

Beth Ann Herrmann
University of South Carolina
Columbia, South Carolina

James V. Hoffman
University of Texas
Austin, Texas

Ned S. Levine
Tucson Unified School District
Tucson, Arizona

Mara T. Lud
Lansing School District
Lansing, Michigan

William McGinley
University of Michigan
Ann Arbor, Michigan

Joy N. Monahan
Orange County Public Schools
Orlando, Florida

David W. Moore
Arizona State University, West
Phoenix, Arizona

K. Denise Muth
University of Georgia
Athens, Georgia

P. David Pearson
University of Illinois
Champaign, Illinois

Charles W. Peters
Oakland Schools
Pontiac, Michigan

Carol A. Power
Lansing School District
Lansing, Michigan

Gayla Preisser
Eastern Montana College
Billings, Montana

Victoria G. Ridgeway
University of Georgia
Athens, Georgia

Laura R. Roehler
Michigan State University
East Lansing, Michigan

Greg P. Stefanich
University of Northern Iowa
Cedar Falls, Iowa

Karen Tripp-Opple
Plymouth-Canton
*   Community Schools*
Plymouth, Michigan

Sheila W. Valencia
University of Washington
Seattle, Washington

PART ONE

A Frame of Reference

PRELUDE

The concept of the middle school is not a new one. It was developed decades ago to meet the special needs of early adolescent students. The chapters in this section provide a perspective on the middle school as it relates to reading and literacy. Chapters 1 and 2 describe the development of the middle school, its unique student population, and its unique instructional function, particularly in terms of literacy development. Chapter 3 suggests that the middle school may not be achieving its unique function, and Chapter 4 describes how the goals of middle school reading are influenced by various classroom management styles. Together, the four chapters introduce you to the middle school generally, and to middle school reading particularly, and provide a frame of reference for the remaining sections of the book.

Middle School Reading: A Historical Perspective

David W. Moore
Greg P. Stefanich

AN UNDERSTANDING of the reasoning and actions that led to the establishment of middle schools enhances an understanding of how reading instruction is conducted in these schools. This chapter presents a broad perspective on both middle schools and middle school reading instruction. We describe apparent differences between recommended and actual practices associated with this institution and suggest explanations for these differences.

Establishment of Schools in the Middle

The organization of American public schools has moved from two levels to three. Most public school students in the early 1900s attended an 8-year elementary program and a 4-year secondary program; however, by the 1980s most students attended a three-level structure as school districts inserted a level of schooling between elementary and secondary. This new middle level grouped grades 4-9 into different patterns. For example, grades 4-6 were grouped and labeled intermediate or upper elementary school. In 1970 the dominant pattern consisted of junior high schools with grades 7-9, but by 1984 the dominant pattern shifted to middle schools with grades 6-8 (McEwin & Alexander, 1987). Thus, most accounts of the establishment of middle schools begin with the founding of junior high schools in the early 1900s (Barton, 1975; Peeler, 1975; Toepfer, 1982).

Junior High Schools

Around the turn of the century, educators began recognizing the value of a distinctive educational program for students in the middle grades. Reports by national committees of educators who studied secondary schooling reflected changes that were occurring and helped shape future changes.

In 1892 the National Council on Education named Harvard University President Charles W. Eliot to chair a committee whose purpose was to recommend a program of studies for secondary schools. Among other things, the influential *Report of the Committee on Secondary School Studies* (National Education Association, 1893/1969) recommended changing the dominant 8 year/4 year structure to a 6-year elementary and 6-year secondary program. To achieve this 6-6 structure, seventh and eighth grade students were to be moved to a secondary environment with specialized course offerings. This recommendation marked a change in the treatment of middle grade students in comparison with primary grade students.

The *Cardinal Principles of Secondary Education* (National Education Association, 1918) explicitly called for secondary education to be divided between junior and senior periods. Among other things, this report called for students in the junior period to explore their aptitudes in order to tentatively choose the type of occupation they would pursue later; students in the senior period were to receive training in their chosen fields.

Another recommendation contained in this report was to broaden the post-elementary school curriculum. The committee stated that secondary schools should do more than prepare students for college. This recommendation paved the way for the life adjustment and vocational guidance functions junior and senior high schools eventually assumed.

The number of junior high schools grew enormously during the first half of the twentieth century. The first junior high schools opened in Columbus, Ohio, and Berkeley, California, in 1910. Fifty years later, about 80 percent of all high school graduates had experienced a 6-3-3 program (Alexander, 1987).

School conditions are rooted in the economic and social situations as well as the psychological theories of the time (Chubb & Moe, 1986; Kliebard, 1986; Wiebe, 1969), and the impetus for junior high schools was no exception. For example, when early reports on secondary schooling were written, U.S. society was moving from an agrarian to an industrial economy. Improved technology reduced the need for chores and responsibilities in the home, and promoted the hiring of specialists in manufacturing and services. Industrialists concerned with education wanted to change the curriculum for middle level students in order to produce citizens and workers educated enough to meet the rapidly changing demands of the new order.

Child labor laws and compulsory schooling laws of the time kept students in school. These laws, and the increasing population and urbanization of the early 1900s, led to the need for a new school structure that would relieve the enrollment pressures on elementary and high school buildings. Another impetus for junior high schools was provided by G. Stanley Hall, who pioneered the study of child development during this period. Hall (1904) published an influential two volume work that emphasized the uniqueness of early adolescents and stressed the importance of considering their special needs when planning educational programs.

In sum, a distinctive school organization for middle level students began with the emergence of junior high schools in the early 1900s. These schools resulted from the work of three influential groups: (1) those who were concerned about efficiently producing good workers and enlightened citizens, (2) those who wanted to relieve overcrowded schools, and (3) those who wanted to provide children with an environment that fit their particular stage of development. The concerns and beliefs of many people were combined in producing this particular school structure.

Middle Schools

The notion of middle schools as an alternative to junior high schools emerged in the 1960s. Educators noted that junior high schools were not serving the educational purpose for which they were intended. As Eichhorn (1980, p. 57) stated, the movement "erupted as a protest against the program, not against the concept, of the junior high school."

The concept of the junior high that middle school advocates wanted to preserve was stated best by Gruhn and Douglass (1947) in *The Modern Junior High School*. They summarized their concept of an optimal educational program for early adolescents by stating the six functions of the junior high school: integration, exploration, guidance, differentiation, socialization, and articulation. The following excerpt from *The Modern Junior High School* describes these functions of middle level education:

Function 1
Integration

To provide learning experiences in which pupils may use the skills, attitudes, interests, ideals, and understandings previously acquired in such a way that these will become coordinated and integrated into effective and wholesome pupil behavior.

To provide all pupils a broad, general, and common education in the basic knowledges and skills which will lead to wholesome, well-integrated behavior, attitudes, interests, ideals, and understandings.

Function 2
Exploration

To lead pupils to discover and explore their specialized interests, aptitudes, and abilities as a basis for decisions regarding educational opportunities.

To lead pupils to discover and explore their specialized interests, aptitudes, and abilities as a basis of present and future vocational decisions.

Function 3
Guidance

To assist pupils to make intelligent decisions regarding present educational activities and opportunities and to prepare them to make future educational decisions.

To assist students to make intelligent decisions regarding present vocational opportunities and to prepare them to make future vocational decisions.

To assist pupils to make satisfactory mental, emotional, and social adjustments in their growth toward wholesome, well-adjusted personalities.

To stimulate and prepare pupils to participate as effectively as possible in learning activities so that they may reach the maximum development of their personal powers and qualities.

Function 4
Differentiation

To provide differentiated educational facilities and opportunities suited to the varying backgrounds, interests, aptitudes, abilities, personalities, and needs of pupils in order that each pupil may realize most economically and completely the ultimate aims of education.

Function 5
Socialization

To provide increasingly for learning experiences designed to prepare pupils for effective and satisfying participation in the present complex social order.

To provide increasingly for learning experiences designed to prepare pupils to adjust themselves and contribute to future developments and changes in the social order.

Function 6
Articulation

To provide a gradual transition from preadolescent education to an educational program suited to the needs and interests of adolescent boys and girls (pp. 59-60).

These functions of the junior high school can be taken as the theoretical foundation of middle level education. Middle level programs were expected to provide a transition between elementary and secondary schooling to meet the needs of early adolescents. These programs were to blend the child-centered nurturing emphasis of elementary schools with the subject-centered competitive emphasis of secondary schools.

As noted previously, middle school advocates asserted that junior high programs were not performing the desired functions of middle level education. Junior high schools were seen to be mere replicas of senior high schools. The rationale for junior high schools might have been based on the lofty functions presented by Gruhn and Douglass and others, but the actual practices in junior

highs were seen to reflect the academic orientation of senior highs.

Modern Middle Schools

In order to clarify how a program could be designed to fulfill the classic functions of middle level education, recent publications list the essential characteristics of middle school programs (Lipsitz, 1984; NASSP's Council on Middle Level Education, n.d.; National Middle School Association, 1982) and describe surveys of the features of exemplary middle school programs (George & Oldaker, 1986). These publications help answer the question, "What makes a middle school a middle school?" After all, simply grouping grades 5-8 or 6-8, attaching a high sounding rationale to the new school organization, and calling it a middle school will not sufficiently fulfill the educational needs of early adolescents. In fact, some junior high schools with grades 7-9 fulfill the needs of early adolescents better than named middle schools (Yoder, 1982).

Recommended Practices

Alexander (1987) examined the literature on middle level education and summarized the essential characteristics of a true middle school program. A paraphrased version of his summary follows:

1. *An interdisciplinary organization with a flexibly scheduled day.* Teachers from academic specialties such as language arts, mathematics, science, and social studies meet regularly in order to coordinate their instruction for a particular group of students. Actual team teaching might occur, but the emphasis is on

Joint planning can help teachers effectively meet students' diverse needs.

mutual planning in order to meet students' needs. For instance, teachers might meet weekly in order to monitor the behavior of students who are acting up or becoming overly withdrawn. Interventions are designed to promote the personal development of such youngsters. During the meetings, teachers might plan lessons that capitalize on what is being presented in one another's classes. Science and social studies teachers might have their students summarize materials according to the guidelines presented by the language arts teacher. With a flexibly scheduled day, class periods of unequal times might be presented. For example, teachers might combine their classes twice a week for large section activities that last twice as long as normal. A homeroom period might be offered that allows students to participate in activities they choose on a daily, weekly, or monthly basis.

2. *An adequate guidance program, including a teacher advisory plan.* Teachers meet regularly with a homeroom or advisory group of students in order to perform various activities and provide guidance. Teachers might publicize and encourage students to participate in different clubs during this time, or they might counsel students individually or in groups about personal, aca-

demic, and vocational issues. For instance, programs that deal with smoking, alcohol, and drugs might be offered in homerooms. Teachers assume a special responsibility for the personal well-being of the students assigned to them.

3. *A full-scale exploratory program.* Exploration is offered in different ways. First, teachers offer short courses in subjects such as foreign languages and the fine and practical arts in order to expose students to their contents. Longer courses in these subjects are offered later in individuals' programs. Second, teachers offer programs and clubs in special interest areas such as photography and aviation. Students are able to participate in these activities because of the flexibly scheduled day. Minicourses on nontraditional topics such as mythology and medicine also could be offered. Finally, teachers encourage students to pursue independent investigations of the topic being studied during the regular course work.

4. *Curriculum provision for such broad goals and domains as personal development, continued learning skills, and basic knowledge areas.* This rather general goal is meant to underlie all the course offerings of a middle school. A curriculum of personal development seeks to promote areas such as physical wellness and decision making. A school that fosters continued learning skills includes attention to higher order literacy and thinking strategies as well as information processing tools such as computers and reference sources. Basic knowledge areas include the concepts and ideas about the world that characterize educated citizens.

5. *Varied and effective instructional methodology for the age group.* Teachers do more than present lectures, conduct recitations, and monitor seatwork with whole-class groups. Instead, they might follow up a large group presentation with small group interaction, use multimedia presentations, and allow peer tutoring or some form of cooperative learning. Teachers present material at rates that are appropriate for particular groups of learners. The methodology is varied to respect the diversity and the increasing sophistication of middle school students.

6. *Continued orientation and articulation for students, parents, and teachers.* Administrators and teachers introduce the middle school program to new students and their parents annually. Provisions are made for the orientation of new families during the year. Ongoing communication is maintained between the school and the home. In addition, teachers participate in staff development activities to refine their skills in carrying out the functions of middle level education.

The first three items noted by Alexander describe entities that are especially important for distinguishing middle schools from other school levels. An interdisciplinary organization, a guidance program with a teacher advisory plan, and an exploratory program are the hallmarks of exemplary middle schools. The other items listed — provisions for broad curricular goals and domains, appropriate instructional methodology, and continued orientation and articulation — seem to fit primary, secondary, and middle grades.

Actual Middle School Practices

In order to determine the extent to which practices characteristic of exemplary middle schools were being implemented, Binko and Lawlor (1986) conducted a small-scale survey. Responses from 237 teachers and 43 school administrators revealed that the recommended practices most evident in actual middle schools were:

- Emphasis on basic skills.
- Differentiation of teaching methods according to student abilities.
- Utilization of media.
- Differentiation of subject area objectives according to ability.
- Encouragement of creative ideas by students.

The practices rated least evident were:

- Interdisciplinary team teaching.
- Single discipline team teaching.
- Ability of teachers to function as counselors.
- Provisions for minicourses.
- Use of a nongraded organization (p.83).

The findings obtained from this small sample of middle schools reveal a discrepancy between recommended and actual practice. Although the respondents reported instructional emphases in some recommended areas, not evident were interdisciplinary cooperation, personal guidance, and exploratory programs. These findings are consistent with those from several dissertations conducted since 1978 (Brown, 1978; Holmes, 1981; Munsell, 1984; Nesper, 1981).

Various explanations are possible for the apparent gap between recommended and actual practice in middle schools. One is that many groups in U.S. society combined to establish this level of schooling, and not all of the groups were motivated primarily by the theoretical considerations of teaching young adolescents according to their particular stage of development.

For instance, concerns about declining enrollment motivated some people to promote middle schools. In the 1960s and early 1970s, comprehensive high schools became underutilized. To remedy this situation, the ninth grade was returned from the junior high to the senior high, and the junior high was called a middle school.

Groups working to racially integrate schools also promoted the middle school structure. Black children and white children typically went to separate schools because they lived in segregated communities. Integrationists respected the need for elementary schools to be located within each community, but they wanted to bring together students from the segregated communities as soon as possible. Seventh grade was considered too late for successfully mixing children from different races, so fifth or sixth grade was chosen, and the new structure was called a middle school.

Even if a middle school was established according to professional recommendations, many forces could work against its continuation. School administrators facing tight budgets have difficulty scheduling classes so that interdisciplinary groups of teachers can meet and plan cooperatively. In addition, teacher education institutions have been slow to develop distinct programs for middle level educators, and state certification standards almost universally allow teachers trained in a senior high model to work in the middle grades. According to Alexander and George (1981), "Probably the greatest problem and need of the middle school movement is the lack of personnel trained for and committed to the education of transescents" (p. 20).

Middle School Reading

This section turns from the general middle school movement to the specific reading instruction methods associated with these schools. Reading instruction is needed that meets early adolescents' requirements in areas such as integration, exploration, and socialization. Appropriate instruction also is necessary in areas specific to reading development. Knowing the general developmental needs as well as the specific reading needs of preteens helps educators plan effective reading programs. When considering the reading needs of this age group, it is important to realize that even average readers differ considerably. Students who achieve the same scores on reading tests have different interests, aptitudes, personalities, backgrounds, and learning styles. Moreover, not all readers are average. Problem readers and superior readers always exist.

Hall and other child development researchers stimulated inquiry into the stages of reading development exhibited by preteens and other age groups (Gray, 1939). By the mid 1930s, authorities such as McCallister (1936), McKee (1934), and Thorndike (1934a, b, c) had

articulated the characteristic reading needs of middle level students. More recent statements about this topic (Early, 1984) have retained most of the initial thinking. In brief, average readers at the end of fourth grade generally have achieved basic fluency. They are able to read in thought units rather than word by word. Average readers also have well developed strategies for decoding unfamiliar words. Long words might stump these students, but the difficulty probably arises because they do not have the words in their listening vocabularies or because the words contain spelling constructions not yet encountered.

Average readers at the end of fourth grade also have basic comprehension strategies. They can answer questions about information stated explicitly in the text, but they have difficulty with abstractions. Because of the limited amount of background information acquired up to this time, these readers frequently misinterpret information and miss allusions to ideas. Finally, average readers at this stage typically have few study strategies. Many students progress readily through reading tasks in primary grades but are frustrated by tasks presented in middle grades. For the first time, students must silently understand and retain quantities of complex written information. Preparing for chapter tests and reporting information synthesized from various materials can be frustrating for these students unless they receive appropriate instruction.

Recommended Reading Practices

In order to determine the features of successful middle school reading and writing programs, the Center for Early Adolescence at the University of North Carolina at Chapel Hill began the Project on Adolescent Literacy in 1985. Investigators visited 32 sites that boasted successful programs and isolated 11 characteristics of their literacy instruction. Defining these features seems to be the most productive way to recommend practices for better reading programs. According to this report, teachers in successful middle level literacy programs:

- Spend a high proportion of time on actual reading and writing.
- Teach skills in the context of actual reading and writing.
- Stress silent reading, reserving oral reading for special activities, such as dramatic readings or sharing students' written pieces.
- Teach strategies for reading comprehension.
- Build lessons on the background information and experience of the students.
- Integrate speaking and listening activities with reading and writing activities.
- Focus on writing.
- Model for students how experienced readers and writers plan and accomplish their goals.
- Give students hands-on experiences that help them understand what they read and write.
- Facilitate discussions rather than lead them by asking open-ended questions that elicit answers requiring critical thinking rather than yes/no answers, and by modeling

the way responsible adults learn through discussion.
- Use varied heterogeneous as well as homogeneous groupings and regroup students around interests as well as ability levels (Center for Early Adolescence, 1987, p. 3).

The exemplary reading practices listed reflect some traditional and some relatively new recommendations from the reading education literature. One of the longest standing recommendations found in the list is to have middle school students spend a high proportion of time reading. To do such reading, students require access to library books, magazines, brochures, and audiovisual kits, rather than being restricted to textbooks and workbooks. Spending a high proportion of time reading helps satisfy general developmental needs for integration and exploration as well as specific reading needs for interest and knowledge of the world.

Another familiar recommendation is to include reading instruction across the curriculum. The idea is for middle school teachers to teach students *how* to read subject matter materials. Teachers of science, social studies, and home economics are not expected to rely on reading specialists to improve students' reading performance. The recommended role for specialists is to support classroom instruction with resources and suggestions and to work with exceptional readers. Finally, two other common recommendations are to group students flexibly according to reading interests and performance and to emphasize comprehension.

Two relatively new recommendations for middle school reading programs involve explicit instruction and writing. One of the practices listed calls for teachers to model how they planned and attained their literacy goals. If students are expected to summarize passages, teachers should summarize a passage first, thinking through the process aloud. A related recommendation is for teachers to teach comprehension strategies. Strategies differ from skills because strategies involve knowing when and why to employ particular processes. To illustrate, students might be skillful at summarizing passages requested by others, but they might not summarize passages when interpreting text by themselves. These students would be skillful but not strategic. The call for explicit, direct instruction to ensure strategic reading mirrors much of the current thinking in the professional literature about teaching reading comprehension (Pearson & Dole, 1987).

The second practice calls for a focus on writing. The Center for Early Adolescence list was derived from literacy programs rather than from programs limited to reading. However, the connection between reading and writing has been well established during the past decade. An emphasis on writing is consistent with much of the current literature about middle level reading programs (Atwell, 1987).

Actual Reading Practices

Recommended reading practices provide goals for program development. They specify what middle level educators should seek in this curricular area.

Knowing the prevalence of these recommended practices during typical daily instruction also is important. Middle level educators who understand the realities of actual practice are better able to implement ideal programs.

Published descriptions of reading practices in grades 5-8 reveal many actual practices that differ from recommended ones (Goodlad, 1984; Shaver, Davis, & Helburn, 1979; Smith & Feathers, 1983; Stodolosky, Ferguson, & Wimpelberg, 1981). According to these reports, students' reading tasks generally were to acquire assigned information contained in textbooks. This information typically was factual, and students generally wrote it on worksheets before going over it in class. The essence of the tasks seemed to be to locate textbook sentences that contained correct answers. Teachers conducted large group recitations based on the assigned readings and frequently elaborated on the text's concepts by explaining selected points and reporting personal experiences related to the information. Students tended to read little connected text during the school day. Many students were able to progress through the day by relying on the comments of teachers and other students to get required information instead of reading for themselves. Practically no time was spent preparing students for reading assignments or teaching specific reading strategies. As Goodlad (1984, p. 105) summarized, "The data from our observations…support the popular image of a teacher standing or sitting in front of a class imparting information to a group of students. Explaining and lecturing constituted the most frequent teaching activities."

One caution is important to remember when considering reading practices. Because a comprehensive, methodologically adequate description of middle school reading practices is not available, the precise nature and extent of practices is difficult to pinpoint. The findings about actual reading practices reported here come from studies that include grades 5-8.

If the description of reading practices presented here applies to most middle schools, there is a clear discrepancy between recommendations and actualities. Having students spend a lot of time reading and writing, building lessons on the background information and experience of students, giving students hands-on experiences, discussing information critically, and grouping students flexibly are missing from the reports of actual practices.

As noted earlier, many forces affect what happens in schools. One that seems responsible for the actual reading practices reported centers around social control. Teachers who conduct whole-class recitations on information contained in a single textbook control the content covered. Middle school teachers perceive pressure from upper grade teachers, administrators, and parents to produce students who have acquired the information customarily presented in school. For instance, most middle level science curricula call for students to learn the steps of the scientific method, the parts of the eye, the life cycle of bean plants, and the stages of mitosis. Text based recitations allow teachers to present this information (and only this information) ex-

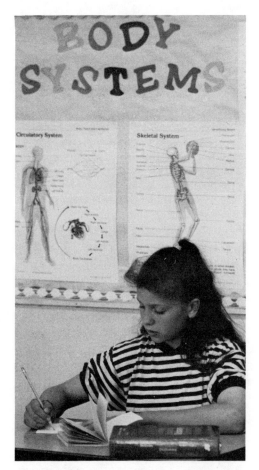

Middle school students must be able to read and understand various technical and scientific materials.

peditiously. In addition, teachers are expected to produce students who exhibit orderly, submissive behavior, and teachers typically desire such behavior during the school day in order to reduce tension. Because recitations allow teachers to control student behavior, their use persists. The persistence of recitations is explained by Doyle (1983, p. 186) as follows:

Some tasks, especially those which involve understanding and higher level cognitive processes, are difficult for teachers and students to accomplish in classrooms. In attempting to accomplish such tasks, students face ambiguity and risk generated by the accountability system. Teachers, in turn, face complex management problems resulting from delays and slowdowns and from the fact that a significant portion of the students may not be able to accomplish the assigned work. As tasks move toward memory or routine algorithms, these problems are reduced substantially.

Conclusions

The recommendations and the realities relative to middle school reading seem to be disparate. Too many middle schools fall short in practices such as providing abundant time and materials for wide exploratory reading, teaching reading across the curriculum through interdisciplinary teaming, teaching comprehension strategies explicitly, providing enriched opportunities for writing, and eliciting thinking.

Implementing recommended practices seems to be the primary issue facing middle level educators. Relatively well-accepted guidelines are available about the type of educational program best suited to the needs of early adolescents. However, there are no simple procedures for effectively instituting and maintaining these guidelines in middle schools. Educators have the task of implementing recommended practices in the face of powerful social, political, and economic constraints. Much progress has been made in defining developmentally appropriate reading instruction for early adolescents. However, in order to avoid past and present criticisms that middle level practices are inadequate, educators must determine how to enter the twenty-first century with the nation's middle schools implementing appropriate teaching practices.

References

Alexander, William M. (1987, Summer). Toward schools in the middle: Progress and problems. *Journal of Curriculum and Supervision, 2,* 314-329.

Alexander, William M., & George, Paul S. (1981). *The exemplary middle school.* New York: Holt, Rinehart and Winston.

Atwell, Nancie. (1987). *In the middle: Writing, reading, and learning with adolescents.* Portsmouth, NH: Boynton/Cook.

Barton, Ronald R. (1975). *A historical study of the organization and development of the junior high and middle school movement, 1920-1975.* Unpublished doctoral dissertation, University of Arkansas, Fayetteville, AR.

Binko, James, & Lawlor, James. (1986, September). Middle schools: A review of current practices—How evident are they? *NASSP Bulletin, 1*(70), 81-87.

Brown, William T. (1978). *A comparative study of middle school practices recommended in current literature and practices of middle schools in South Carolina.* Unpublished doctoral dissertation, University of South Carolina, Columbia, SC.

Center for Early Adolescence. (1987). Adolescent literacy: What schools can do. *Common Focus: An Exchange of Information About Early Adolescence, 8,* 3-4.

Chubb, John E., & Moe, Terry M. (1986, Fall). No school is an island: Politics, markets, and education. *The Brookings Review, 4,* 21-28.

Doyle, Walter. (1983, Summer). Academic work. *Review of Educational Research, 53,* 159-199.

Early, Margaret. (1984). *Reading to learn in grades 5 to 12.* San Diego, CA: Harcourt Brace Jovanovich.

Eichhorn, Donald H. (1980). The school. In Mauritz Johnson (Ed.), *Toward adolescence: The middle school years.* Chicago, IL: University of Chicago Press.

George, Paul S., & Oldaker, Lynn S. (1986). A national survey of middle school effectiveness. *Educational Leadership, 43,* 79-85.

Goodlad, John I. (1984). *A place called school.* New York: McGraw-Hill.

Gray, William S. (1939). Reading. In Guy M. Whipple (Ed.), *Child development and the curriculum.* Bloomington, IL: Public School Publishing.

Gruhn, William T., & Douglass, Harl R. (1947). *The modern junior high school.* New York: Ronald Press.

Hall, G. Stanley. (1904). *Adolescence.* New York: D. Appleton.

Holmes, James F. (1981). *Implementation status of selected middle school principles in named California middle schools: A descriptive study.* Unpublished doctoral dissertation, University of Northern Colorado, Greeley, CO.

Kliebard, Herbert M. (1986). *The struggle for the American curriculum, 1893-1958.* Boston, MA: Routledge & Kegan Paul.

Lipsitz, Joan. (1984). *Successful schools for young adolescents.* New Brunswick, NJ: Transaction Books.

McCallister, James M. (1936). *Remedial and corrective instruction in reading: A program for the upper grades and high school.* New York: Appleton-Century.

McEwin, C. Kenneth, & Alexander, William M. (1987). *Report of middle level teacher education programs: A second survey (1986-1987).* Boone, NC: Appalachian State University Media Services.

McKee, Paul G. (1934). *Reading and literature in the elementary school.* Boston, MA: Houghton Mifflin.

Munsell, William R. (1984). *A study of the extent to which identified programmatic characteristics of middle level education are implemented in the middle schools and junior high schools in the state of Colorado.* Unpublished doctoral dissertation, University of Colorado, Boulder, CO.

NASSP's Council on Middle Level Education. (n.d.). *An agenda for excellence at the middle level.* Reston, VA: National Association of Secondary School Principals.

National Education Association. (1918). *Cardinal principles of secondary education.* Washington, DC: U.S. Government Printing Office.

National Education Association. (1969). *Report of the committee on secondary school studies.* New York: Arno Press. (Original work published in 1893.)

National Middle School Association. (1982). *This we believe.* Columbus, OH: National Middle School Association.

Nesper, David P. (1981). *A study to determine the current level of implementation of eighteen selected critical attributes of middle schools in the United States.* Unpublished doctoral dissertation, Ball State University, Muncie, IN.

Pearson, P. David, & Dole, Janice A. (1987, November). Explicit comprehension instruction: A review of research and a new conceptualization of instruction. *Elementary School Journal, 88,* 151-165.

Peeler, Thomas H. (1975). The middle school: A historical frame of reference. In Gerald G. Duffy (Ed.), *Reading in the middle school.* Newark, DE: International Reading Association.

Shaver, James P., Davis, O.L., Jr., & Helburn, Suzanne W. (1979, February). The status of social studies education: Impressions from three NSF studies. *Social Education, 43,* 150-153.

Smith, Frederick R., & Feathers, Karen M. (1983, December). The role of reading in content classrooms: Assumption vs. reality. *Journal of Reading, 27,* 262-267.

Stodolosky, Susan S., Ferguson, Teresa L., & Wimpelberg, Karen. (1981). The recitation persists, but what does it look like? *Journal of Curriculum Studies, 13,* 121-130.

Thorndike, Edward L. (1934a, October). Improving the ability to read. *Teachers College Record, 36,* 1-19.

Thorndike, Edward L. (1934b, November). Improving the ability to read (part 2). *Teachers College Record, 36,* 123-144.

Thorndike, Edward L. (1934c, December). Improving the ability to read (concluded). *Teachers College Record, 36,* 229-241.

Toepfer, Conrad F., Jr. (1982). Junior high and middle school education. In Harold E. Mitzel (Ed.), *Encyclopedia of educational research* (5th ed., vol. 2). New York: Free Press.

Wiebe, Robert H. (1969, Summer). The social functions of public education. *American Quarterly, 21,* 147-164.

Yoder, Walter H. (1982). Middle school vs. junior high misses the point. *Educational Leadership, 40,* 50.

Understanding Middle School Students

Gayla Preisser

Patricia L. Anders

Peggy Glider

SPEND A DAY WATCHing the immensely diversified students in the halls of a middle school or a junior high. The students you see vary in their physical development, social maturity, cognitive ability, and emotional growth. This diversity presents educators with special challenges that are best met by those who are well grounded in theories of adolescent development and sensitive to the complex nature of this age group. The middle school movement is an example of educators responding to these special characteristics. For example, the curriculum typically provides a broad range of options from which students may sample, thus appealing to their diverse and expansive interests. Options range from opportunities for interdisciplinary study and for making connections between disciplines (Gardner, 1983) to project oriented activities to accommodate their high energy levels and social needs. Likewise, the organization of most middle schools is flexible so that the expanding needs and interests of students in this age group may be encouraged and accommodated.

The aim of this chapter is to provide a global description of early adolescence. Specifically, we (1) present various psychological theories of early adolescent development; (2) summarize physical, cognitive, and affective characteristics of this age; (3) highlight the influences of environmental forces on development; and (4) suggest some general implications of this information for middle school educators.

Theoretical Views of Early Adolescent Development

It is evident from the literature that there are few conceptual frameworks designed to "understand, research, and interpret early adolescent development, learning, and experience" (Thornburg, 1980, p. 216). For the most part, early adolescent researchers have extrapolated insights from the grand theories of human development. While such theories can be used as guidelines, they are limited because they do not address this specific developmental stage. Moreover, while grand theories may consider school-aged adolescent youth, the era in which they were constructed does not reflect accurately the complex and multifaceted world many modern young people are experiencing. Many of the traditional perspectives also are limited to unidimensional views of development, and it is apparent that development is much more complex.

However, theoretical models related specifically to adolescent development have begun to emerge. Recent models have expanded to incorporate the interaction between adolescents and their environment as a factor in their development. For example, some research has focused on the interplay of biological and psychosocial aspects of development among young adolescents (Brooks-Gunn & Peterson, 1983). These studies have given rise to multidisciplinary models of development that address the relationship among biological, psychological, and social factors (Lerner & Foch, 1987) and contextual orientations (Lerner & Kauffman, 1985).

Despite their shortcomings, grand theories do provide insight into adolescent development. Therefore, we present overviews of both the relevant grand theories and more recent approaches to early adolescent development.

Erikson's Industry and Identity

One of the grand theories that is particularly relevant to middle school educators and researchers is Erikson's (1963) theory of personality. It suggests that individuals encounter the following eight developmental stages or tasks throughout life: (1) Trust vs. Mistrust, (2) Autonomy vs. Shame and Doubt, (3) Initiative vs. Guilt, (4) Industry vs. Inferiority, (5) Identity vs. Role Confusion, (6) Intimacy vs. Isolation, (7) Generativity vs. Stagnation, and (8) Integrity vs. Despair. Of these, Stages 4 and 5 are relevant to the early adolescent.

Each age-related stage consists of a "crisis" or turning point that must be resolved. Positive resolution of a crisis aids in the resolution of subsequent crises, and each resolution contributes to healthy personality or ego development. If crisis resolution is not achieved during the appropriate stage, later experiences can provide further opportunity for successful resolution. For example, a teacher who is supportive of a student's activities may help reverse feelings of guilt or inadequacy from a previous stage.

In the Industry vs. Inferiority stage, the school-aged child is engaged in developing a sense of industry that leads to a feeling of competence. It is during this stage, from ages 6-12, that broader skills and knowledge are acquired. For example, prior to age 6, children are committed to learning basic skills such as walking, dressing, and playing cooperatively with peers. As the child reaches early adolescence, these basic skills give rise to greater and more demanding skills, including the ability to demonstrate productive work, increased independence, and greater responsibility. In short, the individual "learns to win recognition by producing things" (Erikson, 1963, p. 259). Consequently, individuals may develop a sense of inadequacy at this age if they are not afforded the opportunity to master these tools and skills, to participate in society in a responsible fashion, and to receive recognition. These feelings of inadequacy or inferiority may discourage students from subsequently establishing a sense of identity, the crisis confronting adolescents.

While exploring a sense of accomplishment and skill, early adolescents also are concerned with others' perceptions of them as well as with their role or place in the broader social context. According to Erikson, this growing concern with the self is a rudimentary step in resolving one's identity, or the beginning of the Identity vs. Role Confusion stage. The adolescent task is one of resolving the identity conflict, either by establishing an identity or by falling into a state of identity diffusion. This state is marked by the increasing need for the individual to balance childhood assumptions and behaviors with the oncoming adult roles as prescribed by cultural surroundings. Many early adolescents begin the initial steps of identity formation in response to bodily changes caused by puberty as well as accelerated social norms and expectations.

Erikson notes that in the struggle to redefine themselves and their roles, adolescents often confront the adults with whom they interact, challenge existing social structures, and adopt idols as role models. Moreover, during this stage young people may temporarily overidentify with the heroes of cliques and crowds. These cliques provide both peer support and the opportunity to test one another's growing sense of identity. Prior to establishing this sense of self, however, adolescents often explore and challenge extremes. These extremes, according to Erikson, often include rebellious, deviant, and self-destructive acts.

In sum, Erikson perceives the early adolescent and the adolescent years as a time in which individuals are seeking new adventures and challenges in order to establish a sense of competency. It also is a time to compare themselves with others and test social limits in order to ascertain a sense of their own identity.

Maslow's Needs Theory

Another viable approach for understanding and working with young adolescents is Maslow's (1943) theory of human motivation. In brief, Maslow argued that all individuals express five basic human needs that must be met or satisfied in order for physical and psychological growth to continue. These needs are hierarchical in nature and include, from the lowest to the highest: physiological needs, safety, love and belonging, esteem, and self-actualization.

From this perspective, early adolescents must first satisfy basic physiological needs such as hunger and thirst. When these needs are not fulfilled, they dominate one's thinking or existence. For example, hungry students are probably more concerned with their empty stomachs than with their academic tasks. Sensitive teachers recognize the increased nutritional needs of their rapidly growing students.

The next need is safety, being free of danger and feeling safe and secure. Maslow suggested that safety needs are especially apparent in young people, who are less able than adults to control their surroundings. According to Maslow, one indication of young people's need for safety is their "preference for some kind of undisrupted routine or rhythm" (1943, p. 377). Maslow further stated that children "generally prefer a safe, orderly, predictable, organized world, which [they] can count on, and in which unexpected, unmanageable, or other dangerous things do not happen" (p. 378). Instances of injustice, unfairness, or inconsistency can make the early adolescent feel anxious and unsafe. Such feelings may manifest themselves in unruly, rebellious, withdrawn, or depressed behavior. Such behavior is an at-tempt by the individual to gain control or feel secure within the environment.

When physiological and safety needs are satisfied, love and belonging become important. For early adolescents, at-tempts to satisfy belonging needs are evident in their friendships, formation of groups or cliques, and identification with role models. Once individuals are secure in their belonging needs, their attention turns toward fulfilling esteem needs.

Maslow defined esteem needs as the "desire for a stable, firmly based, usually high evaluation of [oneself], for self-respect, or self-esteem, and for the esteem of others" (p. 381). Esteem needs are broken into two categories. One category is the desire for feelings of achievement, adequacy, and confidence within oneself; the other is the desire to be recognized and appreciated by others. Similar to Erikson's (1963) idea of Industry, satisfying esteem needs leads to confi-

Friendship and peer acceptance are especially important for early adolescents.

dence and feelings of worth and use in the world. Conversely, not satisfying such needs leads to feelings of inferiority, weakness, and helplessness.

Last in Maslow's hierarchy of needs are those related to self-actualization. These needs spring from the individual's desire for self-fulfillment, to "become everything that one is capable of becoming" (p. 383). Self-actualization is generally associated with older individuals.

Developmental Tasks

Erikson's and Maslow's theories, while providing insight into early adolescence, are not specifically theories of early adolescent development. They are broad perspectives on personality development and human motivation. For these reasons, some (Havighurst, 1952; Thornburg, 1980) prefer to view early adolescent development in terms of developmental tasks.

Havighurst initiated the concept of developmental tasks, arguing that much of human development revolves around learning. For example, individuals learn to walk, talk, read, work, and interact with others. In short, living involves learning a series of tasks or behaviors. Because they must be learned to secure reasonable happiness and success, they constitute the developmental tasks of life. In general, developmental tasks are those encounters or challenges occurring at particular points in the life cycle which, if mastered or resolved, facilitate the successful well-being and development of the individual.

Developmental tasks have roots in several individual and environmental forces. Some developmental tasks result from physical maturation. For example, during adolescence the physical changes of puberty require adjustment to a new physique as well as to a new code of acceptable behavior with those of the opposite gender.

Some tasks stem largely from societal pressures. According to Havighurst, adolescents face the tasks of "achieving a masculine or feminine social role" (p. 37) and "developing intellectual skills and concepts necessary for civic competence" (p. 54). Such tasks are heavily influenced by the views and expectations of one's culture and environment.

Other tasks involve the development of the individual's personality or self. "As the self evolves, it becomes increasingly a force in its own right in the subsequent development of the individual" (Havighurst, 1952, p. 62). Tasks stemming from personal goals include those related to choosing an occupation and developing a philosophy of life. For adolescents, "acquiring a set of values and an ethical system as a guide to behavior" (p. 62) is a developmental task derived largely from one's personality.

In brief, Havighurst recognized six life stages: Infancy and Early Childhood, Middle Childhood, Adolescence, Early Adulthood, Middle Age, and Later Maturity. For each of these stages, Havighurst delineated approximately 6-10 tasks, or 48 developmental tasks in all. Some tasks are universal and invariable from culture to culture (those based on biological maturation), while others vary according to cultural values (those that grow out of societal pressures).

Developmental tasks can be recurrent or nonrecurrent. Recurrent tasks are those that "recur over a long period of time, in varying but closely related aspects" (Havighurst, 1952, p. 31). For example, the task of getting along with one's age-mates occurs within each life stage, although each stage involves different aspects of social integration. Conversely, nonrecurrent tasks are those that, once mastered, no longer represent a developmental issue. Examples include learning to walk and talk.

Havighurst's model, as Thornburg (1980) notes, provides a viable means of understanding early adolescents. There is almost certainly a set of common "developmental, social, and behavioral characteristics [that] are being encountered by early adolescents today" (p. 216). These shared experiences or developmental tasks are important in making a transition into adolescence. Thornburg designated seven such tasks for the early adolescent: (1) becoming aware of increased physical changes, (2) organizing knowledge and concepts into problem solving strategies, (3) learning new social/sex roles, (4) recognizing one's identification with stereotypes, (5) developing friendships with others, (6) gaining a sense of independence, and (7) developing a sense of morality and values (p. 216).

According to Thornburg, it is essential that early adolescents have opportunities to pursue these tasks. Such experiences will enable them to gain a greater understanding of themselves "developmentally, socially, and behaviorally" (p. 217) and to "function better as an adolescent, and subsequently as an adult" (p. 220). Moreover, as these young people often may not know how to approach task-related issues, it is important that adults offer support and guidance toward successful resolution.

Biological/Psychosocial Relations

A more recent model addressing adolescent development is that of reciprocal biological/psychosocial relations (Lerner, 1985). In brief, this model suggests that adolescents, because of their individual physical and behavioral characteristics, elicit different responses from people than do other groups. These reactions by others feed back to adolescents and influence their further development. Thus, adolescents influence their own development by influencing social contexts and socializing agents.

Within this model, there are three ways in which the early adolescent acts as a "producer of his/her own development" (p. 357). First, the adolescent may be a "stimulus," causing different types of reactions from others. Variations in character, physique, temperament, ability, and personality create certain reactions from observers that have an influence on the adolescent's subsequent behavior and/or development.

Second, adolescents act as "processors" of information gleaned from others' reactions. The role of processor is not consistent and predictable; rather, it is affected by environmental cues and other aspects of development such as physical and emotional changes. Nonetheless, the adolescent as processor suggests that development is influenced by the ways information is processed, cognitively and emotionally, and by the ways perceptions of others and others' reactions are processed.

Third, during early adolescence individuals become increasingly able to act as "agent, shaper, or selector" in their development. That is, they are capable of choosing the activities in which they wish to engage, the peer groups to which they want to belong, and the manner in which they want to conduct themselves. This ability to independently shape or select their environment, as well as their behaviors, certainly influences their development.

Embedded within this model is the notion of "goodness-of-fit." This term refers to how closely one's individual characteristics or behaviors match those characteristics or behaviors called for or expected in particular settings or by significant others. The premise is that if there is a good fit between an adolescent's exhibited traits and the traits expected by others, the adaptation to a given setting will be smoother and more successful. Environments characterized by little discrepancy of fit tend to provide more support for the adolescent and to encourage developmental growth.

For example, teachers may react differently to a 13-year-old, early-maturing male who is attractive, tall, and has a well-developed body than to a less developed age-mate (adolescent as stimulus). Teachers may expect advanced cognitive performance, more refined or mature behavior, and greater athletic prowess from the early-maturing male. If the young man demonstrates delayed cognitive function (adolescent as processor), engages in unruly or childlike behaviors, or expresses apathy toward physical activities (adolescent as agent), a discrepancy of fit exists. Consequently, adaptive

interactions may be hindered and subsequent development altered.

In sum, Lerner (1985) argues that early adolescents play an integral and dynamic role in mapping their own developmental courses. Early adolescents' diverse and changing cognitive, social, and emotional processing skills enable them to "provide match or goodness-of-fit with adaptational demands emanating from the social context" (p. 362) in varying degrees.

Applying the Theories

These theoretical perspectives, both the grand theories and the theories designed to describe the adolescent, provide practitioners with assumptions from which to organize schools and develop curricula. It is evident that this period of life is marked by rapid and multiple changes, both individual and environmental, and that these changes interact in a simultaneous and dynamic fashion. Thus, middle level educators who adopt a multidimensional approach are facilitating their students' growth. More precisely, attending to the factors of development—physical, intellectual, emotional, and social—is especially critical while early adolescents are striving to gain a sense of competency, worth, esteem, and identity.

Early adolescents are faced with a number of unique tasks such as adapting to bodily changes, establishing appropriate gender-related behaviors, and discerning the responsibilities associated with greater independence. Similarly, they are experiencing numerous physical, psychological, and social needs. Teachers must be sensitive to these challenges and respect their students' needs and emotions as well as offer guidance and support. Finally, early adolescents are active participants in student development because of their individual characteristics, their processing abilities, and the choices they make. This being the case, adults wishing to facilitate student development will work with them toward a successful transition to a new life stage.

Empirical Views of Early Adolescents

Research on early adolescents and adolescent development and behavior is extensive and varied, and is critical to those who work with these young people. A brief overview of some of the more common topics and general findings within this body of research is presented here.

Individual and Maturational Issues

Physical concerns. The diversity of physical development in this life stage, especially in terms of growth and hormonal change, is more profound than at any other stage of life. Both boys and girls begin a major growth spurt during early adolescence, although females begin earlier (ages 10-12$^1/_2$) than males (ages 12$^1/_2$-16). Puberty is concurrent with this adolescent growth spurt.

Whether early adolescents interpret physical maturation positively or negatively is influenced by how others react to their bodily changes. If significant adults (teachers, parents, club leaders) view pubertal changes with respect and approval and provide ways to express acceptance of the individual's more mature status, the transition into full sexual ma-

turity will be smoother.

Cognitive concerns. Piaget's work (Gruber & Voneche, 1977; Piaget, 1970, 1972) is important in considering research on intellectual functioning among early adolescents. Piaget asserted that cognitive development progresses through four qualitatively different stages: (1) sensorimotor, marked by an infant's concept of space, time, and objects; (2) preoperations, involving the young child's ability to adopt symbol systems, including language; (3) concrete operations, the acquisition of conservation and rule learning skills; and (4) formal operations, characterized by increased logical, hypothetical, and reflective thinking.

Within this framework, 10- to 15-year-olds are in a transitional state, moving from concrete to formal operations. There is great disparity in early adolescents' thought capabilities. For example, Brazee and Brazee (1979) found that of 49 seventh graders, 51 percent operated at the concrete level, 41 percent were functioning at the transitional level, and 6 percent utilized formal operations. This diversity in ability requires that middle level educators be aware of the primary characteristics of each cognitive phase. It also requires that curricula include the presentation of materials for both concrete and formal operational tasks, thus ensuring that all students receive sufficient intellectual success and challenge.

In brief, young people operating in Piaget's concrete stage of thought are capable of relational and combinatorial procedures, including simple and multiple classification (using two or more characteristics), seriation (ordering objects along a given dimension), and class inclusion reasoning (seeing something as an entity in itself and as part of something else). They have a good concept of number (more than, less than), cause and effect, irreversibility, and logical reasoning about concrete problems or actual objects and events (Inhelder & Piaget, 1958).

Keating (1980) has delineated five characteristics to distinguish adolescent formal operational thinking from previous stages of thinking and language. One is that individuals in this stage can think about possibilities or consider alternative solutions to a problem as well as gauge the probability of the success of a given solution. A second characteristic is the ability to generate hypotheses and accept or reject them on the basis of given experiences or information. In addition, formal operational thinkers can plan ahead; they can think through an entire sequence of steps related to a problem and gather necessary information beforehand. Fourth, increased metacognitive or reflective thinking ability is evident. Adolescents can think their own thoughts, evaluate them, and determine ways to use their thinking abilities. The fifth characteristic is an ability to think beyond immediate situations and to reason about hypothetical settings and abstract concepts.

Because of their newly developed cognitive skills, especially metacognition, early adolescents become preoccupied with themselves and their ideas. According to Elkind (1967, 1980), adolescent egocentrism and the imaginary audience phenomenon (adolescents assume that they are the focus of everyone's attention) lead to the heightened self-consciousness apparent in adolescence. Formal operations also give rise to what is known as the "personal fable" concept, a set of idealistic views regarding how valuable, important, and indestructible the self is. For example, early adolescents believe that, while others may get sick and die, they will not.

Individuals in the transitional stage are not capable of consistent formal operational thought. Of course, whether a person in this stage demonstrates concrete or formal thinking largely depends upon the nature of the task (Brazee & Brazee, 1979). Problems that create emotional distress may be approached from a concrete, here-and-now perspective even though abstract reasoning skills are available.

Moral development is related to cognitive growth. According to Kohlberg's (1976) theory, early adolescents are primarily operating within the conventional level. Thus, moral decisions are based on conforming to stereotypes or what pleases others (good boy/good girl orientation), or on rules or authority (law and order orientation). The formal operation stage must be reached before moral judgments can be made on individual rights and social principles (social contract orientation).

In contrast to Kohlberg's theory, Eisenberg's (1982) theory addresses moral development from a prosocial orientation. This involves the conflict in reasoning between satisfying one's own wants or needs and satisfying those of others. Such moral decisions involve helping, sharing, or comforting behaviors. Prosocial research shows that early adolescents' judgments on whether to help another are based on whether they recognize that person's need. As young people move into adolescence, reasoning based on empathy ("I know how she feels") and internalized values ("It's my responsibility") increases.

Other approaches to understanding adolescent intellect or cognition are evident in the literature. One is the information processing approach (Siegler, 1983; Sternberg, 1982), that describes how we mentally attend to, store, retrieve, and reason about information. Another contemporary view of intelligence is that of Gardner (1983, 1985), who contends that seven distinct types of intelligence exist: linguistic, logical-mathematical, musical, spatial, bodily kinesthetic, intrapersonal, and interpersonal. Gardner asserts that individuals may demonstrate different levels of aptitude in these areas. Such a perspective suggests that intellectual growth is more complex than was traditionally believed. Moreover, this view suggests that educators must develop strategies for nurturing many different kinds of intelligence (Gage & Berliner, 1988).

Affective concerns. Early adolescents are inconsistent in mood, beliefs, temperament, and behavior. Such inconsistency often gives rise to personal confusion and brings out numerous and diverse emotions. The emotional upheaval during early adolescence is further "compounded by the fact that adolescents generally mature more slowly emotionally than they do physically, intellectually, and socially" (Thornburg, 1982, p. 71).

Fear is one of the more common emotions within this age group. Broadly, young people are fearful of becoming adolescents, in part because they do not know what to expect. More specifically, because of their strong desire to belong, early adolescents are fearful of being rejected, of being inadequate, and of failing. Because of increased reflective and hypothetical thinking ability, these fears often are exaggerated as middle school students begin to imagine events, reactions, and outcomes. Thornburg suggested that educators can help alleviate adolescents' fears by role playing to highlight differences between real and imaginary states and by providing opportunities for students to openly discuss their apprehensions.

Anxiety also surfaces in adolescence. It develops from continued apprehensions or fears. Such an emotional state is characterized by prolonged irritable, depressed, unhappy, or uneasy behavior and sudden mood shifts. We can help early adolescents reduce anxiety by creating situations that lead to positive feelings and by providing accurate information about anxiety-producing events.

Other emotions that intensify during early adolescence are guilt, which stems from lack of congruence between values and behavior; grief, or understanding the loss of a significant person (for early adolescents, grief is often felt in losing a pet or breaking up with a boy/girlfriend); jealousy, caused by feelings of insecurity (being treated unfairly, being surpassed in athletics, being less attractive); and shyness, or fear of talking to or meeting others (usually prompted by fear of rejection). Early adolescents also experience heightened levels of affection, love, and happiness (Thornburg, 1982).

Finally, early adolescents experience new dimensions in anger, often manifested in outward attacks on someone or something. At this age, individuals typically get angry when they are teased, treated unfairly, or lied to, or when things go wrong (Thornburg, 1982). Our goal in helping young people to cope with anger is not to make them feel as if they should not get angry but, rather, to guide them toward constructive emotional outlets.

In summary, early adolescents are contending with an array of emotions and are trying to learn appropriate ways of controlling these feelings. While it is difficult to prescribe acceptable emotional outlets or settings in which such outbursts are appropriate, educators can help adolescents build emotional skills. For example, teachers should allow individuals to express their feelings without guilt or shame, thus facilitating self-reflection and opening up alternative feelings, reactions, or behaviors.

Context or Environmental Issues

Parents, family, and peers. As children begin to appear more adultlike, they gain greater independence and engage in more diverse social interactions, and family relationships take on a new dimension. This occurs, in part, because early adolescents must define themselves independently of the family unit, while still maintaining familial bonds. Teachers can aid this process by providing students with opportunities to discuss developing and changing relationships, by teaching effective communication skills, by modeling democratic adult-adolescent relationships, and by providing guidance or resources.

Key in the transition from family to independence is the role of friendship and peers. Two major developments occur in this area: the emergence of individual friendships with members of both genders and the formation of groups or cliques. Both types of interactions are important because interpersonal skills are developed, values are explored, competitive and cooperative behaviors are learned, sex roles are developed and explored, and perspectives are broadened (Thornburg, 1982). Such experiences help promote healthy social maturation.

Both parents and peers influence the adolescent, but in different ways. For example, peers are more influential in status approval concerns such as mode of speech, clothing style, and meeting places. Parents have greater influence on decisions regarding educational, occupational, or life goals (Sebald & White, 1980).

The school. Schools are a major socialization agent for many adolescents. Schools teach academic skills and content, help students realize their identity and potential, and provide ways for students to integrate and interpret their society. The ideal middle school offers a vital and relevant curriculum including content, skills, direction, and learning experiences that both enhance individual development and foster academic interest and confidence.

Providing these functions is important to adolescent development for several reasons. Nearly all early adolescents demonstrate both the capability and the willingness to learn. Factors within the school, however, can lead students to become disheartened. For example, when academic content is outdated or unrelated to the students' real world, assignments are boring, or the school climate is sterile or nonreceptive, early adolescents may develop negative attitudes toward school. Eventually, such attitudes lead to underachievement, and many young people simply give up and drop out of school. In fact, approximately 25 percent of our nation's students drop out of school before receiving a high school diploma, most during the ninth grade (National Center for Educational Statistics, 1980).

Students ages 10 to 15 are acquiring values and perceptions of themselves and their abilities that often last into adulthood, and middle level education can greatly influence these perceptions. To this end, middle grade teachers and administrators need to provide experiences leading to academic accomplishment, esteem, and positive attitude.

Not surprisingly, some studies suggest that junior and senior high schools serve more social functions than scholarly ones (Coleman, 1965). For example, star athletes are likely to receive greater public recognition than star pupils, and being named king or queen of the spring dance is apt to draw more attention than winning a blue ribbon at the state science competition. However, other studies indicate that students link school settings with academics. Mitman and Packer (1982) found that early adolescent students are more concerned with academic issues than with popularity, athletics, or social issues. Moreover, most students reported that learning content material, getting good grades, and doing well in school are important. In fact, students overwhelmingly reported academic achievement as the most important aspect of school. Educators must find ways to make school achievement challenging and satisfying to students.

Media. Mass media, including television, radio, music, film, and literature, has a great impact on students' development. This influence stems from two factors. First is the pervasiveness of the media. On the average, students in fourth through ninth grades watch 4-7 hours of television a day (Murray, 1980). The media is also influential because it provides common or shared experiences that often determine adolescent fads or standards.

Television is a powerful and broadening tool providing messages about virtually every concept, but it is difficult to know how much it affects emerging adolescents. Existing research on children and adolescents suggests that, to some degree, ideas presented in the media are assimilated into individuals' world view, thus influencing their perspectives and attitudes. The degree to which attitudes and behaviors are learned through television viewing varies with a number of factors, including how closely a program matches reality, individual cognitive processing skills, amount of viewing, and the level of interest and attention invested (Bandura, 1977).

Teachers and parents should monitor early adolescents' television viewing and help them interpret what they see. While teachers have little control over what their students watch, read, or listen to, they can offer guidelines for productive, healthy, and realistic use of our society's mass media.

Delinquency, substance abuse, and suicide. In the past 10-15 years, a significant increase in juvenile delinquency has been recorded within the early adolescent and adolescent populations. At least 2 percent of adolescents have a record of juvenile court cases, but the actual number of those engaged in delinquent behaviors is assumed to be significantly higher since many such behaviors go unpunished by the justice system (Santrock, 1987).

Gold and Reimer (1975) found that nontrivial delinquent behaviors increased between 11 and 18 years of age, with the greatest acceleration occurring at around age 15. Hypothesized causes for delinquency are varied. Ross (1980) suggested that juvenile delinquents fail to develop sufficient behavioral controls, while Gold and Petronio (1980) see delinquency as part of the adolescent's search for identity. Research has found significant correlations between delinquency and family variables such as parental monitoring, discipline, and family stress (Patterson & Stouthamer-Loeber, 1984).

Substance abuse also is on the rise among early adolescents. In a recent study, suspensions for substance abuse in junior high schools were approximately equal to senior high school suspensions in the same metropolitan school district (Glider, Kressler, & McGrew, 1988). Nicotine and alcohol remain the leading substances abused by early adolescents, with inhalants and marijuana gaining in

prevalence. While harder substances such as cocaine and amphetamines are not as common among early adolescents as they are among older adolescents, experimentation at this level is on the rise. Factors leading to substance abuse have been studied for years. Research has linked such abuse to both peer pressure and parental substance use (Chassin, Presson, & Sherman, 1984).

Suicide among adolescents is increasing at an alarming rate. This rate has tripled since 1950 to make suicide the second leading cause of death for adolescents (Smith, 1980). Depression, which increases significantly from childhood to adolescence (Sroufe & Rutter, 1984), is the primary factor correlated with suicide. These depression-based suicides can be caused by family problems (Weiner, 1980); by a belief that one is "bullet proof" (Lipsitz, 1983); or by such common occurrences as failing grades, breaking up with a boy/girlfriend, or not making the ball team (Santrock, 1987).

In all three of these behavioral areas (delinquency, substance abuse, and suicide), teachers must be sensitive to the signs that their students are in need of help. Strong intervention and prevention programs in the schools have been shown to reduce many of these high-risk and potentially dangerous behaviors (Evans, 1983; Wodarski & Hoffman, 1984).

Implications for Middle Level Education

According to Gage and Berliner (1988), the instructional process involves a number of primary tasks. One of these is a clear understanding of student characteristics. Thus, understanding developmental growth and capabilities, differences and commonalities, concerns and interests, and physical and emotional states of students is a major challenge. For example, Braun (1985) suggests that early adolescents are learning to negotiate or interact successfully among peers, striving to handle the pressure to conform, and seeking ways to establish friendships and intimacy as well as to understand their own emerging sexuality. Teachers must be sensitive to these needs and demonstrate competence in positive communication skills. Teachers also need ample opportunity to master active listening skills, responses to difficult questions (e.g., "Why should I care about math? It won't help me get a job."), democratic approaches to problem solving, and ways of addressing sexuality-related comments or questions.

In essence, through greater understanding of middle school students, teachers will be better able to educate and to support early adolescent growth and socialization within the school environment. Instruction can be designed to provide for individual learning levels, incentives, examples, and interactions.

Middle school teachers have many opportunities to positively influence early adolescent development. Thornburg (1980) has offered a number of general guidelines. One is that teachers should not compete with their students' friends. Instead, they should encourage reciprocal respect between themselves and their students. Similarly, teachers must be constantly aware of how important friendships are to early adolescents. This component of adolescent development challenges teachers to devise ways in which they can incorporate companionship and social discourse into classroom learning and management and help students learn how to make and maintain friendships.

It is also important for educators to understand that much early adolescent behavior is related to gaining status with friends. In considering academic achievement, they must remember that some students may underachieve to keep friends who would feel threatened by their accomplishments. Conversely, many times students may excel in an area or work harder on a task in order to gain or maintain peer status. Teachers must be able to recognize instances where student performance is affected by peer influence and respond accordingly.

Finally, teachers should not expect students to conform entirely to the mannerisms or standards advanced in the classroom. Young people are diverse and creative in expressing their growing sense of self. They need guidance in learning about their world, about others, and about themselves. However, in aiding early adolescents through this process, teachers should not demand that they accept another person's views or beliefs.

Conclusions

Among the maturational and environmental theories that relate to adolescent development, of special note is Lerner's (1985) model, which postulates interrelationships among adolescents, the people with whom adolescents interact, and the environment. This interdependency captures the complexity of this age group and the tremendous importance of moral, social, and environmental factors as they relate to home, school, and community life.

The middle school student is in the midst of dynamic and extreme change. The metaphor of a swinging pendulum is apt: One moment middle school adolescents are in love with themselves, with everyone around, and with everything they are doing—the next minute they are in hate with those very same people and activities. Concurrent with these physical, emotional, and psychological changes, the student is trying new areas of interest and gaining new perspectives. Such exploration may result in unpredictable and sometimes unpleasant behavior. Hence, adults in the adolescent's life need to be consistent and solid so that testing can occur within safe boundaries.

References

Bandura, Albert. (1977). *Social learning theory*. Englewood Cliffs, NJ: Prentice Hall.

Braun, J.A., Jr. (1985). Transescent interpersonal needs and the preparation of middle school teachers. *Transescence*, *13*(1), 30-33.

Brazee, Edward N., & Brazee, Phyllis E. (1979). Cognitive development in the middle school. *Colorado Journal of Educational Research*, *19*(1), 6-8.

Brooks-Gunn, Jeanne, & Peterson, Anne C. (Eds.). (1983). *Girls at puberty: Biological and psychosocial perspective*. New York: Plenum.

Chassin, Laurie, Presson, Clark C., & Sherman, Steven J. (1984). Cigarette smoking and adolescent psychosocial development. *Basic and Applied Social Psychology*, *5*(4), 295-315.

Coleman, John S. (1965). *The adolescent and the schools*. New York: Basic Books.

Eisenberg, Nancy. (1982). The development of reasoning regarding prosocial behavior. In Nancy Eisenberg (Ed.), *The development of prosocial behavior*. New York: Academic Press.

Elkind, David. (1967). Egocentrism in adolescence. *Child Development*, *38*(4), 1025-1034.

Elkind, David. (1980). Strategic interactions in early adolescence. In Joseph Adelson (Ed.), *Handbook of adolescent psychology*. New York: Wiley.

Erikson, Erik H. (1963). *Childhood and society* (2nd ed.). New York: Norton.

Evans, Richard. (1983). Deterring smoking in adolescents: Evolution of a research program in applied social psychology. *International Review of Applied Psychology*, *32*(1), 71-83.

Gage, Nate L., & Berliner, David C. (1988). *Educational psychology* (4th ed.). Boston, MA: Houghton Mifflin.

Gardner, Howard. (1983). *Frames of mind*. New York: Basic Books.

Gardner, Howard. (1985). *The mind's new science*. New York: Basic Books.

Glider, Peggy, Kressler, Harry, & McGrew, Gustavo. (1988). *Early intervention through peer support retreats*. Paper presented at the annual meeting of the American Educational Research Association, New Orleans, LA.

Gold, Martin, & Petronio, Richard J. (1980). Delinquent behavior in adolescence. In Joseph Adelson (Ed.), *Handbook of adolescent psychology*. New York: Wiley.

Gold, Martin, & Reimer, David J. (1975). Changing patterns of delinquent behavior among Americans 13 through 16 years old, 1967-72. *Crime and Delinquency Literature*, *7*(4), 483-517.

Gruber, Howard, & Voneche, J. Jacques (Eds.). (1977). *The essential Piaget: An interpretive reference and guide*. New York: Basic Books.

Havighurst, Robert J. (1952). *Developmental tasks and education* (2nd ed.). New York: Longman, Green.

Inhelder, Barbel, & Piaget, Jean. (1958). *The growth of logical thinking from childhood to adolescence*. New York: Basic Books.

Keating, Daniel P. (1980). Thinking processes in adolescence. In Joseph Adelson (Ed.), *Handbook of adolescent psychology*. New York: Wiley.

Kohlberg, Lawrence. (1976). Moral stages and moralization: The cognitive-developmental approach. In Thomas Lickona (Ed.), *Moral development and behavior: Theory, research, and social issues*. New York: Holt, Rinehart & Winston.

Lerner, Richard M. (1985). Adolescent maturational changes and psychosocial development: A dynamic interactional perspective. *Journal of Youth and Adolescence*, *14*(4), 355-372.

Lerner, Richard M., & Foch, Terryl T. (Eds.). (1987). *Biological-psychosocial interactions in early adolescence*. Hillsdale, NJ: Erlbaum.

Lerner, Richard M., & Kauffman, Marjorie B. (1985). The concept of development in contextualism. *Developmental Review*, *5*(4), 309-333.

Lipsitz, Joan. (1983). *Making it the hard way: Adolescents in the 1980s*. Testimony presented at the Crisis Intervention Task Force, House Select Committee on Children, Youth, and Families, Washington, DC.

Maslow, Abraham M. (1943). A theory of human motivation. *Psychological Review*, *50*, 370-396.

Mitman, Alexis L., & Packer, Martin J. (1982). Concerns of seventh-graders about their transition to junior high school. *Journal of Early Adolescence*, *2*(4), 319-338.

Murray, John P. (1980). *Television and youth: 25 years of research and controversy*. Boys Town, NE: Boys Town Center for the Study of Youth Development.

National Center for Educational Statistics. (1980). *Projections of educational statistics: 1938-1984*. Washington, DC: National Center for Educational Statistics.

Patterson, Gerald, & Stouthamer-Loeber, M. (1984). The correlation of family management practices and delinquency. *Child Development*, *55*(4), 1299-1307.

Piaget, Jean. (1972). Intellectual evolution from adolescence to adulthood. *Human Development*, *15*(1), 1-12.

Piaget, Jean. (1970). Piaget's theory. In Paul Mussen (Ed.), *Carmicheal's manual of child psychology* (3rd ed., vol. 1). New York: Wiley.

Ross, Alan O. (1980). *Psychological disorders of children: A behavioral approach to theory, research, and therapy* (2nd ed.). New York: McGraw-Hill.

Santrock, John W. (1987). *Adolescence: An introduction* (3rd ed.). Dubuque, IA: Wm. C. Brown.

Sebald, Hans, & White, Becky. (1980). Teenagers' divided reference groups: Uneven alignment with parents and peers. *Adolescence*, *15*(60) 980-984.

Siegler, Robert S. (1983). Information processing approaches to development. In Paul Mussen (Ed.), *Handbook of child psychology* (4th ed., vol. 1). New York: Wiley.

Smith, Donald F. (1980). Adolescent suicide. In Rolf E. Muuss (Ed.), *Adolescent behavior and society* (3rd ed.). New York: Random House.

Sroufe, L. Alan, & Rutter, Michael. (1984). The domain of developmental psychopathology. *Child Development*, *55*(1), 17-29.

Sternberg, Robert J. (1982). Reasoning, problem solving, and intelligence. In Robert J. Sternberg (Ed.), *Handbook of human intelligence*. New York: Cambridge University Press.

Thornburg, Hershel D. (1982). *Development in adolescence* (2nd ed.). Monterey, CA: Brooks-Cole.

Thornburg, Hershel D. (1980). Early adolescents: Their developmental characteristics. *High School Journal*, *63*(6), 215-221.

Weiner, Irving B. (1980). Psychopathology in adolescence. In Joseph Adelson (Ed.), *Handbook of adolescent psychology*. New York: Wiley.

Wodarski, John S., & Hoffman, Susan D. (1984). Alcohol education for adolescents. *Social Work in Education*, *6*(2), 69-92.

What Have We Done with the Middle?

Richard L. Allington

A GENERATION AGO we did not have middle schools. As Moore and Stefanich (this volume) point out, early adolescents attended junior high schools or K-8 elementary schools, depending on whether they lived in rural or urban communities. As American society shifted from an agricultural to a manufacturing economy, urban and suburban communities grew, and the rural population declined. The organization of school districts changed (particularly in rural areas), with widespread consolidation that created fewer, but larger, school districts. In the midst of these changes, dissatisfaction with the emerging junior high school organizational structure resulted in the entity we call middle school. Today most school districts call the school that houses early adolescents a middle school, and, in that sense, the shift has been completed.

However, though most early adolescents attend a middle school, one might ask, "What is this place we call middle school?" The question seems important since middle schools are less frequently studied than elementary or secondary schools. Middle schools also have received less attention in current calls for educational reform.

In the following analysis, a description is provided of the middle school from a perspective of the academic work that early adolescents experience in middle school instruction. A number of questions are raised concerning the policies that shape these experiences—questions about why we create the instructional environments we offer students and about whether these environments meet the goals of the middle school as described in Chapters 1 and 2 of this volume.

The data for analyzing practices are

drawn from the experiences of 12 middle school participants. These students attend three schools in two states and represent advanced placement, regular class placement, and regular class placement with either remedial or special education resource room services. The majority of the participants were observed—some for a week, others for one day—as they attended classes. All were interviewed about their classes. It is from these data that the descriptions and questions are generated.

A Day in Middle School

A surprising aspect of the study of these 12 students is the remarkable similarity of their instructional experiences. The students attend school for about $5\frac{1}{2}$ hours a day and have six or seven different classes during that period. Classes in the three schools are between 43 and 54 minutes long, but all classes within each school are the same length. All students attend classes called English/Language Arts, Math, Science, Social Studies, and Physical Education. Some have classes called Wood Shop, Technology, Health, Keyboarding, or Writing Lab, but there is a consistency to the experiences of all 12 children because of the similarity of their classes. The only noticeable differences in the experiences of these students lie in the success (or lack of success) they have in completing the academic work assigned.

In order to provide a context for the middle school experience, Figure 1 offers a sketch of the whole-day experiences of one eighth grader. Lisa's day was selected because it was representative of those of all 12 students. Examples are presented of the academic tasks of other students, but to understand middle school, the whole-day perspective is necessary.

The most striking aspect of the experiences of students in middle school is the frequent reliance on worksheets and textbooks to teach. In the sense of teacher explanation or modeling (Duffy et al., 1986), instruction occurred rarely, and then typically as corrective feedback after a student (or a group) responded incorrectly to a question or an assigned seatwork task.

Lisa's day is fairly typical of the school day experiences of any of the 12 students. She did attend remedial reading instead of a foreign language class, but it was participation in foreign language instruction that differentiated high-achieving students from low-achieving students. Regardless of which "track" students were in, reliance on text material and low-level task worksheets dominated their instructional experiences. In each case, students were assigned to tracks, even if it was not officially acknowledged. That is, students typically attended classes with other students with similar achievement levels. These achievement levels (particularly reading achievement) determined which sections and courses students attended.

As noted, the primary difference in the instructional experiences of these students was their success or failure at the tasks assigned. The academic work was largely undifferentiated, although some tracks used different texts. When remedial or mildly handicapped students were in regular education courses, invariably they were held to the same task require-

Figure 1
Lisa's Instructional Day

8:27	Homeroom	Attendance and announcements.
8:35	Social Studies	T asks questions about assigned text, L cannot answer questions, T has Ss open text and read aloud, L asked to read definition from glossary, quiz given with 10 multiple-choice items.
9:15	Writing Lab	T assigns "Spelling Demons" sheet with 24 fill-in-blanks and T-made ditto with sentence fragments to be expanded, topic is "Growing Corn."
10:00	Science	T assigns workbook unit on "Oceans," 6 paragraphs and 6 pages of multiple-choice, fill-in-blanks, incomplete sentences, and crossword.
10:45	Language Arts	T assigns "Scope" while Ss write in journal (3 minutes), vocabulary pronounced, play read aloud, questions assigned, T corrects.
11:40	Lunch	
12:05	Health	T reviews 5-step problem solving method, assigns unit on "Family," Ss read aloud, write answers to 3 questions.
1:00	Math	T presents geometry lesson on overhead, Ss copy in notebook, discussion/T questions, T assigns worksheet, monitors.
1:45	Remedial Reading	Assigned worksheet, 1 paragraph and questions, T corrects, spelling test, match definitions, cloze worksheet.
2:30	Dismissal	

T = Teacher   L = Lisa   Ss = Students

ments, with no instructional differentiation, as were the more able students. A frequent complaint of the teachers was the inability of these students to fit the curriculum demands.

Academic Work in Middle School

The instructional experiences of these 12 middle school children were more similar than different. Most of the academic work required students to work alone, reading a text and responding to tasks that required them to simply locate or remember literal information from the test base. With the text in front of them, these students performed a variety of tasks ranging from "copying out" text information to supplying missing words, selecting the appropriate multiple-choice response, spelling from memory, computing math problems, or answering teacher questions about the text. The students were as likely to read these texts aloud as silently. The texts read, which tended to be short, dominated the instructional tasks. The instruction these students experienced gave the image that learning meant reading and remembering, and that thinking or understanding played a minor role. Tasks were assigned, rather than content taught; tasks were corrected, rather than explained. The fragmentation of the curriculum was nearly complete, with rare evidence of instruction in one class being linked with that in another. These students had spelling tasks that were unrelated to any curriculum area, they did various unrelated writing tasks, they were assigned vocabulary study without instruction, and they completed worksheet after worksheet.

The 12 students complained that they did not understand their assigned tasks, that they were not taught, that texts were difficult, and that they were tested on subjects they had not covered. Their complaints were similar, regardless of achievement — some students just had fewer complaints.

Important to these students were their friends, their social relationships, and their own self-images. None wanted to be seen as a "geek," too heavily invested in the academic work of school. All tried to make their teachers happy and not make waves. It was easier for some than for others. All did homework, but some did more than others. While the type of academic work seemed substantively similar, the quantity seemed to differ. The more able students simply had a larger amount of the same work assigned to the less able students. The less able students seemed to work as diligently and as long as the more able students, but with less success.

Questions about Middle School

These schools do not seem to be the unique, vibrant places of learning for early adolescents that the visionaries described as the middle school movement emerged. What happened along the way? Several issues seem critically influential.

The middle school today seems more like the secondary education model than the elementary school model. That is, an array of classes is offered, and each is taught by a separate teacher. Many of these teachers are subject matter specialists, and current trends seem to be moving even further in that direction. An unfortunate result is that most middle school teachers see 100-150 students a day and know none of them well. As content specialists, they demonstrate expertise in their respective disciplines but not in adolescent reading or writing development.

The school day is segmented into a number of brief periods, each period standing alone, with little coherence between the lessons. The brevity of the periods and the number of students seem to create instructional sessions that emphasize breadth of topic coverage rather than depth, and low-level single word locating and remembering rather than comprehension or understanding. Doyle (1984) suggested that a primary task of teachers is constructing class sessions around activities that fit into the time constraints allowed and managing the behavior of students during that period. As in his study of middle school teaching, the lessons here relied on activities derived from texts or worksheets, with oral reading, questions, and tests intermingled to fill the time and keep students on task. The dominance of commercially prepared curricular materials also was evident. As Doyle observes, "Most whole-class presentations were introductions to specific seatwork assignments rather than more broadly construed discussions of content and its meaning" (p. 272).

The proliferation of worksheet tasks seems related to teachers' concepts of instruction as "getting through the material." A seeming contradiction is that the material often was selected by the teacher rather than mandated by a curriculum plan. Nonetheless, completing the tasks presented by the commercial material was equated with teaching the content. However, unlike teachers in some reports of elementary school instruction (Duffy, Roehler, & Putnam, 1987), these teachers rarely used teachers' guides or curriculum guides in their daily instruction. The tasks assigned were generally completed during the class period and corrected or turned in to the teacher. In either event, low-level tasks were more easily corrected; the students could correct one another's multiple-choice responses but probably not essays (had they been assigned). Teachers could correct more low-level assignments than essays in the single planning period each was allotted. Goodlad (1984) noted that students seemed to favor the low-level tasks and had more difficulty with longer, higher level tasks, such as compositions, summaries, or analyses. Thus, a variety of influences shaped the assigned academic work.

The fragmentation of the instructional experiences across the school day re-sulted in students working at a variety of tasks on a variety of topics. Sizer (1984) contends that the trend toward curriculum specialization in teaching is the primary contributor to this fragmentation. With each teacher or each curriculum area adopting its own curriculum plan and curricular materials, fragmentation of instruction seems bound to occur. The result is not a middle school curriculum but an array of curriculum areas taught in middle school.

In an earlier paper, Allington, Boxer, and Broikou (1987) addressed the issue of fragmentation of remedial instruction from regular class instruction and argued for the coordination of middle school remedial and resource room tasks with tasks students found difficult in the core curriculum classes. However, the 12 students examined here experienced fragmentation across the day, not just between regular and remedial or resource room instruction. While the types of academic demands were similar across the classes, the reading and writing strategies needed to accomplish these tasks rarely were addressed or integrated.

Issues and Questions

In the three schools these early adolescents attended, the organization was like that of a junior high school. The relatively brief daily class periods, content specialist teachers (most with secondary school certification), and the grouping of students by achievement levels all mirror common practice in secondary schools (Goodlad, 1984). Perhaps such a plan is what the profession has come to accept as the most appropriate for the education of early adolescents. Acceptance of this organizational plan has several consequences that deserve attention—consequences that may have been underestimated.

Standardization of the School Day

Scheduling all classes for the same length of time denies differences in individuals' learning rates and accelerates differences in individual achievement. In more flexible scheduling plans, different learning rates can be accommodated by scheduling some learners for larger amounts of instruction when needed. Learners seem to differ primarily in terms of rate of acquisition of new understandings, assuming there is similar instruction and prerequisite learning. In most middle schools, learners arrive with different prerequisite knowledge and different achievement levels in several basic skills areas. The use of standard instructional periods for all students denies this commonly accepted fact and results in a steady acceleration of differences in ability. This, in turn, results in an earlier, and unnecessary, sorting of students.

Achievement Tracks

In response to the differences in student achievement levels, these schools responded with de facto ability tracks, even in the face of substantial evidence regarding the negative effects on student achievement and the resultant inequality of educational opportunities for students (Oakes, 1985). In one middle school, nearly 20 percent of the students had been identified as "mildly handicapped" (primarily learning disabled), and these students were often segregated even for content area classes, assigned to resource rooms for science, language arts, and math. This school did not officially acknowledge "tracking" students, but it offered advanced placement courses, remedial courses in reading, writing, and math, and special education resource room courses. The organization mirrored that of the other schools but was notable for the proportion of learners assigned to special education classes.

The issue here is simply whether a child's future should be assigned by age 12, based crudely on previous school experience. Are we satisfied with organizational plans so inflexible and unforgiving that learner differences are viewed as barriers so substantial that they must be accepted as immutable? Standard periods and ability grouping deny that schools can make much of a difference; together they shape instruction so that barriers are enforced, not overcome.

Fragmentation of Instruction

The fragmentation across the school day is made overwhelmingly evident by looking at curricular maps of the instructional experiences of these students. We attempted to determine how this fragmentation affected learners, particularly the least prepared learners, but no definite answer emerged. Even within class periods, instructional activities often were impossible to link. These activities focused on different topics, required different cognitive strategies, and involved texts that varied across several levels of difficulty. Instructional activities observed across several observational days almost appeared to be selected at random from any number of methods texts, teachers' guides, or commercial materials. Curriculum is understood (in perhaps a too academic sense) to mean a coherent array of organized instructional activities selected to facilitate the acquisition of mutually agreed upon knowledge, skills, and understandings. Observed practices rarely matched this concept.

Something resembling a curriculum plan assumed previous mastery of all reading, writing, and speaking skills, strategies, and operations necessary to complete the assigned instructional tasks. It was unclear whether any larger curriculum plan was in effect for the instructional activities experienced across the various content classes in a single school day (much less a week, semester, or year). The notion of an integrated middle school curriculum plan should not be rejected without serious consideration. For the least prepared students, learning is facilitated when instructional activities build on each other and expand and extend the opportunity to learn. There even seems to be an economy of effort for both learners and teachers in such situations. Fragmentation, on the other hand, makes it more difficult for the least prepared students to learn.

Doing versus Learning

In these schools there were far more instructional tasks that required little, if any, comprehension than tasks that promoted understanding. Students were likely to be doing tasks rather than learning skills or acquiring understandings. Much of this may be attributable to (1) the lack of any clear direction from a curriculum plan, (2) the brief instructional periods that prohibited anything but brief selections and brief assignments, (3) the preferences of the learners to not invest too heavily in academic work, (4) the large student load that the scheduling scheme assigned to teachers, and (5) the intensity of the management concerns that seem to drive much of teachers' planning (Doyle, 1984).

Obviously, as Dreeben (1987) has noted, decisions made at the state, district, and building levels exert substantial influence on the nature of instruction in classrooms. Nonetheless, administrative decisions are not completely responsible for fragmentation. While in many instances the teachers had not selected the texts they used, they did create or select much of the instructional activity. The use of grammar dittoes, the transcription tasks displayed on the chalkboard, the teacher-made study guides, the round robin oral reading of materials, the "hot-seat" question and answer formats, the assignments without explanations, and the emphasis on locating rather than understanding were choices made by teachers. When listening to some of the teacher interviews, one gets the impression that the plan is to keep students busy for 43 to 54 minutes a day, with little suggestion of any larger instructional goal.

Researchers left these middle schools with a sense that something had gone incredibly awry, that means and ends had been confused, that doing had been substituted for learning. It was enormously depressing.

A Different Middle School Model

The previous description of several middle schools is offered here in an attempt to portray the nature of the middle school instructional environment. There is a feasible alternative structure.

In the alternative middle school, the students would spend longer periods of instructional time studying topics, themes, and issues that were collaboratively organized across curriculum areas. For instance, one might select a topic such as *plants*, a common science topic in middle school, and organize a 6- or 10-week unit of study. However, this would be an all day instructional session planned cooperatively by faculty from the science, English, math, and remedial reading areas. The unit would include instruction and academic work that revolved around the topic but that was integrated into a long term learning activity. A variety of composing tasks would be designed, along with appropriate instruction. First, students would receive instruction in keeping observational records of plants, relating descriptions to the various forms of plant life. Texts of various sorts would be used, some primarily for reference information and others as models for particular types of writing or reading demands. The measuring and recording of plant growth and environmental conditions would develop several sorts of needed mathematical skills. Groups of students would study and learn together, often in cooperative groups, sometimes in whole groups, and perhaps in tutorials with any of the teachers involved. This curriculum would require more than simply reading and copying out. In addition, the teachers would better know the students they were attempting to teach and could design instructional sequences and tasks that extended beyond the 45 minute standard period.

Social studies, English, and resource room teachers might develop and deliver a similar unit on colonialism. In other words, this middle school would have an integrated curriculum, collaboratively planned and taught by teachers from several disciplines. Depth of understanding, rather than breadth of content covered, would be the focus of the instructional plan. Even if fewer topics were addressed, they would be explored in greater depth, and the academic work would present an integrated emphasis.

Where to from Here?

Obviously, the three middle schools and 12 students observed do not constitute any sort of representative sample of middle schools across the country. Unfortunately, what is known about middle schools suggests that these schools are not simply worst case example. In the students' minds, these schools were not bad places to spend some time. Their friends were there, and that is what seemed to matter. The 12 students all seemed boisterous, social, shy, worried, eager, and adept—in short, like average early adolescents. All were under control.

What do we want from our middle schools? If only safe, fairly friendly sites for adolescents to bloom with their social destiny rigidly determined, then the schools we observed fill that request. If, however, middle schools are to provide more, to narrow the inequities in academic achievement, to refine and foster the abilities necessary for students to become more independent as learners, and to nurture an understanding of the social and physical world, then a substantial rethinking of the middle school idea is required. In this age of calls for reform of the educational process, the future of the middle school cannot be ignored.

References

Allington, Richard L., Boxer, Nora, & Broikou, Kathleen. (1987). Jeremy, remedial reading, and subject area classes. *Journal of Reading*, *30*, 643-645.

Doyle, Walter. (1984). How order is achieved in classrooms: An interim report. *Journal of Curriculum Studies*, *16*, 259-297.

Dreeben, Robert. (1987). Closing the divide. *American Educator*, *11*, 28-35.

Duffy, Gerald G., Roehler, Laura, Meloth, Michael, & Vavrus, Linda. (1986). Conceptualizing teacher explanation. *Teaching and Teacher Education*, *11*, 197-214.

Duffy, Gerald G., Roehler, Laura, & Putnam, Joyce. (1987). Putting the teacher in control: Basal reading textbooks and instructional decision making. *Elementary School Journal*, *87*, 357-366.

Goodlad, John. (1984). *A place called school: Prospects for the future*. New York: McGraw-Hill.

Oakes, Jeannie. (1985). *Keeping track: How schools structure inequality*. New Haven, CT: Yale University Press.

Sizer, Theodore R. (1984). *Horace's compromise: The dilemma of the American high school*. Boston, MA: Houghton Mifflin.

The Influence of Classroom Management

Mark W.F. Condon

James V. Hoffman

LIKE OTHER CLASS-rooms, middle school classrooms offer a context for literacy instruction. The immediate classroom context is nested within a larger institutional context that includes a school setting, a district structure, and a state system for education. This larger context presents certain constraints for teachers in terms of both curricular and organizational decision making. It is the individual teacher's responsibility to create a classroom environment that fits into the larger system as well as maximizes opportunities for teaching and learning. As Allington (this volume) suggests, classroom environments in the middle school do not always reflect the unique purpose of middle schools. In this chapter, we explore the issues related to classroom organization and management that can influence literacy instruction at the middle school level and present alterna-tive middle school class-room environments.

Before investigating these issues in detail, we discuss the assump-tions and understandings about classroom management that undergird our treatment of the topic. First, the term *management* is used to refer to the classroom teacher's sys-tem for engaging students in curricular tasks on a day to day basis. In its simplest terms, management is a teacher's solution to the problem of how to ensure an orderly learning environment. Second, good man-agement is a necessary prerequisite for ef-fective instruction. Research over the past two decades clearly documents the critical role effective teachers play in planning, in-troducing, and maintaining a well-man-aged classroom environment (Doyle, 1986). Third, it is important to remember that by itself good management is *not* a sufficient basis for a literacy-rich class-room. Fourth, there is no single best management system. Teachers must create systems that take into account the characteristics of the surrounding context, their own instructional philosophies and theoretical orientations, and the needs of the learners. Finally, skills of classroom management are learned and refined over time through exposure, practice, and reflection.

In this chapter, three teachers are introduced to provide examples of alternative systems for organizing and managing a reading program at the middle school level. These teachers represent different backgrounds, philosophies, approaches, and institutional contexts. In no way is one teacher regarded as more effective or more ideal than another. Although they clearly represent different levels of management sophistication, each works in a different way to solve the problem of creating an orderly learning environment.

Throughout the chapter are illustrations of typical middle school students. Their behaviors represent needs common to middle school children, including the need for diversity, self-exploration, meaningful participation in the school and community, positive social interaction with peers and adults, physical activity, the development of competence and achievement, and structure and clear limits (Dorman, 1981; Dorman, Lipsitz, & Verner, 1985; Lipsitz, 1979; Preisser, Anders, & Glider, this volume). The essence of classroom management is that teachers respond appropriately to students' needs, developing their strengths and helping them work through their weaknesses.

Pat's Seventh Grade

Pat teaches seventh grade reading and language arts in a public middle school.

Her certification is 7-12 English. She has done advanced work in reading instruction while working on her master's in education. She seldom teaches English and American literature, even though she would like to. Pat says that teaching reading allows her to feel effective and needed.

The rambling building accommodates more than 300 students in the seventh grade, with similar numbers in sixth and eighth. There are 12 classes of seventh grade students, and Pat is involved directly with no fewer than 157 young people each day. Some of these children are mainstreamed from special education classes. She teaches more advanced students in two honors sections.

Pat's school is administratively organized to conform to the latest trends in middle school education (Alexander & George, 1981). This educational structure means she shares these students with her "family" of four other colleagues, each of whom specializes in English, math, science, or social studies. The physical education, music, and art teachers are shared by all of the families of teachers in her building. Each week, her team of teachers plans the weekly schedule together in extensive work sessions after school. They work together on some units, such as "African Adventure" and "The Animals in Town," and in isolation on others. The team has a good rapport, and the members generally feel that the team's curriculum choices and instructional activities do not diminish the individual teacher's particular areas of effectiveness. Pat sees her role as a skills teacher, supportive to all classes, and for the most part she follows the direction of the group. Generally, the team attempts to provide a "small school within a large school" atmosphere for their students.

The team's curriculum is determined initially by the school district. The instructional materials with which Pat is provided were selected for their strengths in offering tasks to promote the skills demanded by the state-mandated tests and the school curriculum. Within that framework, she attempts to become involved with the rest of the teachers in their content units. She is not responsible specifically for teaching content area reading; however, in her team-coordinated instruction, she offers lessons to help her students develop mastery of the texts for their other courses.

When Pat teaches reading, she attempts to use techniques from the magazines and journals she reads for her classes at the university, These materials often are found in the teacher's lounge. For example, she has recently included in her lessons metacognitive skills objectives like K-W-L (Ogle, 1986) and other study techniques. Usually she teaches directly, using a straightforward approach based on teacher effectiveness research (Cummings, Nelson, & Shaw, 1980; Hunter, 1976). She does some oral reading with her students and many exercises on grammar and punctuation to aid composition and boost test scores, which is the goal of the district administration. Her evaluation procedures are based on individual effort, objective tests, and reading skills quiz grades.

Pat's teaching style results from 12 years of practice. She endorses a basic skills orientation to the curriculum and understands the management system she uses. When her system works, it is because the content and her classroom management complement one another. Each year, she improves in many areas of her teaching as she attempts to respond to the needs of her students, the changing curriculum in reading and language arts, and the challenges of teaching in this particular middle school.

When Pat's system fails to work, it is because her teaching and her management objectives conflict. Her sense of the problems in this conflict results in questions that she asks herself about improving her own teaching and classroom. This kind of response reflects the natural tendency of professionals to consider themselves to be in need of improvement. Though some are perennial issues, Pat's most burning questions for this year are: "How do I promote reading with the generally unskilled and uninterested readers throughout the class's range of achievement levels, but especially at the lower end of that range?" "How can I ensure that the top students get as much attention as the lower ones?" "How might reading be better incorporated with content area instruction and with the newly mandated emphasis on writing?"

In answering these questions, there are five basic areas Pat must attend to each year in attempting to ensure that the class will run smoothly and that learning will be maximized. Classroom management and the complementary problem of student discipline can be addressed in these five large categories (Emmer et al., 1982; Mangieri, 1980; Wayson & Pinnell, 1982).

1. *Organizing the Room and Materials.* The work Pat has done to prepare the physical arrangement of the room and the ways materials are stored and distributed help to ensure a smoothly running classroom. Pat stores materials used daily on shelves where they can be reached easily. She stores other items, those needed later in the year or only on rare occasions, away from the center of activity. This organization is facilitated by a system of student helpers who take turns distributing, collecting, and sorting materials. This arrangement is beneficial for the large number of middle school students like Jessica who need physical activity and find it immensely difficult to remain seated throughout the entire instructional period.

Pat has found that developing small "up and doing" tasks, which are assigned systematically to the largest possible number of her students each day, helps students like Jessica get the activity they need. When a lesson section is completed, no fewer than half a dozen jobs are assigned on a rotating basis up and down the rows of chairs. Most of these jobs require the students to get up, move, write, count, or distribute things, and return to their chairs. Students anticipate their responsibilities and enjoy the 30 seconds of moving about. It is not a perfect system, but Pat feels that her students are more attentive as a result.

Pat's bulletin boards reflect her flair for art and a pride in her classroom. She uses the boards for displaying class rules, "perfect" papers, and usually a motivational expression of the importance of literacy or some other generally positive theme, with a seasonal touch.

Pat's neat rows of chairs face the largest of the two chalkboards behind her desk. She takes some pride in the tidiness and symmetry of this arrangement, which, in her estimation, maximizes on-task behavior in her students. All in all, her room reflects her perception of an efficient classroom.

2. *Planning for Self-Discipline.* The rules of the school, stated in the handbook students receive during orientation, are included on a poster in Pat's room. She wishes to emphasize what is considered appropriate in general terms within the school. Her class rules echo and embellish the school's general guidelines and reflect a consistency within her teaching team. She thought long and hard about rules, how to communicate and enforce them, and how to express them in ways that do not confuse her students. Expectations for the duties required during homeroom, class start-up, bathroom and library passes, tardiness and absence, the proper format for assignments, and discussion and movement during instruction are laid out clearly and colorfully on her largest bulletin board. Pat has been diligent over the years in adding, editing, and altering the displays of expectations in her classroom.

3. *Beginning the Year.* The basic structure of her classroom is in place almost immediately. Pat spends much of her time during the first week of classes ensuring that students understand and can respond well to her guidelines and rules. With each new activity, Pat adds to the students' understanding of how the structure and the instructional activ-

One classroom management style emphasizes orderliness and consistency.

ity work together.

She began day one last fall with her Four A's routine, which would be consistent throughout the year: Attention, Attendance, Administrative tasks, and Assignments. Having initiated the class period this way, she could conduct whatever lesson she had planned with confidence that the class was "with" her. The class ended with another set of activities that became a daily routine.

During that first week, she wanted to make the students feel comfortable and successful in her room. Therefore, she made every effort to keep the classes in-

teresting, with each student's success being the focus of her activities. Having developed a generally positive attitude in the first five days of school, her job for the rest of the year will be easier if she maintains the controlled atmosphere she has established.

If Pat has a problem here, it is with students like Teddi who might be characterized as *groaners*. Teddi gets bored easily with routine, a common quality of middle schoolers. Despite Pat's efforts to keep things positive, her room does seem to have a regularity that grates on Teddi. However, routine is one of the qualities of

Pat's room that she works hard to establish. To keep the interest of students like Teddi, while still implementing her established standard procedure, Pat must emphasize their interests and successes as well as the routine.

4. *Grading and Evaluating.* Pat has been careful to promote a positive attitude about the work required in her classes. Along with posting samples and guidelines for assignments, she has determined the frequency with which she needs to grade students and the regularity with which she will give feedback to members of the class about their progress. During class discussion, for example, she works hard to include everybody in the activity.

Grading generally is based on a percentage of the total number possible. Pat is as objective as possible in her grading so the students know that their personalities and attitudes do not affect their grades. Students are given progress reports every three weeks during each grading period, and phone calls and conferences with parents are a regular part of Pat's planning period.

Pat's students are familiar with her disciplinary system, which makes her handling of off-task or disruptive behavior minimally intrusive into teaching and learning. The assertive disciplinary procedures (Canter, 1976) she uses include a visible record of each day's infractions and clear consequences for each. She recently added incentives for consistently high marks and good conduct. As with the more negative consequences in her system, these incentives are fully comprehended by the students. Pat has a controlled classroom, focusing on the students, the curriculum, and her own instruction.

5. *Maintaining a Management System.* The key to maintaining Pat's system is consistency after the system is established. This is not to say that fine tuning is not allowed or encouraged, because that is a necessary part of anything that goes on in schools. New students, fire drills, team field trips, or whole team activities that alter the day's schedule require Pat to adjust the way she handles the class. However, by carefully monitoring her students when they are in her class, by identifying and stopping misbehavior, and by focusing on governance by the rules, not the teacher, she manages her classroom effectively. This management style has allowed her to teach her reading and language arts lessons in a manner with which she is comfortable and effective.

Pat begins each class period 15 seconds after the bell, allowing time for settling in. Having gotten the attention of the class, she takes attendance, discusses or hands out materials from the office or team, indicates exactly what materials the students will need for the period's activities (spending time to give her "look" to those who indicate that a needed item is not in their possession), and then presents a summary of the class agenda.

She presents the concept, skill, or reading materials that will be the focus of the lesson and attempts to elicit responses from the students. She uses an overhead projector for all of the board work she does with her classes, which allows her to maintain eye contact while she writes and leads the discussion. It also allows her to have a record of what she wrote that day. Pat uses questions to shape the discussion and is patient with students who must fumble about in their materials to come up with a response. She tolerates no calling out, and calls on students randomly, sometimes when hands are raised, sometimes not. She tolerates some whispering and mumbling if she feels it indicates involvement in the topic, and while she moves about the room, she often allows students to work quietly in pairs if the written work is ungraded. Pat can cover quite a lot of material in a short period of time, and students know they've been working hard when the end of the period arrives.

Summary of Pat's Seventh Grade

In reflecting upon Pat's classroom management, her professional preparation is a good place to begin (George & Lawrence, 1982). Pat was trained as a secondary English teacher. Although she is a member of a team and now focuses on reading, she is basically more oriented toward English and American literature than she is toward the reading problems of students who enter her classroom. It is safe to say that regardless of the individual needs of the students who walk in the door, Pat is likely to conduct her instruction, management, and discipline in substantially the same way.

Each year, Pat works to improve her management style to best suit her teaching style. Part of Pat's professional responsibility is to stay current in her field and in her teaching. As education research and Pat's own reflections on classroom experiences challenge her initial training, she alters her teaching and management styles.

Pat's classroom is good for certain things and not so good for others. For example, metacognitive skills that grow out of students monitoring their own learning cannot be taught effectively in a classroom like Pat's where the teacher monitors everything. By the end of the year, Pat may sense this and make new adjustments in her program. Although Pat has not sensed it, there is also a problem with leadership in her classroom. Frederica, for example, seems to have some leadership ability among her gum popping crowd of hair combers in the back corner. Channeling Frederica's strength of personality into academically productive action is a challenge Pat will soon face in the ongoing development of her classroom.

David's Eighth Grade

David initially was trained as an elementary teacher. His early visions of his career were of working with first and second graders, helping young children learn the basics of language and literacy. When he was first certified, he was fully prepared to handle the entire curriculum for a class of 28 students. However, his vision did not include students with the kinds of interests and needs that his eighth graders have—sex, the freedoms and responsibilities of adulthood, and ethical issues. Yet he has worked hard to be the best middle school teacher he can be.

David's class is a group of eighth graders in a parochial school. He has attended to many of the same issues Pat has worked on to ensure that his class runs smoothly and efficiently. However, both the appearance of David's classroom and its activities are immensely different from Pat's.

In his school, a single teacher is responsible for the entire curriculum for the eighth grade. Because the school lacks the resources available in public schools to convene and pay curriculum committees, it defines the curriculum as "the textbook content." Therefore, there is little variation in what students are supposed to learn. How well and in what manner they learn are the prerogatives of the teacher. There are no "reading" books as such, so David provides reading instruction in content areas, vocabulary, and study skills. David thinks these areas are requirements of each discipline, and he puts them together with writing and oral language when implementing his literacy program.

Last summer David attended workshops on cooperative learning and student teams in the classroom (Glasser, 1987; Johnson & Johnson, 1975; Johnson et al., 1984; Slavin, 1982). In his classroom, students are involved in most decisions about what particulars in a given discipline will be pursued and about how the class will conduct itself to learn and master the knowledge in those areas. David is convinced that his team approach helps him meet the needs of all the youngsters in his heterogeneous group, and that it will serve to support the literacy program he has planned. Although the reality of his classroom is immensely different from Pat's, David's approach to creating a management system is not much different from hers. The five critical areas of classroom management focus on how his approach differs.

1. *Organizing the Room and Materials.* David has carefully arranged the writing, resource, and other materials so that when one group sends a student to get supplies or conduct business, no other group is bothered. Since students stay in the room for most of the day, David can have his students store most books and supplies in their desks, while Pat cannot.

David's bulletin boards include much the same content as Pat's. However, they lack the mature artistry and slick professional look one sees in most classrooms. This is because everything put on the walls (class rules, published writing, book reviews, and even the standard seasonal or thematic encouragement) is planned, produced, and displayed by students.

The importance of this style of management is clear when one reflects upon questions like the three Pat asked. To meet identified needs of this age group, for example, David is interested in giving everyone opportunities for meaningful participation in their school, physical activity, and self-exploration (Dorman, Lipsitz, & Verner, 1985; Emmer et al., 1982). By arranging the room in a manner that stresses sharing, either through placement of chairs in circles or through other peer-to-peer working arrangements, students assume roles as equals in the ways they use reading, writing, and conversation to communicate with one another and the teacher.

In more traditional classrooms like Pat's, students with high energy levels need provisions to allow them to move about. The teacher who assigns students responsibility as distributors, collectors, or maintainers of the instructional materials also is trying to provide time to get up and move about and an opportunity to assume and execute responsibility. These are identified needs of children this age (Dorman, 1981). However teachers do this, and however well-intentioned those managerial moves are, the arrangements must be evaluated on the basis of whether they complement the general instructional approach of the teacher.

2. *Planning for Self-Discipline.* The classroom is a sea of movement and sound. David believes that in order for language and literacy to be taught in a way that is both meaningful and effective, the classroom must be filled with communication. He has established an orientation at the beginning of each day, with decisions being made under his supervision on the amount of time to be spent on each of the various projects and on study in the curricular areas. Students then begin their various group and individual tasks. Furniture is moved, within-group assignments are made, and lessons designed by David to meet the needs of specific groups or subgroups are begun. Students take roll, collect or distribute money or communications from the office, and place all appropriate documents and other items in the various In/Out boxes on David's desk. It is easier to see how *self*-discipline is developing for David's students than it is in Pat's room. Movement to and from the library, bathroom, and other areas of the building and campus are all coordinated so that David can be available as needed and informed about everything.

3. *Beginning the Year.* David must be more careful than Pat in initiating his year. Most students are accustomed to teachers being completely in charge and telling students precisely what to do. Therefore, David must be careful how to initiate his students into a different role than they expect. The introductory teaching of group process roles, the art of generating a consensus, shared decision making, and cooperative attitudes of "positive interdependence" (Glasser, 1987) takes much longer than Pat's first week; yet David's task must be accomplished early to ensure that the classroom will run productively and smoothly during the year.

During the first weeks of school, Lena was a management challenge for David. Like many middle schoolers, Lena had a problem understanding the structure and limits in David's classroom. She asked a lot of technical loophole kinds of questions that pulled the class or group away from the content of a task and into critical discussions of what was a legitimate process within David's class. It was several weeks before the statement of class rules was composed in a way that allowed the class to respond to Lena's queries and allowed her to become a productive group member.

4. *Grading and Evaluating.* In nearly every subject there is some form of grouping that puts students in cooperative work patterns rather than in individual competitive patterns. Grades are awarded to groups. Like Pat's, David's grading is objective, but the focus is on the correctness of the group's critical consensus rather than on an individual right answer. Even tests are group ef-

forts. These procedures are no less well-defined and understood by David's students than they are by Pat's. However, the relationships between people in David's classroom during most instructional experiences are quite different from those found in Pat's class. The focus of attention is more on what the students are doing than on what David does. He is positive in questioning his students about both their production and their procedures. He makes points about proper and improper group procedures, the value of productive initiative, and the results of poor planning or irresponsibility on the part of groups or group members. Students ask for advice about procedure, information on the location of and access to resources, and clarifications about the objectives of the curriculum and potential benefits of their experiences with the content.

This does not mean that all students naturally benefit from David's system. Pete is a top student who rails against working with his less able peers, whom he calls "ding-dongs." He wants to strike out on his own, intent on finding the "right answer," which he has been taught will bring him recognition and success. Rae, on the other hand, is so quiet she often seems to become lost in the group. She is well liked and seems pleasant, but she never responds critically to reading, to experiences within the classroom, or to the opinions of her peers, even when some of them offer relatively non-threatening opportunities for self-exploration and independence.

David's desire to respond to these natural differences in personalities, while at the same time helping students feel competent and successful, forces him to read about and discuss his system with colleagues daily. He is not dissuaded from the approach he has taken, for his commitment to the theoretical underpinnings of cooperative learning is strong. He is aware, however, that managerial responses consistent with that theory and supportive to these children are constantly under development.

5. *Maintaining a Management System.* David's maintenance system is more complex than Pat's. Initiation during the first few weeks of school represents the beginning of a process. Every week some new aspect of cooperation, communication, and group process must be addressed and handled. Because of David's strong beliefs in communication and literacy, issues must be discussed and "composed" by the entire class. David asks a doubting colleague, "How else will they learn to think and respond critically in a literate manner?" New students, disruptions, feedback on performance, and grading are individual in their impact, but the entire class has been given a share in the determination of disciplinary procedures and record keeping.

Today, David began his day with reports from the chairpersons of his various social studies groups, each of which is studying a different Middle Eastern country. One group found the addresses of most of the consulates for the countries under study and prepared a list to place on the bulletin board for the other groups to use. They are clearly proud of their "find," and all members of the group seem to need to add a comment to their chair's report. David announces that the librarian has requested that no more than two groups come to the library at one time, since the size of her collection on the Middle East is rather limited. After a brief discussion about sending only representatives from each group, the groups quickly decide who needs to go early and which groups can wait until later in the day or until tomorrow. David begins to consider aloud the question of determining a due date for this large group project and consults with the groups about their progress. Students observe David as he "juggles" aloud the needs of six groups that have operated well or poorly. Some of the groups are waiting for data from the library or the mail. One group is beset by a member's illness, and another by a total lack of direction.

David observes to the class that some of the groups will finish ahead of others, and the class discusses how early groups could most productively spend their time on preparing their presentations and beginning to plan their science projects on solar energy while waiting for the others. When they arrive at a date, most of the students write the date on their project folders and begin mumbling about their plans for the day. In spending time on such matters, David is demonstrating his desire to lead his students to manage their time well across many different curriculum areas, rather than requiring them to meet his due date.

Summary of David's Eighth Grade

As with Pat, some of David's curriculum and some of his teaching styles do not coincide with the way he conducts his classroom management. In a demo-

cratically oriented classroom, the entire text (the stated curriculum) cannot be covered. Neither can David guarantee that the basic skills arranged into grade-level–specific, end-of-year tests will be covered in a lesson dedicated to their mastery. David accepts that his class's scores vary on the skills tests. Scores seem to go up and down according to the enthusiasm he can generate within his group activities for the kind of precision and right answer orientation on which the tests dwell. Still, David fervently believes that if all teachers embrace the same orientation to literacy that he does, all the really important skills will be learned and will be learned better than in classes like Pat's. This is not to say that Pat can or should emulate David, only that David's orientation to literacy and dedication to his students as language learners are most productive when expressed in the management style he creates.

Just like Pat, David knows halfway through each academic year that his room is an imperfect place in which to teach the reading, language, and attitudes about literacy that he treasures. Differences in David's initial preparation as an elementary teacher set him apart from Pat's departmentalized orientation. Differences in their assigned teaching positions, in their inservice work, in their university course work, and in their classroom experience have brought them to different places as professionals.

Although many differences exist, there is a similarity in the needs of Pat's and David's students and in the teachers' concerns with student achievement. David is interested in the same three questions

Regardless of their classroom management styles, all teachers hope that their students will develop the reading habit.

that Pat asked herself. Pat's classroom management restricts the choices she feels she can make to promote achievement in her classes, while David's exposure and subsequent commitment to empowering students in a group-oriented classroom have led him to establish a much different management system.

Judd's Multigrade Classroom

Judd was trained as a middle school teacher. He knows much about the characteristics of middle school students and their educational needs (Johnston & Markle, 1986), and like Pat, he is in complete control of his classroom. Also like Pat, Judd is the reading and writing teacher on a team of teachers. However, instead of seeing his role as a supportive one, he feels in many ways that his classroom is a haven from all the other classes. What he does is not isolated from his other team members' activities, but he believes that reading and literacy deserve more than support status. In Judd's mind, communication and the uses of language allow students to reason through and record their thoughts, which are worthy objectives for children of any age, particularly middle schoolers. Judd expects his team members who specialize in a single subject to teach the children the content area reading and writing that support development in those disciplines. He offers a place where students from his sixth/seventh grade team can coordinate and integrate learning both from other classes and from their own lives through their self-selected reading and writing.

Judd participates in all of the experiences through which he leads his students. When students are engaged in freewriting, library research, publication, or careful reading, they can look up to see that Judd also is doing this activity. Each student experiences readership, authorship, and critical analysis of compositions in both reader and author roles. As a result of these experiences, children become involved in discussions about how authors decide to publish and how they determine what to revise. Judd is a student of the process school of literacy and runs what he would call a whole language classroom (Altwerger, Edelsky, & Flores, 1987). As a veteran of writing process training in his graduate work, Judd has read most of the books published on this student-oriented approach to developing the thinking and language skills necessary to read and write well in any discipline (Atwell, 1987; Calkins, 1986; Graves, 1983; Hansen, 1987; Stock, 1983). The entire class does not focus on one set of reading or writing objectives at the same time. The curriculum is driven by the approach called kid watching (Goodman, 1978).

Teachers can respond in a variety of ways to the three questions that have been identified as ongoing challenges for reading teachers. The curriculum teachers choose, the instruction they offer, and the management/discipline they attempt to develop must all work in concert to maximize reading and literacy competence. Judd's managing style differs from both Pat's and David's, as an evaluation of the five categories of management shows.

1. *Organizing the Room and Materials.* Judd's room doesn't look like a normal classroom. There are desks in the middle of the room, but around the outside are cubby holes where small groups of students can "scooch" up to the wall and read one of the several books they have going, write a letter to an author or an editor, or discuss some issue of literary substance with one another without bothering their classmates. The room has an abundance of reference materials, hundreds of adolescent literature paperbacks, and crates of folders with students' names. The bulletin boards are full of student work, and scattered throughout the room are quotations, both from famous reading and writing experts and from the not-so-famous ones who are Judd's students. Rules, general and few in number, are posted in Judd's rough printing near the front of the room. Judd is not much of an artist, and adornments in the room seem more serendipitous than planned. There may be a play advertisement, a movie poster (Hollywood's rendition of one of his favorite adolescent novels), student writing, and notes from students to Judd or to other students that are particularly telling about their experiences in developing literacy. Judd's room looks like a cross be-

tween a busy, bustling place and Pat's orderly room.

2. *Planning for Self-Discipline.* Judd's class is a structured environment for only a small part of the six instructional periods each day. Most of the time, it is a workshop for readers or writers. With all of these different activities going on, Judd runs the class the way it makes sense to him. The rules he uses are designed less to promote order than to ensure productivity. The organization of the management of this class is an outgrowth of students working productively and trying to keep out of one another's way. Still, some students require more encouragement than others because they are less sure of themselves and their roles. Judd spends a few minutes each day in a whole class meeting, finding out exactly what all students are doing and what their plans are for the class period. He also checks on their need for individual conferences or inclusion in group lessons (Atwell, 1987). Through this short meeting, Judd can inform everyone about others' work and about his expectations for all class members. Individual conferences give him an opportunity to meet with each student at least once a week. These 5 or 10 minute conferences are amicable and task-oriented times for communication and reflection. The culture of communication and literacy that Judd wants to develop for his students is unmistakable.

3. *Beginning the Year.* Judd begins the year with demonstrations of how he and his students will be working within the class. For example, he shows students that he values communication and liter-

acy by conducting short daily coaching lessons, by discussing the ways in which reading and writing may be done, and by praising the wide range of behaviors that constitute literate conduct. He also provides them with direct experiences in communicating appropriately with other students and with the teacher, using writing (through notes placed in one another's files) and brief on-task discussions on matters such as an author's style, identification of one's audience, or the manner in which engaging books include the author's voice. Throughout, Judd emphasizes productivity, confidence in each student's ability to be productive, and the expectation that students serve their peers well as both reading audiences and producing authors. All students read and write from the first day, regardless of how they have previously considered themselves in the realm of literacy.

Critical analysis of a peer's writing (a poem or longer work), conferences about issues that trouble the reader or writer, and sharing of production and literary experiences are introduced during the first week. By the second week, some students are beginning to ask about forming book discussion groups, selecting library materials, writing topics, and coauthorship.

4. *Grading and Evaluating.* In Judd's opinion, competitive grading is neither informative nor productive in a setting that focuses on process. His grading is a combination of subjective and objective judgments about effort and productivity. Determinations of productivity are generally related to publication, panel mem-

bership, or some other kind of sharing or performance that displays the composed ideas of the student.

Since there is so much natural individualization within this class, some students find themselves uncomfortable in the academic spotlight. It is especially distressing for students like Lamar to be asked to write about things they know when they may not have learned much about the world and academics in five years of schooling. Judd commonly asks his students to write about what they know best, and that is themselves. Lamar was unwilling to take the social and psychological risk of displaying his knowledge (and ignorance) of himself until he discovered that Judd was more than willing to publicly take that risk, and that the class tended to be supportive and often complimentary.

Talk is a valuable commodity in Judd's class. Those who converse too little are as liable to be corrected as those who like to gab. Judd develops a discipline focused on managing the talk to optimize literacy. In Judd's view, a quiet class silences literacy learning.

Expectations are high for all of Judd's heterogeneously grouped students because he feels that no nonreaders or nonwriters walk through his door, only those who may not have begun to read and write. Absences or lack of intensity during the class only mean that the student must be productive at home or in other settings where supervision is available to verify that time is spent reading, working on research, or preparing manuscripts. As should be clear from this description, Judd tolerates neither illiteracy nor aliteracy in his students.

5. *Maintaining a Management System.* As students become accustomed to the workshop atmosphere and schedule, they generally are eager to get to class and disappointed when it ends, even through the work is hard. In this respect, Judd's class echoes David's experience. Middle school students working on their own projects tend to be more dedicated to efficient classroom operation than when working under other circumstances. Of course, rules occasionally must be reviewed and reinforced, but this is usually done one to one between Judd and the students. Managerial adjustments still must be made daily for some students. Tucker, for instance, is a big boy who tends to bully his way around the school, displaying little ability to communicate. Judd's classroom is set up in such a way that Tucker has been forced to become conversant, initially with Judd and eventually with other students, about their attempts to make sense of their lives with reading and writing. Tucker has falteringly produced responses to articles, books, and analyses of writing that pertain to nuances of vocabulary selection and sentence construction. Judd is certain that over time Tucker will learn to conduct his academic and social affairs outside the classroom with more than just physical strength.

Certainly, Judd must accept the leadership of the classroom, and just as certainly, these students are open to all of the silliness and seriousness that beset middle school students. They are efficient and effective in most of the lessons, workshops, and conversations within Judd's class.

This morning, Judd began as he always does, with his gradebook open. He uses four or five gradebooks a year because every day he records in them the students' daily plans, along with grades given that day. The roll call is not answered by "here," but by a brief statement of each of the student's intentions for the class period. Examples of their reports (and Judd's responses) include: "Finishing a first draft of a poem" (Okay.), "Library to take this dumb book back" (That's three this week; bring back five.), "Writing an article for the *Flame* (school newspaper) with Clarice" (That's due Friday; can you make it?), "Can we do our panel today?" (How much time will you need?), "Could I see you today?" (Yep, we're due.), "Chapter 16 in my book" (Three days is too many for one chapter; do we need to discuss this?). This takes perhaps four minutes. Then as Judd writes the time schedule for the day, the class begins to break up.

Some students work alone with a sharp pencil and a pad of paper; others begin chatting. Judd clears his throat pointedly, and they get down to business. Judd then settles in at his desk with the four students who are sharing their understandings about *Where the Red Fern Grows* (Rawls, 1973). This period he will spend 20 minutes with this group, 20 more in 5-minute segments with various students who need conferences, and the remainder of the time overseeing the panel and ensuing discussion.

Summary of Judd's Multigrade Classroom

By focusing on developing a culture of communication and literacy, Judd matches his teaching style to his class-room management system. He learns about the inadequacies of his management system from his students as an intregal part of his daily duties. Therefore, his refinements in management and instruction occur daily, not yearly. Judd responds to his students' efforts and assists them in troublesome areas. His "workshop" classroom provides a medium for individual students to explore, discuss, and improve their writing and reading (Atwell, 1987; Hansen, 1987).

Like David, Judd has created a social support system for his students. Unlike David, Judd has his students create individual products. Judd has generated a classroom that builds on nearly all the qualities identified as supportive of children of this age.

Student needs and teacher concerns are the same in Judd's class as in Pat's and David's. The questions he asks are the same. The difference is that the students in this setting are working as hard as the teacher to answer the questions. Sharing the load among 30 interested parties in each class is an efficient and effective way to handle the individualization in which everyone is interested.

The Future

There is no single way to manage middle school teaching contexts. The middle school represents a transition between the traditionally student-centered, self-contained elementary school and the content-oriented, 50-minute instructional periods at the secondary level. Tradition has yet to take hold in the relatively young middle school movement. This places great demands for creativity on teachers like Pat, David, and Judd.

These teachers have addressed the important instructional questions through differing approaches to classroom management.

How *does* one promote reading with the generally unskilled and uninterested readers at the lower end of the achievement range? Pat does it through a focus on basic skills and strict grading of assignments with immediate feedback from the teacher. David does it through group membership and responsibility. The more advanced readers and writers work hard with the less accomplished members so that the group grades will be as high as possible. Judd assists his students in selecting reading materials and writing topics, demonstrates his own reading and writing efforts, and maintains one to one contact.

How *can* a teacher ensure that the top students get as much attention as the lower ones? Pat uses the traditional methods of grades and rewards to let her top students know how they are doing. She then attempts to enrich her assignments to challenge all of her students on their level. David sometimes places these students throughout his groups as potential leaders and resources, and at other times places them together to learn from one another. He spends time ensuring that group tasks are as challenging to them as to their less advanced peers. Judd's work with higher performing students is identical to his work with the lower functioning ones. The individualization in the workshop provides a natural place to seek the level of challenge appropriate to the student.

How *might* reading be better incorporated with content area instruction and integrated with an emphasis on writing? Pat is working hard to include more selections from the content textbooks from her students' other classes. Pat also is considering using her class as a place for developing leadership for some of the activities and experiences in her teaching team's larger content units. Writing, which builds on the class's daily lesson, is more likely to occur in short sessions at the end of her class. It comes in the form of learning logs that children use to reflect daily on their learning. David is attempting to do more with less (Sizer, 1985) by focusing on larger issues in science and social studies (abandoning a significant amount of the text content) and then studying the large issues more deeply. This can mean doing social studies to the exclusion of science for three weeks at a time (and vice versa). It includes a lot of content-specific writing and reading, however, and that is what David is striving for. Judd attempts to develop a closer connection between all of the disciplines all of the time. He encourages many real world kinds of projects in individual research and inquiry: eulogies, advertisements, oral histories, commentaries or reviews, and correspondence with practicing scientists and historians. Through these projects Judd enriches the content of his fellow teachers as well as the competence of his students.

Middle school teachers who teach reading can address these kinds of enduring concerns by orchestrating their general instructional orientation, their manner of responding to individual middle schoolers (and to the ubiquitous social groups that constantly evolve within any given class), and the classroom management that forms a teaching context.

If the teacher wishes to teach preparation for standardized testing, the classroom management style should parallel and complement those instructional objectives. Teaching children to give the right answer to skills questions would not work well in a classroom that asks for student group decisions. Similarly, teaching communication skills and critical response will not be very successful in a classroom that is quiet, subdued, and full of students working on their own activities. Only certain combinations of curricular emphasis, instructional approach, and classroom management work well together. At one time or another all teachers find themselves in the position of having a less than optimal combination of these three dynamics of teaching. In fact, because of frequent changes in curriculum, managing styles, and the instruction they wish to offer, teachers are constantly reminded that their classrooms are less than perfect. Changes must be implemented, and teachers must recognize that effective management is a means, not an end. Literacy, not full-time engagement in academic tasks, is the ultimate goal.

The context teachers provide for their classes defines the experiences of the students. Teachers who are comfortable with giving instruction in reading and learning skills that are discipline specific, teachers who work to integrate several disciplines while distributing the responsibilities of teaching and learning, and teachers who work alongside students in a workshop full of demonstrations about literacy may have different orientations when it comes to maximizing achievement within their curricula. However, all these teachers are motivated by the same kinds of concerns about their students. Good teachers are constantly working to respond by changing their classroom contexts to meet those needs that dictate the conditions of their students' growth in reading and literacy.

References

Alexander, William M., & George, Paul S. (1981). *The exemplary middle school*. New York: Holt, Rinehart and Winston.

Altwerger, Bess, Edelsky, Carol, & Flores, Barbara. (1987). Whole language: What's new? *The Reading Teacher*, *41*, 144-154.

Atwell, Nancie. (1987). *In the middle: Writing and reading and learning with adolescents*. Montclair, NJ: Boynton/Cook.

Calkins, Lucy M. (1986). *The art of teaching writing*. Portsmouth, NH: Heinemann.

Canter, Lee. (1976). *Assertive discipline: A take charge approach for today's educators*. Santa Monica, CA: Canter & Associates.

Cummings, Carol, Nelson, Cliff, & Shaw, Dian. (1980). *Teaching makes a difference*. Edmonds, WA: Teaching, Inc.

Dorman, Gayle. (1981). *Middle grades assessment program*. Chapel Hill, NC: Center for Early Adolescence.

Dorman, Gayle, Lipsitz, Joan, & Verner, Pat. (1985, March). Improving schools for young adolescents. *Educational Leadership*, *42*, 44-49.

Doyle, Walter. (1986). Classroom organization and management. In Merlin Wittrock (Ed.), *Handbook of research on teaching* (3rd ed., pp. 392-431). New York: Macmillan.

Emmer, Edmund T., Evertson, Carolyn M., Sanford, Julie P., Clements, Barbara S., & Worsham, Murray E. (1982). *Organizing and managing the junior high classroom* (R & D Center Paper No. 6151). Austin, TX: Research and Development Center for Teacher Education.

George, Paul S., & Lawrence, Gordon. (1982). *Handbook for middle school teaching*. Glenview, IL: Scott, Foresman.

Glasser, William. (1987). *Control theory in the classroom*. New York: Harper & Row.

Goodman, Yetta. (1978). Kid watching: An alternative to testing. *The National Elementary School Principal*, 57, 22-27.

Graves, Donald H. (1983). *Writing: Teachers and children at work*. Portsmouth, NH: Heinemann.

Hansen, Jane. (1987). *When writers read*. Portsmouth, NH: Heinemann.

Hunter, Madeline. (1976). *Improved instruction*. El Segundo, CA: TIP.

Johnson, David W., & Johnson, Roger T. (1975). *Learning together and alone*. Englewood Cliffs, NJ: Prentice Hall.

Johnson, David W., Johnson, Roger T., Holubec, Edith J., & Roy, Patricia. (1984). *Circles of learning*. Alexandria, VA: Association for Supervision and Curriculum Development.

Johnston, J. Howard, & Markle, Glenn C. (1986). *What research says to the middle level practitioner*. Columbus OH: National Middle School Association.

Lipsitz, Joan. (1979, September/October). Adolescent development: Myths and realities. *Children Today*, 8(5), 2-7.

Mangieri, John N. (1980). Characteristics of an effectively organized classroom. In Diane Lapp (Ed.), *Making reading possible through effective classroom management* (pp. 10-26). Newark, DE: International Reading Association.

Ogle, Donna. (1986). K-W-L: A teaching model that develops active reading of expository text. *The Reading Teacher*, 39, 564-570.

Rawls, Wilson. (1973). *Where the red fern grows*. New York: Doubleday.

Sizer, Theodore R. (1985). *Horace's compromise: The dilemma of the American high school*. Boston, MA: Houghton Mifflin.

Slavin, Robert E. (1982). *Cooperative learning: Student teams*. Washington, DC: NEW.

Stock, Patricia. (1983). *Forum: Essays on theory and practice in the teaching of writing*. Upper Montclair, NJ: Boynton/Cook.

Wayson, William W., & Pinnell, Gay Su. (1982). Creating a living curriculum for teaching self-discipline. In David L. Duke (Ed.), *Helping teachers manage classrooms*. Alexandria, VA: Association for Supervision and Curriculum Development.

PART TWO

Curriculum and Instruction in Reading

PRELUDE

Central to middle school reading are the questions "What should I teach?" "How should I teach?" and "How should I evaluate whether I was effective?" This section attempts to answer these questions. Chapter 5 provides a framework for literacy instruction; Chapters 6 and 7 suggest what should be taught in the cognitive/metacognitive and affective domains, respectively; Chapter 8 deals with instruction; and Chapter 9 focuses on evaluation. You will note that all five chapters place emphasis on writing as well as on reading. This reflects our twin beliefs that we are engaged broadly in literacy development rather than narrowly in the development of reading acquisition, and that reading and writing are reciprocal language modes best conceptualized and taught in integrated ways.

Content Knowledge in Reading: Creating a New Framework

Charles W. Peters

A FUNDAMENTAL GOAL of middle schools is comprehension of content knowledge in areas such as English, science, and social studies. The purpose of this chapter is to propose a conceptual framework for balancing the goal of content knowledge and strategy application.

Factors Influencing Reading Instruction

Despite theoretical advancements in how reading and learning are conceptualized, middle school reading instruction has remained largely unchanged for decades. The hope for a major curricular reorganization generated when junior high schools were first converted to middle schools has almost disappeared. An outdated structure for reading remains. This section examines four interrelated factors that contribute to this lack of progress in reading.

5

Using Outmoded Organizational Structures

The way middle school reading is taught has been influenced by how it has been organized. Typically, middle school reading programs are organized in one of two ways. The first reflects an elementary perspective in which reading is taught as a separate subject. Frequently, the basal reader is the primary means of instruction, and formal developmental reading instruction is usually completed by the end of sixth grade. If students need additional or special help in reading, it is generally offered in the form of a separate remedial class. When this perspective dominates, a skills-in-isolation approach to reading instruction often results. Instruction moves from one reading selection to another driven by the need to cover the next set of skills; thus skills are often presented in a nonintegrated context. As a result, reading is viewed as static, and content or domain knowledge is minimized or ignored.

The second organizational approach incorporates reading into the language arts curriculum. As students move from elementary to middle school, a separate class for reading usually is dropped after the sixth grade and merged with the language arts/English curriculum in the seventh or eighth grade. While it is better than the elementary perspective, reading as language arts/English has two limitations: (1) systematic transfer of learning strategies to other disciplines is minimized, and (2) narrative materials are the prevailing form of text. While language arts instruction can include how to read other types of materials in other disciplines, often it does not. Further, this approach assumes that the language arts/English teacher has knowledge of reading processes and has full responsibility for teaching students how to apply reading strategies to other disciplines. In fact, language arts/English teachers seldom possess knowledge of reading processes, and even when they do, they cannot be expected to assume total responsibility for reading because they have their own content to teach.

If learning across the curriculum is to occur, all content teachers must share responsibility for teaching reading strategies within their disciplines. This means we must offer a model for learning that views reading/writing in a broader context. Without such a perspective, middle schools will continue to provide limited literacy instruction.

Emphasizing Isolated Skills

A second factor influencing middle school reading is that reading is frequently viewed as a static, skills-driven process. This perspective assumes that determining the main idea of a poem is the same process as determining the main idea of a passage on the causes of the Civil War. Not only are there major structural differences between these two types of materials, but the prior knowledge required to interpret the two is much different. In other words, a skills-driven approach to reading ignores how the purposes of learning, the type of materials used, and the assigned task all influence strategy selection.

This static perspective is in sharp contrast to the current interactive view of reading in which readers build knowledge from previous experiences and use that information in conjunction with knowledge about the reading process to construct a holistic representation of a text. To do this, readers must be sensitive to the relationships among the various elements of information within a text so they can integrate new and old information into a complete whole. Inherent in this view of reading is the notion that readers construct meaning for a text as a function of the interaction among the reader, the text, and the context of the reading situation (Anderson et al., 1985; Wixson & Peters, 1984).

Much of what is taught about reading at the middle school level is not consistent with precepts that underlie the interactive view of reading. Peters (1984) examined some of the more widely recommended instructional activities (vocabulary enhancement, graphic organizers, questioning strategies) to ascertain how they addressed comprehension in light of the changing nature of comprehension instruction. He found that skills often were presented in isolation. And when some activities did utilize factors such as prior knowledge, text structure, and metacognitive knowledge, they were limited to one or two of these factors. For example, a teacher might explain graphic organizers but say nothing about varying this strategy as purpose, text, and task change.

Deemphasizing Domain Knowledge

Middle school reading also has been influenced by a tendency to minimize the role of domain knowledge, the transfer of knowledge to new learning situations, and the flexible use of knowledge. This is particularly significant at the middle school level since what students should be learning is how to apply strategies to a variety of content areas.

Research is increasingly pointing to the importance of domain knowledge in the learning process. As Rabinowitz and Glaser (1985) point out, people who exhibit highly competent performance have easy and fast mental access to relevant information, are able to view problem situations in qualitatively distinct ways, can use strategies effectively and flexibly, and have good metacognitive skills. Therefore, to construct meaning efficiently, readers must be able to access appropriate domain knowledge. Voss

(1986) corroborated this view by demonstrating that the level of one's domain knowledge influences its assimilation and retrieval. It seems clear that teachers should spend more time helping students acquire knowledge.

To this end, Spiro et al. (1987) recommended traversing or crisscrossing a topic from many different perspectives. Presenting information from multiple perspectives allows students to acquire a more integrated knowledge base, helping them move beyond surface level interpretations to deeper levels of understanding. However, implementing the notion of traversing selected topics in a systematic manner requires a different view of reading instruction; it means moving from a skills or a narrative-based approach to one in which content knowledge plays a greater role.

The role of domain knowledge is even more important in the transfer of knowledge to new learning situations. As Chi (1987) points out, transfer is impeded without a well-integrated knowledge base. If knowledge acquisition and integration are ignored in favor of teaching isolated skills or generic strategies, strategies do not transfer. For transfer to be enhanced, teachers must continually restructure domain knowledge under different types of learning situations. Consequently, domain knowledge plays an extremely important role in the application of strategies because transfer from one type of material to another is unlikely if students' domain knowledge is skimpy or poorly organized.

Pressure from National Reform Movements

A fourth factor inhibiting progress in middle school reading is the national reform movement for excellence in education that began in the early 1980s with reports such as *A Nation at Risk* (National Commission on Excellence in Education, 1983). The pressure created by these reports pushes the middle school curriculum in divergent directions. One type of reform calls for a predominantly content-oriented curriculum; another type wants to move the curriculum toward generic learning, where content knowledge is subjugated to a process approach. The first sees domain or content knowledge as the target; the second views development of the learning process as the goal. Each has potential implications for middle school reading and learning.

Content reform movement. In a series of recent national reports, the importance of teaching strategies is being reexamined. One of the more influential studies is the *Report on the First National Assessment of History and Literature* (Ravitch & Finn, 1987). In their report, Ravitch and Finn point out that many high school students lack basic history and literature knowledge. Because this information plays such an important role in interpreting human experience, they argue for a curriculum in which history and literature are more prominent and in which strategies are given a relatively low priority.

Some critics also believe there is a deficiency in what students are asked to read. In a study by Sewall (1987), a group of historians, authors, editors, and journalists examined fifth, eighth, and eleventh grade American history textbooks and found them to be poorly written and, in most cases, lacking substantive information about American history. They concluded that what these materials produce is a curiously disembodied style of history that describes what happened but not why. These findings are even more critical when one considers the dominant reliance on a single textbook at the middle school level (Sewall, 1988). While this may not be a startling finding for those who are familiar with the research on learning from text (Anderson & Armbruster, 1984; Britton & Black, 1985; Otto & White, 1982), it does provide additional ammunition to those who advocate a return to a predominantly content-oriented curriculum.

The arguments expressed in these studies are further bolstered by the works of Bloom (1987) and Hirsch (1987), who are critical of not only what but also how subjects are being taught at all levels of education. Hirsch advocates learning a body of culturally approved information that will enable students to live successfully as adults. The presumption is that by digesting bits of sanctioned knowledge, students will be better prepared to deal with the ambiguity, contradiction, and complexity of adult life. To Hirsch, skills have been overemphasized and information that constitutes our literate national culture has been underemphasized.

General skills movement. At the other end of the curricular reform continuum are those who advocate the use of generic learning strategies (Beyer, 1987,

1988; Chance, 1986). Those who support this perspective believe skills and strategies can be uniformly applied across a variety of content areas. In other words, skills are taught in a decontextualized manner where the goal is to learn skills without consideration for differences within and across the various content disciplines. Some of those who support this position believe that more time should be spent learning generic strategies such as problem solving so they can be applied to a variety of learning situations both inside and outside the classroom.

Striving for a Balanced Approach

The ultimate focus of middle school reading and writing must be more consistent with what Katz (1982) calls "critical literacy," in which a student builds knowledge from previous experiences and uses that information in conjunction with other knowledge (i.e., knowledge about strategy use and domain-specific knowledge) to interpret new learning situations. The key here is the learner's ability to use content and strategy knowledge in a flexible manner and to transfer it to new learning experiences. An approach that integrates both process and content facilitates this kind of knowledge acquisition.

When content teachers relinquish responsibility for teaching process, "appropriate" information is emphasized without regard for what Paris, Lipson, and Wixson (1983) call strategic learning. That is, students get little opportunity to apply learning strategies (process) across a variety of curricular areas. But when teachers emphasize strategy to the exclusion of content, they ignore the fact that domain knowledge influences strategy selection. A balance is needed between content and process.

A balance requires teachers to avoid separating the acquisition of knowledge from the process or strategy. For instance, most reading specialists view social studies as if it were a monolithic structure rather than as many different disciplines (anthropology, economics, geography, government, history, psychology, sociology) possessing structural, conceptual, and methodological differences (Peters, 1982; Peters & Hayes, 1989). History and geography, for instance, are two important social studies courses at the middle school level. While geography may deal with some of the same topics as history, it also involves examination of the earth's surface, the environment, and the people who inhabit various regions of the world. Two major features are involved: the natural or physical features and the cultural and human features (Backler & Stoltman, 1988). History, on the other hand, includes the study of conflicting forces such as wars and revolutions—violent upheavals of nations interpreted in a human context of causations often explained in terms of impact on institutions and on policies (Hegel, 1899, 1956; White, 1973). In short, historians look at causation differently than do geographers.

Since historians examine events in a human context of causations that are explained in terms of their impact on institutions and policies that exist within a specific historical context, these events are considered unique. Consequently, to some historians the past does not predict the future, and it is this uniqueness that explains historical phenomena. This is not necessarily true of physical geography, where events such as the formation of and the climate in certain regions are controlled by natural laws that are invariant and, as such, predictable.

The climate in Africa is different from the climate in Antartica but the factors that control these differences are not the same as those that control historical events. Therefore, causation is not viewed in the same manner. Another difference between the two is the methodology historians and geographers use to interpret the past: historians use diaries, documents, journals, newspapers, and letters, and geographers use maps, graphs, charts, demographic data, and measurement devices. This usually means examining the relationship between culture and the physical features of the earth.

Such distinctions are important because each implies a different approach to strategy. Different strategies are shaped by the thinking patterns typical of the various disciplines in social studies (Anderson & Armbruster, 1984) and require different approaches to the development of instructional support activities (Peters & Hayes, 1989). Students must be taught to see the differences in the structural composition of various disciplines and to make adjustments in how they read and think about topics within those fields. Thus, reading in social studies should not merely entail getting information from the printed page but also learning how to adjust for various structures when reading history, geogra-

phy, or government materials. Once students realize that these distinctions exist, they can use different strategies when reading history, biology, mysteries, or poetry.

If reading is taught from a generic skills perspective or if content is decontextualized to emphasize skills, however, content teachers conclude that their job is to take care of the content without worrying about teaching process because students will learn process from the reading teacher. If middle school reading programs are to improve, this must change.

Reconceptualizing the Reading Program

This section describes five recommendations for balancing reading programs and the instructional guidelines that emerge from these assumptions. The recommendations serve as a framework for restructuring middle school reading.

1. *Base reading programs on sound theoretical views of reading and learning.* One of the major weaknesses of the middle school reading program is its structure. To be consistent with what we know from research, the reading program must be more than another language arts course of which reading is one component. Learning across the curriculum (Katz, 1982) must be its primary focus so that the full range of topics and materials students encounter is supported. Most of the reading material will be informational rather than narrative because narrative is not the major type of material read at this level.

However, materials do not determine

program structure. Structure comes from the theoretical assumptions underlying reading as an interactive process. An interactive framework suggests that one must first establish a clear purpose for learning, which then dictates the type of material and strategies to be used. Goals must be placed in a larger context, one that reflects a recursive rather than a linear approach to learning. When learning is linear, students move through skill hierarchies; when learning is recursive, students accumulate and integrate knowledge.

2. *Integrate domain knowledge (content) with strategies when developing a reading program.* Domain knowledge is an important component in middle school reading and writing. Without sufficient domain knowledge, comprehension is impeded, strategies cannot be used appropriately, learning is fragmented, and transfer of knowledge is impaired. More attention needs to be given to how domain knowledge influences strategy usage, rather than focusing on either generic skills or skills that are applied to primarily literature-based materials.

Reading topics should be selected from content areas pertinent to the curriculum. By doing so, we avoid using contrived or irrelevant materials. The goal is to make a direct connection between the content areas students are pursuing in other courses and the reading class. Failure to make this connection relegates reading to an insignificant position. In contrast, the goal should be to create a reading environment that helps students shift their view of reading from a restricted perspective to one resem-

bling an integrated instructional environment. To do this, reading teachers must work more closely with content area teachers. Such collaborative efforts are important in order to help students apply strategies systematically across their many different subject matter classes.

A reading teacher adhering to this strategy would not select a nonfiction piece of material merely to expose students to that particular type of text. The teacher would address what topics students are likely to encounter in their other content classes, what type of nonfiction or informational text would best address these topics, the variety of purposes for which they might read this particular type of material, the types of strategies required to read the material, and how strategies change as assigned tasks change.

The instructional process would begin by selecting a topic frequently discussed in one of the middle school curricular areas. The goal is not to turn reading teachers into content teachers but to take familiar topics and plan activities that demonstrate to students how domain knowledge influences strategy usage and how to think about learning in a variety of contextual settings that link to students' other subject area classes.

The next step in the instructional planning process is the selection of materials. If the topic is plate tectonics in earth science, the material should come from an earth science textbook representative of the level students encounter in their earth science class. The selection can be the same or different from the one students already use in the regular earth science class, but the material should be used after the topic has been covered in their regular science class. There are two advantages to using a selection that students have previously encountered. First, it provides an opportunity to approach a topic from multiple perspectives. Students can read, write, and think about the topic from new vantage points. Topics used in this manner facilitate the integration of knowledge. Second, this technique allows students to explore how content influences the processes used to comprehend. While content determines process, this approach emphasizes how the two are inextricably linked.

Both content goals and process goals are important. Content goals focus on the important information in the text, thus helping the reading teacher avoid decontextualizing. Examples of content goals for a selection on plate tectonics are (1) understanding what is meant by plate tectonics, (2) understanding various theories that describe plate tectonics, and (3) understanding the strengths and weaknesses of each theory. Note that these goals focus on the global level of learning and emphasize holistic understanding of material. Process goals focus on the cognitive operations that underlie the student's interpretation of the reading materials. They are designed to help reading teachers make explicit some of the steps students must go through to understand content goals. Examples of process goals related to the content goals are understanding how to link evidence to a theory, how to compare various theories, and how to use adjunct aids to interpret theories. Content and process goals are important because they become the focal point around which all instruc-

tional activities are organized.

The next step is to transform the content and process goals into a series of integrated instructional activities. To facilitate student learning, these activities are divided into three phases: (1) before reading activities, where the emphasis is on the evaluation and activation of prior knowledge; (2) during reading activities, where the reading teacher models or guides students in the attainment of the identified goals; and (3) after reading activities, where additional application, evaluation, and transfer strategies are modeled (see Chapter 6, this volume). In the following paragraphs, each phase is described in the context of a lesson on plate tectonics.

Before reading. In the before reading phase, students engage in reading and writing activities designed to assess and activate prior knowledge. An example of such an activity is ACCESS (Peters & Hayes, 1989), in which students are asked to supply a variety of information about key concepts relating to a passage on plate tectonics (plates and boundaries) and to provide information about concepts related to the process goals (e.g., theory and evidence). (See Figure 1.) Each category at the top assesses different but related types of knowledge. Collectively, they assess each student's knowledge about plate tectonics. Consequently, the activity is more than a vocabulary test of unfamiliar terms; it is an assessment of students' understanding of the central points of the material.

A writing assignment also can be used to activate prior knowledge. Since plate tectonics deals with proving a scientific theory, students can be asked to write

Figure 1
Prior Knowledge Assessment

Words	Words that describe each term	Examples of the word	Give a definition of the word	How are the following words related?
Plates				Plates and Boundaries
Transform				
Boundaries				Transform and Plates
Theory				
Evidence				Theory and Evidence

Figure 2
During Reading Activity
Linking Evidence and Theory

A. *Claim*   Magnetic reversals support Plate Tectonic Theory.

   Reason

   Result

   Result

   Result

1. Molten rocks cool and harden with magnetic fields locked.

2. Iron particles in rocks become a permanent record.

3. Iron particles form series of stripes.

4. Each stripe presents a different period of time.

5. Each stripe can be dated.

Conclusion

B. *Claim*   The ocean floor is spreading.

   Reason

   Reason

   Reason

   Reason

Evidence

1. Older rocks further from ridge.

2. Plates are separating.

3. New molten rock pushed to the surface.

4. The age of the rock can be measured.

Conclusion

---

about one of their theories or views (e.g., boys are better at sports than girls or girls are more intelligent than boys) and to provide evidence to support their theory. Such activities can be the basis for discussion of theory and evidence. For example, is the statement "Girls are more intelligent than boys" a theory or a belief? What distinguishes the two, and why is it important to differentiate between them? What type of evidence do you need to prove a theory? Finally, why is it important to know terms like *theory* and *evidence* before reading a selection on plate tectonics?

During reading. During reading, content processing guides can be used. Their primary function is to juxtapose content with process by providing students with an explicit plan for how to read content materials (Peters & Carlsen, 1989; Peters & Hayes, 1989). Because the guides are structured to go from those that provide assistance to those that expect students to operate at a higher level of independence, they allow a gradual progression from teacher control to independent student control. They provide procedural steps that allow students to better understand the strategies used to generate responses and how those strategies vary as purpose, text, and task vary.

The first during reading content processing guide is shown in Figure 2. Its purpose is to help students understand how to causally link evidence to theory. Students are provided with an explicit plan that models the steps involved in this process, and are asked to tie together a sequence of reasons and results that support a claim made by the theory. Once students have placed the evidence in its proper causal

sequence, they must formulate a conclusion about how well the evidence supports the theory. Keep in mind that teaching causal reasoning is modeled because it is an important part of scientific reasoning. The activity is designed to help students make this connection.

Another example of such a during-reading guide is seen in Figure 3. The activity that focuses on evaluating theory about plate tectonics is designed to have students identify at least four claims that have been made to support the theory, find evidence from the text that supports the theory, identify any weaknesses associated with the evidence, make a judgment as to whether they believe the claim, and provide written justification to support their judgments.

This activity guides students through a process fundamental to understanding how scientists establish support for a theory. Thus, it provides a balance between content and process that is fundamental to an interactive model of reading.

After reading. This balance is further exemplified in three types of after reading activities. The first activity is designed to help students synthesize important ideas presented in the selection; the second asks students to evaluate the utility of the guide and make modifications to correct any of its inadequacies; and the third asks students to transfer strategies to a new learning situation. An example of an after reading activity is seen in Figure 4. Students are able to analyze two illustrations from the text after comprehending the plate tectonics theory in the during reading phases. They then interpret the illustrations, determine how they are similar

Figure 3
During Reading Activity
Evaluating Theory

Theory   At one time a supercontinent existed; but because the land was divided into plates, it began to move. As the plates separated, new continents were formed.

Claims made to support the theory	Evidence used to support the theory	Weakness of the evidence	Do you believe the claim?	Provide justification to support your judgment
1.				
2.				
3.				
4.				

Figure 4
After Reading Activity
Evaluating Graphic Data

Text illustrations	What claim is made in the illustration?	How are the illustrations similar?	How are the illustrations different?	What conclusions can be reached about the theory of plate tectonics?
A				
B				

and different, and reach a conclusion about whether the data support the theory of plate tectonics. To do so they must evaluate the extent to which the two illustrations support the theory, combining reading and writing processes in a manner consistent with interactive views of reading.

A second after reading activity is a modification of the content processing guides used in both the during and after phases of reading, in which students consider one basic question: "How useful are activities in helping students attain their purpose?" With respect to plate tectonics the question would be "How useful was the causal sequencing activity in helping you understand the theory of plate tectonics?" In answering this question, students must identify why the guide worked or why it was inappropriate. For example, if students did not find the content processing guide helpful, they would propose ways to correct it. By focusing on why they used a practical guide and whether it was useful in attaining their goals, students consciously monitor, regulate, and modify their strategies.

A third after reading activity helps transfer the strategies used with the plate tectonic materials to another earth science chapter. Students begin by identifying the goals for reading; then they identify important information in the material that meets their goals (e.g., Does it explain a theory? Does it describe how an object functions?). Next, they determine whether the material is organized as it was in previous selections. Finally, they identify strategies they would use to read new materials.

The purpose is to help students identify ways to prepare to read another chapter. This is important because students are doing more than completing a guide; they are thinking about the process used to attain their goals. They must identify the circumstances under which they would use the strategies modeled in the guides, make a judgment about their utility, and explain how they might be modified. In other words, students come to understand when, why, and how they would apply these strategies in another context.

3. *Build an integrated strategic knowledge base by exploring topics that allow systematic transfer across and within the various disciplines of the curriculum.* The context in which strategies are taught is crucial. The goal is for readers to use their cognitive resources in a manner that demonstrates purpose and intention (Garner, 1987). To build this into the reading curriculum, teachers must do more than merely teach skills-in-isolation or strategic knowledge. They must teach students to transfer strategic knowledge to new learning situations across a variety of disciplines. This means teaching students that as subject matter changes, so must strategy selection. Therefore, a variety of topics and text structures must be used to show students how to use strategies flexibly (Chi, 1987).

To help illustrate that strategies are not generic and must be adapted as the content area changes, consider the differences that exist between reading a chapter on plate tectonics and reading the story *To Build a Fire* (London,

1980). While causal reasoning strategies are required to comprehend both texts, there is a big difference between using causal reasoning in the context of a short story and using it in an earth science selection. For one thing, a story has a plot structure that requires the reader to causally link a problem, a conflict, and a resolution to understand the thematic focus (Brooks, 1984; Leitch, 1986). It requires knowledge about story schemas, story grammars, and human actions (Mandler, 1984; Voss & Bisanz, 1985). This literary knowledge is different from scientific knowledge. Scientific knowledge is a logical and rational approach to explaining the natural world, with the explanation based on a coordination of theories and evidence that provides a framework for the organization and interpretation of natural phenomena (Himsworth, 1986; Kuhn, Amsel, & O'Loughlin, 1988).

To further illustrate the point, compare the content goals developed in the plate tectonics activities with the content goals developed for *To Build a Fire*. In the earth science selection, the content goals focus on understanding theory and evidence in the context of plate tectonics. To understand *To Build a Fire*, readers must use a narrative structure to interpret human actions; for instance, to understand how one's feelings can prevent a person from making rational judgments. In the plate tectonics selection, causal reasoning was framed by theories and evidence. But stories are not organized in this manner. As literary theorists point out, a story is transformed by causally linking the events to its plot structure (Segre, 1988). In science, therefore, theories and evidence are tied together by causal links; in literature, causal reasoning transforms the plot into a story.

Consequently, a different set of processing goals is necessary for *To Build a Fire*. Examples of such goals are understanding how character traits are causally linked to the thoughts, feelings, and actions, and understanding that identifying character traits is a good strategy for identifying the theme of a story. To transfer a strategy like causal reasoning across disciplines, students need to be shown how to adjust and adapt strategies from one reading selection to another.

Let's examine how this would be done in a middle school program. The transfer can be handled in two ways: one is within the same discipline and the other is across disciplines. Both occur in the after reading phase, when students engage in synthesizing the ideas in the selection, evaluating the effectiveness of the content processing guides, modifying the guides if necessary, and transferring the strategy to a new learning situation. The first approach is to focus on transferring strategies to new material in the same field (perhaps the next chapter in the same book, as was described in the plate tectonics after reading phase). In the second approach, students are guided through a series of questions that direct their attention toward the similarities and differences between how they approached reading the plate tectonics material and how they read a story. Specifically, they would be asked:

- How are the two selections organized differently?

- Why are they organized differently?

- What do these differences suggest about how one reads these selections?

- How are the processing guides organized differently?

- Why are the processing guides organized differently?

- What do the differences suggest about how you read the two selections?

- Are the selections similar in any way?

- What accounts for the similarity?

The emphasis is on understanding the differences and similarities in strategy selection and usage so that students will realize that their strategy must change when content changes.

This activity could be taken one step further by asking students to think about how they would use the story and plate tectonic selections to help them develop a plan for reading a history chapter on the causes of the American Civil War. First, before students even looked at the chapter, they would be asked to think about the historical context and circumstances that influence historical events and to compare these with the earth science and story selections. Second, students would preview the chapter, developing content and process goals based on what they believed to be the central purposes of the chapter. Third, they would develop a plan for reading the chapter, predicting the types of knowledge and strategies they would need in order to comprehend the passage. They

would need to consider whether causal reasoning will be the same in a historical context as in a scientific or literary context, whether they have to modify their reading strategies to accommodate the differences imposed by domain knowledge, and whether the information in a historical context affects meaning. The intent is to get students to understand that there is a relationship among the content, the structure of the text, and the strategies used to read it. This is the essence of becoming a strategic reader.

Activities like these create bridges that lead to an integrated knowledge base. A key element is traversing the terrain, not merely covering topics but spending time integrating the information through a combination of reading and writing activities that focus on topics from a variety of perspectives.

4. *Base instruction on a holistic interpretation of materials that require students to synthesize information rather than concentrate on discrete bits of information.* Instruction should focus on a more global level of learning and move away from activities that tend to trivialize information or that are overly analytic in nature. The primary focus is to move toward a perspective similar to the one described in the plate tectonic activities where major instructional decisions were influenced by the extent to which they reflected the content and process goals. For example, the plate tectonics activities tried to get students to focus on the central purpose by having them think about the major theories presented and the evidence associated with each. They did not deal with discrete components of the theories. The reading teacher cannot

assume that a particular line of questioning will allow students to pull the information together. Instruction must be orchestrated carefully through a series of activities that have a holistic focus. When left to chance, most students get only fragmented bits of information as opposed to significant information. The rule of thumb should be that information should not be considered significant unless it contributes to students' understanding of the content and process goals.

5. *Provide explicit instruction that identifies the essential steps necessary for completion.* Teachers cannot assume that traditional question asking and discussion help students understand complex mental operations. As the during and after reading activities on plate tectonics illustrate, teachers must guide students through the steps that accomplished readers go through when answering certain questions. Guiding students is an extremely important part of showing students how to transfer strategies to other content areas. In the past, reading teachers assumed that if students completed skills worksheets they would be good readers. Current research, however, demonstrates that direct, explicit instruction is essential if students are to improve comprehension performance.

Summary

Reading has undergone a significant transformation, moving away from a static, isolated skills orientation to an interactive orientation. Consistent with this changing perspective, middle school reading programs must shift from being extensions of the language arts/English program to focusing on learning across the curriculum, with equal emphasis on domain knowledge and strategies. This chapter provides a rationale for achieving a balance between content and strategies. Subsequent chapters suggest that the conceptual frame for middle school reading also should include balanced consideration of cognition, metacognition, and affective dimensions of reading, and attention to writing as well as reading.

References

Anderson, Richard C., Hiebert, Elfrieda H., Scott, Judith A., & Wilkinson, Ian A. (1985). *Becoming a nation of readers: The report of the Commission on Reading*. Washington, DC: National Institute of Education.

Anderson, Thomas H., & Armbruster, Bonnie B. (1984). Content area textbooks. In Richard C. Anderson, Jean Osborn, & Robert Tierney (Eds.), *Learning to read in American schools: Basal readers and content texts*. Hillsdale, NJ: Erlbaum.

Backler, Allen, & Stoltman, Joseph. (1988). *Global geography*. Bloomington, IN: Agency for Instructional Technology.

Beyer, Barry K. (1988). *Developing a thinking skills program*. Boston, MA: Allyn & Bacon.

Beyer, Barry K. (1987). *Practical strategies for the teaching of thinking*. Boston, MA: Allyn & Bacon.

Bloom, Allan. (1987). *The closing of the American mind*. New York: Simon & Schuster.

Britton, Bruce K., & Black, John B. (1985). *Understanding expository text: A theoretical and practical handbook for analyzing explanatory text*. Hillsdale, NJ: Erlbaum.

Brooks, Peter. (1984). *Reading for the plot: Design and intention in narrative*. New York: Knopf.

Chance, Paul. (1986). *Thinking in the classroom: A survey of programs*. New York: Teachers College Press.

Chi, Michelene T.H. (1987). Representing knowledge and metaknowledge: Implications for interpreting metamemory research. In Franz E. Weinert & Rainer H. Kluwe (Eds.), *Metacognition, motivation, and understanding*. Hillsdale, NJ: Erlbaum.

Garner, Ruth. (1987). *Metacognition and reading comprehension*. Norwood, NJ: Ablex.

Hegel, Georg Wilhelm Friedrich. (1899, 1956). *The philosophy of history*. New York: Dover.

Himsworth, Harold. (1986). *Scientific knowledge and philosophic thought*. Baltimore, MD: Johns Hopkins University Press.

Hirsch, E.D., Jr. (1987). *Cultural literacy*: *What every American needs to know*. Boston, MA: Houghton Mifflin.

Katz, Marilyn. (1982). Critical literacy: A conception of education as a moral right and social ideal. *The public school monopoly*. Cambridge, MA: Ballinger.

Kuhn, Deanna, Amsel, Eric, & O'Loughlin, Michael. (1988). *The development of scientific thinking skills*. San Diego, CA: Academic.

Leitch, Thomas M. (1986). *What stories are*: *Narrative theory and interpretation*. University Park, PA: Pennsylvania State University Press.

London, Jack. (1980). *To build a fire*. Mankato, MN: Creative Education.

Mandler, Jean Matter. (1984). *Stories, scripts, and scenes*: *Aspects of schema theory*. Hillsdale, NJ: Erlbaum.

National Commission on Excellence in Education. (1983). *A nation at risk*: *The imperative for educational reform*. Washington, DC: National Commission on Excellence in Education.

Otto, Wayne, & White, Sandra. (1982). *Reading expository material*. New York: Academic.

Paris, Scott, Lipson, Marjorie, & Wixson, Karen K. (1983). Becoming a strategic reader. *Contemporary Educational Psychology, 8*.

Peters, Charles W. (1984). *An analysis of content reading strategies*: *Interactive or static*? Paper presented at the National Reading Conference, St. Petersburg, FL.

Peters, Charles W. (1982). The content process model: A new approach for conceptualizing content reading. In Judythe Patberg (Ed.), *Reading in the content area*: *Application of a concept*. Toledo, OH: University of Toledo.

Peters, Charles W., & Carlsen, Marilyn. (1989). Using a literary framework to teach mysteries. In K. Denise Muth (Ed.), *Children's comprehension of text*: *Research into practice*. Newark, DE: International Reading Association.

Peters, Charles W., & Hayes, Bernard. (1989). The role of reading instruction in social studies classrooms. In Diane Lapp, James Flood, & Nancy Farnan (Eds.), *Content area reading and learning*: *Instructional strategies*. Englewood Cliffs, NJ: Prentice Hall.

Rabinowitz, Mitchell, & Glaser, Robert. (1985). Cognitive structure and process in highly competent performance. In Frances D. Harowitz & Marion O'Brien (Eds.), *The gifted and talented*: *Developmental perspectives*. Washington, DC: American Psychological Association.

Ravitch, Diane, & Finn, Chester E. (1987). *What do our 17-year-olds know*? *A report on the first national assessment of history and literature*. New York: Harper & Row.

Segre, Cesare. (1988). *Introduction to the analysis of the literary text*. Bloomington, IN: Indiana University Press.

Sewall, Gilbert T. (1987). *American history textbooks*: *An assessment of quality*. New York: New York Educational Excellence Network, Columbia University.

Sewall, Gilbert T. (1988). American history textbooks: Where do we go from here? *Phi Delta Kappan, 69*(8), 552-558.

Spiro, Rand J., Vispoel, Walter P., Schmitz, Ala S., & Boerger, A.E. (1987). Knowledge acquisition for application: Cognitive flexibility and transfer in complex content domains. In Bruce K. Britton & Shawn M. Glynn (Eds.), *Executive control and processes in reading*. Hillsdale, NJ: Erlbaum.

Voss, James F. (1986). Social studies. In Ronna Dillon & Robert J. Sternberg (Eds.), *Cognition and instruction*. New York: Academic.

Voss, James F., & Bisanz, Gay L. (1985). Knowledge and the processing of narrative and expository texts. In Bruce K. Britton & John B. Black (Eds.), *Understanding expository text*: *A theoretical and practical handbook for analyzing explanatory text*. Hillsdale, NJ: Erlbaum.

White, Hayden. (1973). *Metahistory*: *The historical imagination in nineteenth century Europe*. Baltimore, MD: Johns Hopkins University Press.

Wixson, Karen K., & Peters, Charles W. (1984). Reading redefined: A Michigan Reading Association position paper. *Michigan Reading Journal, 17*, 4-7.

Cognitive and Metacognitive Goals in Reading and Writing

Beth Ann Herrmann

MORE THAN TWO DEC-
ades of research has shown
that reading is a complex
process involving much more than mastery and application of isolated skills.
Expert readers are metacognitive; that
is, they are aware of and in control of the
cognitive reasoning processes associated
with constructing meaning from text.
This chapter focuses on the cognitive
reasoning processes associated with effective reading and provides a general
plan for organizing a middle school
reading curriculum that allows students
to learn how to be in metacognitive control of their reading while maintaining an
emphasis on content, as specified in the
previous chapter.

Background

Today, we know more than ever before
about the reading process. In this section, traditional and current views of

6

reading are contrasted to illustrate how much has been
learned about reading in
the past 20 years.

Traditional Views of Reading

Traditionally, reading has been described as a linear, procedural, routinized activity. Expert readers have been
viewed as those who can master a discrete set of competencies or skills and,
with little effort, automatically apply
them when reading.

Traditional views of reading assume
that skills to be mastered range from the
smallest to the largest components of
reading. For example, to become efficient readers, students must first learn
the alphabet letters and their associated
sounds, followed by learning how to
blend sounds into syllables, words,
phrases, and sentences. "Real" reading
results from the mastery of these sep-

arate parts. Consequently, the typical reading curriculum has focused on isolated reading skills, such as letter/sound associations, structural analysis skills, and a series of comprehension skills. As a result, reading instruction emphasis has been on skill-and-drill practice — such as worksheets — geared toward helping students master skills. Little emphasis has been placed on the cognitive reasoning processes associated with constructing meaning from written text.

Current Views of Reading

In the past 20 years, research on the strategic nature of reading and research on metacognition have established that real reading does not occur in a linear, routinized fashion, and involves much more than the application of isolated skills. Instead, expert readers engage in constructive thinking; they begin by constructing an interpretation of written text (Paris, Lipson, & Wixson, 1983; Pressley et al., 1985).

Current views of reading reflect that expert readers are aware of and in control of cognitive reading processes. As in Chapter 5 (this volume), a before, during, and after reading structure can be used when analyzing the reasoning processes used by readers. For example, before reading, expert readers consciously engage in strategic reasoning when they access appropriate background knowledge to make initial predictions about the text meaning. During reading they consciously construct meaning by combining prior knowledge with new text information, monitoring comprehension and modifying initial predictions when necessary. When an obstacle to comprehension (e.g., an unknown word) is encountered, expert readers solve the problem by consciously selecting and applying "fix it" strategies to "repair" comprehension blockages. After reading, expert readers reason about the significance of what was read and about conclusions to draw and judgments to make about the content. In short, expert readers are metacognitive (Baker & Brown, 1984; Barr et al., 1987; Flavell, 1981).

Consider the following example. Suppose two middle school students, one who is in metacognitive control of her reading and another who is not, are assigned to read a short story in their literature book. The student who is not in metacognitive control of her reading approaches the text in a nonstrategic, mechanical manner. For example, she sets "getting done" as her goal for reading and immediately begins reading with little thought given to what the story is about. During reading she pays too much attention to each word encountered, ignoring the overall message. She makes little effort to systematically monitor comprehension, and on several occasions she skips over difficult words she cannot pronounce and continues on without returning to figure out the unknown words. Frequently, she becomes confused, but she keeps on reading because the goal is to get done. At the end of the story, she closes her book, breathes a huge sigh of relief, and mutters something like "Well, I don't know what it says, but I got it done."

In contrast, the student who is in metacognitive control of her reading approaches the text in a strategic manner.

Expert readers approach text with the goal of constructing meaning rather than "getting done."

For example, her goal is to construct meaning from the text. Before reading, she surveys the text to get a general idea of information contained in each subsection. At the same time, she thinks about what she knows about the topic and uses that knowledge, as well as headings, subheadings, and graphic aids, to make initial predictions about the text meaning. During reading she consciously evaluates how closely the text information matches her initial predictions by combining her prior knowledge with new text information. When an unknown word disrupts the meaning-getting process, she slows down and uses fix-it strategies to figure out how to pronounce the word. Whenever the author's message does not match her initial predictions, she stops to modify or change the predic-

tion. After reading, she reasons about the significance of the text information by drawing conclusions about the author's message.

Unfortunately, many middle school students do not learn how to be in meta-cognitive control of their reading because their instruction focuses primarily on isolated reading skills. For example, many students enrolled in developmental reading classes spend much of their time completing workbook pages designed to help them master individual skills. For the most part, the teacher plays an incidental role, ensuring completion of assignments. Little or no instructional time is devoted to helping students become aware of and assume control of the reasoning processes that could help them read more effectively.

Summary

Reading is no longer thought of as a linear activity requiring the mindless application of a set of isolated skills. Today, reading is defined as purposeful construction of an interpretation of written text.

Despite our changing views of reading and recent research findings, there have been few changes in reading instruction practice (Allington, this volume; Pressley et al., 1989). For example, in many middle school developmental reading classrooms, little or no emphasis is placed on cognitive or metacognitive reasoning processes. If students are to learn how to be in metacognitive control of their reading, instruction must focus more on cognitive reasoning processes while also striking the balance between process and content that Peters describes (Chapter 5, this volume). Such instruction must be well grounded in a reading curriculum that emphasizes cognitive and metacognitive aspects of reading.

Cognitive and Metacognitive Elements of Reading

A reading curriculum that focuses on cognitive and metacognitive aspects of reading helps students understand the reading process and control cognitive reasoning processes associated with effective reading and studying. These aspects of the reading curriculum are described in the following sections.

Reading

Understanding the reading process. A portion of the middle school reading curriculum should focus on helping students understand how the reading process works. First, students must understand that the basic function of reading is communication and that effective reading is a meaning-getting, sense-making, problem-solving process requiring effort, enthusiasm, perseverance, thinking, and strategic reasoning. Such conceptual understandings form the basis of comprehension.

Second, students must understand the role of prior knowledge in effective reading, how to evaluate their prior knowledge, and the extent to which they use their prior knowledge when reading. For example, a student assigned to read a chapter on the United States Constitution must first evaluate what is known about the Constitution and how to use this knowledge when reading to better comprehend the text message.

Third, students must understand their general thinking ability when it comes to completing reading tasks. For example, a student assigned to read the Constitution chapter must maintain attention on the reading task, plan before acting, and relate the task to previous reading encounters about similar topics.

Controlling the reading process. A major portion of the middle school reading curriculum should focus on helping students develop metacognitive control of the cognitive reasoning processes associated with effective reading. Three types of cognitive reading strategies should be taught.

First, before-reading strategies are used to activate prior knowledge, to set goals for reading, and to make initial predictions about the text meaning. For example, a student assigned to read a chapter on the United States Constitution activates the appropriate background knowledge by thinking about what is already known about the topic. He or she sets goals for what is to be learned and makes initial predictions about the text's meaning by examining the vocabulary, sentence structure, chapter length, subsections, graphic aids, sequence of information, and complex associations embedded in the text.

Second, during-reading strategies are used to construct an interpretation of the author's message. Two types of during-reading strategies can be taught. Monitoring strategies are used to check the accuracy of previously made predictions and to keep track of newly acquired information. For example, a student reading the Constitution chapter actively evaluates how well the text information matches initial predictions made about the author's message. If the text information matches the predictions, the author's message makes sense and the meaning-getting process continues. Newly acquired information about the Constitution is temporarily stored in the student's short term memory. Since the student's short term memory can hold only a small amount of information, new chunks of information are transferred by connecting them to existing chunks of information stored in the student's long term memory. Whenever text information does not match initial predictions about the author's message, the student slows down and pays closer attention to the text information. A conscious effort is made to connect prior knowledge about the Constitution with the text information. At this point, either the initial prediction is modified or a new predic-

tion is generated. In either case, meaning is restored and the meaning-getting process resumes.

Fix-it strategies are used when an unknown word or a difficult segment of a sentence is encountered and the author's message is temporarily obscured. For example, suppose that when reading the Constitution chapter the student comes across the word *proclamation* and is unable to pronounce it. A combination of word identification strategies is used to figure out how to pronounce the word. One type of word identification strategy that may be used is a context clue strategy. Using what is already known about the topic, the student figures out interrelationships between text clues (definitions, experience clues, sentence structure clues, mood clues) and key concepts presented in the text. If such information is sufficient, the student makes a reasonable guess at the word. If, however, sufficient clues are not included in the text, another kind of word identification strategy—structural analysis—may be tried to break the unknown word apart by its structural units (prefixes, root word, suffixes, inflectional endings). While doing this, the student combines prior knowledge with useful context clues. A second guess is made at the word. If the structural analysis clues are not sufficient, the student uses a third type of word identification strategy—phonics—to identify and blend known letter/sound associations located at the beginning, middle, or end of the word.

Although a reader may be able to pronounce all the words contained in the written text, middle school readers frequently find their reading disrupted because of difficult associations at the paragraph level (analogies, complex comparisons, figurative language, ambiguous statements, causal relations, difficult sequence of events, anaphora). When this happens, several comprehension fix-it strategies are used to restore meaning. For example, suppose the student reading the Constitution chapter is confused by an implied cause and effect relationship contained in the text. As soon as the confusion occurs, the student stops and pays closer attention to causal clues (e.g., "because") and to the interrelationships between information provided before and after the clues. Using what is already known about the topic, the student makes an inference about the causal relationship and tests the inference against the predictions previously made about the author's message. If the inference makes sense, the meaning-getting process resumes. If it does not make sense, the student consults a reference source or outside authority.

Finally, after-reading strategies are used to organize and restructure the author's message and/or to make judgments about the author's credentials, use of facts, and potential bias or intention (propaganda), as well as the validity of the message. Such postreading reflection requires strategic reasoning about text information relative to what is already known about the topic.

In sum, teaching students how to use before-reading, during-reading, and after-reading strategies helps them become aware of and understand the cognitive reasoning processes associated with effective reading and, through this awareness and understanding, to assume control of the meaning-getting process. Students in control of this process are more likely to be successful than students who do not know how to use these strategies.

Studying

Understanding and controlling the studying process. A portion of the middle school reading curriculum should focus on helping students study more effectively. Understanding the cognitive reasoning processes associated with effective studying and assuming metacognitive control of these processes are important goals. Three study strategies should be taught: notetaking, locating, and remembering.

First, notetaking strategies are used to record and organize useful notes for the purpose of sorting out complex information and/or combining material from several sources so the information can be remembered. For example, to organize important facts about the Constitution, the student in the example uses background knowledge to identify and condense relevant information into note form and to organize these notes into a series of major headings with more detailed subheadings.

Second, locating strategies are used to identify specific information in different types of books. For example, after reading the Constitution chapter, the student locates and verifies facts in an encyclopedia about when and where the Constitution was written by using three reading rates. First, a skimming rate is used to obtain the gist of the author's message in the encyclopedia selection. After learning that the encyclopedia selection has to do with the development of the Constitution, a scanning pace is used to find specific information. Finally, after finding the section that deals with when and where the Constitution was developed, a careful reading rate is used to understand the information.

Third, remembering strategies are used to integrate new concepts into existing schemata. For example, to remember facts about the Constitution, the student combines background knowledge with new text information to construct interrelationships between new and old concepts.

Teaching students how to use notetaking strategies, locating strategies, and remembering strategies helps students study more effectively because they understand how to obtain and remember important information. Students who understand and control the cognitive reasoning processes associated with these strategies are more effective learners than those who do not know how to use these strategies.

Summary of the Reading Curriculum

Effective middle school reading instruction puts students in metacognitive control of their reading. Such instruction is grounded in a reading curriculum that includes planned learning experiences that help students understand and control both the reading process and studying. In the next section, similar curricular elements are described as they relate to the teaching of writing.

Cognitive and Metacognitive Elements of Writing

Like reading, writing is an active, strategic process requiring constructive thinking that begins with a desire to convey a meaningful message (Flower & Hayes, 1981; Hayes & Flower, 1980; Scardamalia & Bereiter, 1986a, 1986b). Just as expert readers are in metacognitive control of their reading comprehension, expert writers are in metacognitive control of their writing.

A writing curriculum should emphasize the cognitive and metacognitive aspects of writing, including planned learning experiences that help students understand the writing process and understand and control the cognitive reasoning processes associated with effective writing. Descriptions of aspects of the writing process follow.

Understanding the Writing Process

A portion of the writing curriculum should focus on helping students understand how the writing process works. First, students must understand that the basic function of writing is to convey a message and that effective writing, like effective reading, is a constructive, problem-solving process requiring effort, enthusiasm, perseverance, thinking, and strategic reasoning ability. Second, students must understand the role of prior knowledge in effective writing and how to evaluate their prior knowledge when writing. For example, students must learn how to use prior knowledge to select relevant pieces of information to include in written text. Finally, students must understand their general thinking ability when it comes to completing writing tasks. For example, students must learn how to apply strategic approaches to writing tasks, check writing performance, maintain attention on writing tasks, plan before acting, and relate current writing situations to previous writing encounters. Such conceptual understandings serve as a foundation for effective writing.

Controlling the Writing Process

A major portion of the middle school writing curriculum should focus on helping students control the cognitive reasoning processes associated with effective writing. Three types of cognitive writing strategies should be taught: planning, translating, and reviewing.

Planning strategies are used before writing to activate prior knowledge about the topic, to identify the intended audience, and to set goals for writing. Three kinds of planning strategies are used. The first type is used to retrieve from long term memory any relevant information about the topic. For example, if the students assigned to read the Constitution chapter also are assigned to write a summary of the chapter, they retrieve from long term memory relevant information about the Constitution. How well organized and developed the retrieved information is depends on how much knowledge students have stored in long term memory and how the knowledge is organized. A second strategy is used to identify the intended audience. For the student in our Constitution example, the intended audience is the teacher, who probably has a lot of background knowledge about the Constitution. A third strategy is used to set goals for writing. Goal-setting involves deciding on the best way to approach the task by thinking about the level of difficulty of

the text to be written and the amount and form of information retrieved from long term memory. In the case of the student in our example, the goal for writing the summary is to organize and learn factual information about the Constitution.

Translating strategies are used to translate meaning into a linear piece of written text that contains organized, meaningful ideas. Two types of translating strategies are used. The first is used to organize important ideas about the topic. Ideas are organized by thinking about higher-order relationships among them. For example, the student writing the chapter summary interconnects ideas about the Constitution by creating sentences equivalent in meaning, creating cause and effect relationships, sequencing information, and creating anaphoric relationships. A second type of strategy is used to manipulate all the special demands of written English to figure out the best way to express, in visible language, interconnections between important ideas.

Reviewing strategies are used to determine the extent to which the written message makes sense. Two types of reviewing strategies are used. The first is used to determine whether goals have been met for writing the text. For example, the student in our example analyzes the written draft of the chapter summary to determine whether important facts are well organized. A second type of strategy is used to systematically revise the message and goals as a means of further translating the ideas contained in the written text. For example, if the student decides that some of the facts are not well organized, those statements are rewritten to better convey the message.

Summary of the Writing Curriculum

The middle school writing curriculum is similar to the reading curriculum because it includes planned learning experiences that help students understand the writing process and understand the cognitive reasoning processes associated with effective writing. Such a curriculum enables teachers to put students in metacognitive control of their writing. Developing cognitive and metacognitive elements of writing aids in developing the same elements of reading. In the next section, specific suggestions are made for how to teach students to be in metacognitive control of their reading.

Metacognitive Control of Reading

Regardless of what kind of middle school teacher you are, you have a responsibility to teach your students how to be in metacognitive control of their reading. How much daily instructional time you spend on this task depends on your content area.

Helping students learn how to be more metacognitive begins with modifying your curriculum to include planned experiences that emphasize cognitive and metacognitive aspects of reading. For example, if you are a developmental reading teacher, decide which skills can be taught as cognitive reading strategies (context clues, structural analysis) and which skills should be taught as memorized routines or procedures (letter sounds, sight vocabulary). If you are a content area teacher employing expository text, decide which checkup exercises, enrichment activities, grammar

exercises, and literature selections are most appropriate for helping students practice using newly learned reading strategies.

In addition to modifying your curriculum, you will need to incorporate two types of instruction into your daily routine. The first is indirect instruction that emphasizes activities. During indirect instruction, students interact with the activities. In contrast, direct instruction requires teacher explanations and mental modeling (Duffy, Roehler, & Herrmann, 1988). During direct instruction, the teacher explains *what* is to be learned, *why* what is learned is useful, and *how* to learn it, and verbalizes cognitive reasoning processes. Materials may be used, but the teacher plays a dominant role in giving information and shaping students' interpretations of the information.

Both direct and indirect instruction are necessary for teaching students how to be in metacognitive control of their reading. The following sections focus on how to incorporate both types of instruction into a regular instructional routine.

Teaching the Reading Process

All middle school teachers can use both indirect and direct instruction to help students understand the reading process. First, use direct instruction to show students how the reading process works and indirect instruction to provide interesting reading experiences that reflect the essential message-sending and message-getting concept of reading. For example, explain that reading is a complex, problem-solving process that requires effort, enthusiasm, and strategic reasoning, and show the students how you construct an interpretation of written text. Then provide reading encounters that highlight the fact that text is produced by a writer who has a message to convey and that reading involves constructing an interpretation of the writer's message.

Second, use indirect instruction to teach students how to evaluate their worldly knowledge. For example, create a risk-free environment (small group instructional situations) in which students feel comfortable discussing the extensiveness of their experiences with and prior knowledge about various topics, how well organized their knowledge is, and if (or how) they use their prior knowledge when reading. Help students expand their worldly knowledge by providing a variety of hands-on experiences with new topics (field trips, sharing sessions, guest speakers).

Finally, use both types of instruction to teach students how to evaluate their ability to use general thinking strategies. For example, provide small group activities during which students share various aspects of their general approach to reading tasks. Then explain the various approaches that expert readers take to complete reading tasks. Explain verbally to students the invisible thinking that occurs when one looks for strategic approaches to reading tasks.

Teaching Metacognitive Control of Cognitive Reasoning Strategies

Developmental reading teachers and English teachers should assume major roles in teaching students when and how to use the cognitive reasoning processes associated with effective reading. Other content area teachers also must help by emphasizing effective reading daily and by spending a portion of instructional time weekly on helping students learn how to strategically read and understand content area materials.

Before-reading strategies. Developmental reading teachers should use a modified think aloud technique to show students how to prepare to read text material. First, using a selection from a textbook, verbalize what you know about the topic to show students how to activate appropriate background knowledge. Second, talk about vocabulary, sentence structure, chapter length, subsections, graphic aids, sequence, and complex associations embedded in the text to show students how to set goals for reading and how to make reasonable predictions about the author's message. Note how the following developmental reading teacher shows her students how to use before-reading strategies.

Teacher: I'm going to use your civics book today to show you how to prepare to read text material. Some of you jump right into reading when you're given an assignment, and there are some things you should do *before* you read that will help you better understand the author's message. Watch what I do to get ready to read the first part of this chapter called "Economics and Economic Systems." The first section title is What Is Economics? I already know that economics has to do with money and that it's important to our country, so I'm guessing that the author is going to give me some general information about economics. There are five subsections here, though, and all of them have to do with an economic system. That makes me think that the author is going to focus on specific information about economic systems.

If you are a content area teacher, use a combination of direct and indirect instruction to help students become more proficient at using before-reading strategies. Use direct instruction to show students how to use these strategies before reading literature selections or textbook materials and use indirect instruction to provide ample opportunities for students to practice using these strategies in small group instructional situations.

During-reading strategies. Develop-

Teachers can work with students to help them develop effective reading strategies.

mental reading teachers also should use a modified think aloud technique to show students how to use monitoring and fix-it strategies. Using a selection from a textbook, explain to students how you monitor your comprehension when reading. Note how the English teacher in the following excerpt models the cognitive reasoning processes associated with comprehension monitoring.

Teacher: I have your literature book here and I'm going to use it to show you how to keep track of your comprehension when you read selections from this book. I'll talk to show you what is going on in my mind as I read part of this story called "The Anchor Man." I've already surveyed the story and I predict that it will be about a swim team or swim meet because of the pictures here. I'm going to stop after each page and see if the information matches my prediction. (The teacher reads the first page aloud and stops.) The author is introducing the main characters on this first page, and both boys are swimmers who are trying out for their school swim team. So far, that matches my initial prediction so I'll read on to see if the author mentions anything about a swim meet.

Developmental reading teachers should use three elements of direct instruction to show students how to use fix-it strategies when a comprehension breakdown occurs (Duffy et al., 1986, 1987). First, introduce lessons by making explicit statements about the strategy to be learned, why it is important, and when it is useful. Note how the teacher in the following passage introduces a context clue lesson.

Teacher: Now I'm going to teach you how to use a strategy for figuring out words you don't know how to pronounce. This strategy is important because some words are crucial to understanding the author's message, and if you can't figure them out, you will have trouble understanding.

Second, use mental modeling to show students how to use the cognitive reasoning processes associated with the strategy. Talk to make invisible mental processes visible, as shown in the following excerpt.

Teacher: Watch me use our context clue strategy. I'm going to pretend that I don't know this word, *cannonading*. Watch what I do to figure it out. (Reading) He took the medicine ball from Stan, reared back, and sent it can...can ...blank at me. My arms went up, the mass of the ball smacked into them, and I went over backwards. Hmmm. I can't pronounce that word and I'm confused. There must be some clues here to help me. I know what a medicine ball is. It's heavy and some people use one to exercise. Stan must have thrown it at the other boy, because he said it hit him in the arms. Let me think about that as I reread the sentence. (Reading)... sent it can ...cannon. Hmmm. A cannon ball is heavy and it does lots of damage to things it hits. That's a good clue. (Reading)... sent it cannon "add" ...ing, cannon ..."aid" ...ing. I don't know which way to pronounce it, but I think I know what it means. The ball was heavy and it was thrown hard—like a cannonball is shot out of a cannon. Stan was lucky he wasn't hurt. Let's check the glossary now to see if I'm right.

Finally, shape the information by asking students to explain or show you how to use the strategy and, on the basis of the students' responses, provide reexplanation, remodeling, analogies, or other elaborations. Note how the teacher in the following lesson excerpt checks students' understanding of the context clue strategy and provides additional instructional information in the form of reexplanation and remodeling when students have trouble understanding the strategy.

Teacher: O.K. Someone tell me what I did to figure out that hard word. Jerry.

Student: You tried to sound it out.

Teacher: Well, I did try to pronounce it, but I did something else. What did I look for in the story?

Student: Clues.

Teacher: That's right. I was looking for clues to help me figure out that word. I did something else, too. What was it?

Student: (no response)

Teacher: Let me help you. After I found some clues in the story, I thought about what I already knew to help me figure out what the clues had to do with what was going on in the story. Watch me use our strategy again.

If you are a content area teacher, your primary responsibility is to provide ample opportunities for students to practice using fix-it strategies in a variety of reading materials. For example, if you are an English teacher, help students use the context clue strategy as they read literature selections and periodically ask students to explain how they used the strategy. A portion of your instructional time every day should be spent showing students how to use strategies when reading textbook and other types of expository materials.

After-reading strategies. Developmental reading teachers should use direct explanation to show students how to reflect on the author's message after reading. Note how the teacher in the following lesson excerpt shows students how to strategically reason about information contained in the selection by drawing conclusions about the author's message.

Teacher: The author has a message for me in this selection. Watch what I do to figure out what it is. On almost every page the author incorporated clues into the text about how difficult it is being on a swim team. On this page it talks about how much time it takes; on this page he talks about how much work it is; and on this page he talks about what happens if you don't put this kind of time and work into it. That's a lot like some other sports I know about. I think what the author is trying to tell me here is that being a successful, contributing member of a swim team takes total commitment.

If you are a content area teacher, set aside a portion of your instructional time daily to allow students to reflect on literature and textbook selections. Provide assistance as necessary; allow students to work in pairs.

Teaching Metacognitive Control of Study Strategies

Middle school teachers share responsibility for teaching students how to study and learn from text. Use direct instruction to teach students when and how to use the study strategies described earlier, and use indirect instruction to provide ample opportunities to apply the strategies.

First, using real textbooks, show students how to identify and condense relevant information into note form and how to organize written notes into outline form. Note how the history teacher in the following excerpt shows students how to organize complex information about the Civil War.

Teacher: We've been reading about the Civil War for a few weeks now, and we've found out that this chapter is loaded with details about the war (refers to information about the Civil War written on the chalkboard). It will be hard for you to learn all of this unless we somehow organize it. Watch what I do to organize this information. Let's see, what I want to do here is categorize all this information. The chapter subheadings will help me. I'll start with *Weapons* — that's an easy word. Guns, knives, cannons, and bayonets all fit into the weapons category, so I'll list them under weapons. *Reasons Why the War Was Fought* is the next subheading, so I'll group all the things that have to do with that topic.

Next, use direct instruction to show students how to use various reading rates to locate information in different types of books. Note how the history teacher in the following lesson shows students how to scan to find information about diseases during the Civil War.

Teacher: (Reading) What types of diseases did soldiers suffer from during the Civil War? Watch what I do to find the answer to this question. I already know that disease means sickness and may lead to death, so I'll think about that as I look through each chapter subsection to find relevant information about sickness or disease. I'm looking at this first subheading for major concepts about disease. All of this information seems to be about weapons, so I'll skip over the rest of this section.

Last, use direct instruction to show students how to remember new text information. Using a textbook, talk to show students how to integrate new concepts into their existing schemata about specific topics. Note how the history teacher in the following excerpt uses a semantic mapping technique before and after reading to show students how to sort complex material and figure out interrelationships between new and old concepts about the Civil War.

Teacher: Before we read this chapter, let's see how much we already know about the Civil War. I'll put Civil War right here in the center of the board. Now, tell me some words or concepts that you know have to do with the Civil War and I'll list them.

Student: North and South.

Student: Slavery.

Student: Weapons—cannons, guns, and bayonets.

Teacher: OK. Good. Now, watch what I do to put some order to all of this. I already know that cannons, guns, and bayonets are weapons, so I'll group them all together and draw a line from Civil War to *Weapons*. (Teacher continues until several categories have been developed.) Now I want you to think about these categories as you read to yourselves the first five pages of the chapter. When you finish I'll ask you to list some more concepts about the Civil War. (Students read.) OK. Did you find more weapons?

Student: Swords.

Teacher: Good. I'll include swords under our *Weapons* heading.

Summary

Helping students learn how to be in metacognitive control of their reading begins with modifying curriculum to make room for cognitive and metacognitive aspects of reading. The next step is to incorporate both direct and indirect instruction into your teaching routine.

Developmental reading teachers are primarily responsible for teaching students when and how to use cognitive reading strategies, and content area teachers are responsible for helping students apply these strategies when reading literature and content area materials.

All middle school teachers are responsible for helping students understand how the reading process works and when and how to use study strategies.

Conclusion

Teaching middle school students how to be more metacognitive is a difficult task. You must be patient. Adapting and modifying your curriculum and instructional practices takes time and is a frustrating endeavor. Try not to take on too much at one time, and do not be afraid to make mistakes. Start small. Make only one or two small changes at a time and make only those changes you think you can realistically accomplish. Wait until you feel confident with those changes before incorporating more changes. Above all, trust your own judgment and intuition as a teacher and try to resist the urge to start all over. Before long, you'll begin to notice your students trying to implement strategic thinking. When that happens, you will know you are on your way to helping your students become more metacognitive.

References

Baker, Linda, & Brown, Ann. (1984). Metacognitive skills and reading. In P. David Pearson (Ed.), *Handbook of reading research*. New York: Longman.

Barr, Rebecca, Blachowicz, Camille, Johnson, Barbara, Morris, Darrell, Mosenthal, James, & Ogle, Donna. (1987). Editorial. *Journal of Reading Behavior, 19,* 213-222.

Duffy, Gerald, & Roehler, Laura. (1987). Improving reading instruction through the use of responsive elaboration. *The Reading Teacher, 6,* 514-521.

Duffy, Gerald, Roehler, Laura, & Herrmann, Beth Ann. (1988). Modeling mental processes helps poor readers become strategic readers. *The Reading Teacher, 42,* 24-28.

Duffy, Gerald, Roehler, Laura, Meloth, Michael, Vavrus, Linda, Book, Cassandra, Putnam, Joyce, & Wesselman, Roy. (1986). The relationship between explicit verbal explanation during reading skill instruction and student awareness and achievement: A study of reading teacher effects. *Reading Research Quarterly, 21,* 237-252.

Duffy, Gerald, Roehler, Laura, Sivan, Eva, Rackliffe, Gary, Book, Cassandra, Meloth, Michael, Vavrus, Linda, Wesselman, Roy, Putnam, Joyce, & Bassiri, Dina. (1987). The effects of explaining reasoning associated with using reading strategies. *Reading Research Quarterly, 22,* 347-367.

Flavell, John. (1981). Cognitive monitoring. In Patrick Dickson (Ed.), *Children's oral communication skills*. New York: Academic.

Flower, Linda, & Hayes, John. (1981). A cognitive process theory of writing. *College Composition and Communication, 32,* 365-387.

Hayes, John, & Flower, Linda. (1980). Identifying the organization of writing processes. In Lee Gregg & Erwin Steinberg (Eds.), *Cognitive processes in writing*. Hillsdale, NJ: Erlbaum.

Paris, Scott, Lipson, Marjorie, & Wixson, Karen K. (1983). Becoming a strategic reader. *Contemporary Educational Psychology, 8.*

Pressley, Michael, Forrest-Pressley, Donna, Elliott-Faust, Darlene, & Miller, Gloria. (1985). Children's use of cognitive strategies, how to teach strategies, and what to do if they can't be taught. In Michael Pressley & Charles Brainerd (Eds.), *Cognitive processes in memory development*. Berlin and New York: Springer-Verlag.

Pressley, Michael, Symons, Sonya, Snyder, Barbara, & Cariglia-Bull, Teresa. (1989). Strategy instruction research is coming of age. *Learning Disability Quarterly. 12*(1), 16-30.

Scardamalia, Marlene, & Bereiter, Carl. (1986a). Research on written composition. In Merlin Wittrock (Ed.), *Handbook of research on teaching*. New York: Macmillan.

Scardamalia, Marlene, & Bereiter, Carl. (1986b). Writing. In Rona Dillon & Robert Sternberg (Eds.), *Cognition and instruction*. Orlando, FL: Academic.

Affective Goals in Reading and Writing

Donna E. Alvermann
K. Denise Muth

AS SEEN IN THE PRE-vious chapter, educators have at their disposal a variety of strategies for improving the cognitive and metacognitive processes related to reading and writing. By contrast, relatively little information is available on the affective domain of reading and writing, which is concerned with emotional feeling and activity (Harris & Hodges, 1981). Yet affect energizes the cognitive domain (Athey, 1985) and plays a major role in the development of middle school readers and writers.

How to develop positive feelings toward reading and writing is the focus of this chapter. Specifically, four affective dimensions—motivation, attitudes, interests, and values—will be examined by drawing upon research and the implications of that research for reading and writing. According to Tonjes and Zintz (1987, p. 50), "Promoting the affective dimensions of motivation, attitudes, in-terests, and values of transescent...students is crucial for content teachers if relevant learning is to take place."

Before discussing the affective dimensions of literacy in detail, a brief discussion of the emotional development of early adolescents, or transescents, and the differences between learning and performance goals is necessary. It is difficult for a teacher to plan effective activities for transescents without considering how students' emotional development might affect the outcome of these activities. As noted in Chapter 2 (this volume), the emotional problems of students in this age group frequently override any interests students might have in their school work.

Emotional Development of Transescents

Transescence, especially the emotional development that occurs during this early adolescent period, is one of the least studied areas of human development. Research into the emotional development of transescents has found that many of the widely held notions about this age group are untrue (George & Lawrence, 1982).

First, the idea that most transescents go through a period of tremendous emotional pressure is not quite true. Many transescents are faced with emotional problems, but severe emotional trauma is a reality for only a small percentage of students (Lipsitz, 1977).

Second, the belief that peer groups are formed from strong emotional bonds is not really true of transescent friendships. Peer groups do exert a tremendous amount of power at this age, but friendships within the peer groups are not as strong as was once believed (Gallatin, 1975). As a result, membership in particular peer groups changes frequently, often for superficial reasons.

Third, advertising notwithstanding, there is no stereotypical transescent. Students in this age group are individuals with their own interests, problems, and ways of coping with their problems.

Fourth, the idea has been refuted that transescents turn away from adults to turn toward one another. Elkind (1967) explains that it is more likely that transescents, being egocentric, turn away from adults believing that adults are aware of and critical of their every move.

However, certain notions of the emotional development of the middle school student hold true. They include a need for peer recognition, a need for minimizing the gap between transescents' ideal-ized selves and their actual performance, and a need to channel emotional energies into creative activities to fulfill self-assertion and self-concept.

For example, transescents need to be accepted by their peers and at the same time recognized as individuals with unique qualities and abilities. This dual need might be satisfied in reading by providing opportunities for students to discuss their assignments in small groups of their own choosing before engaging in large group discussion. In writing, students might be given individual responsibilities within a group project, such as editing a class newspaper. Various editors would have individual responsibilities, but the success of the newspaper would depend on all students effectively doing their jobs.

It is important for early adolescents to work toward realistic goals that are also challenging. In terms of reading, low ability students should participate in higher level as well as lower level reading activities. Failure to teach the necessary higher level reading skills to low ability students may account for much of the achievement deficit among less able readers (Brown, Palincsar, & Purcell, 1984). In terms of writing, students need to write for a variety of audiences and purposes. One example could be writing scripts for plays, a challenging task that is also appropriate for students' interests and abilities.

Finally, transescents must be given opportunities to channel their emotions into creative activities and yet feel secure by doing routine tasks. In reading, this balance can be achieved if opportunities for reading new and challenging information are prefaced by activities that help students relate what they are about to learn to what they already know. Journal writing, where writers serve as their own audience, is an example of a creative activity couched within a familiar routine.

Implications for Teaching Reading and Writing

George and Lawrence (1982) summarized general criteria for teachers based on the emotional needs of transescents. Three of the criteria are presented here with specific examples of their implications for teaching literacy.

1. *Providing opportunities for peer recognition is essential at the middle school level.* Such opportunities should be provided in cooperative, rather than competitive, learning situations. For example, transescents need opportunities to discuss ideas they have learned through both leisure and school related reading. Building a safe environment for discussing these ideas can lead to positive recognition among peers. A safe environment for sharing also can be provided by having transescents write on self-selected topics for a peer audience.

2. *Setting realistic goals is essential to minimize the chances of gaps occurring between transescents' idealized selves and their actual performance.* For example, transescents need to understand that full comprehension may require several readings and that good writing may require several revisions.

3. *Channeling emotional energies into creative activities is especially important.* Such activities fulfill the self-assertion and self-concept needs of transescents. For example, creative readers develop strong self-concepts as a result of being able to challenge ideas for the purpose of improving them. Similarly, creative writers are capable of developing logical arguments for the purpose of persuading others, and feel empowered as a result.

Learning Goals versus Performance Goals

Given the emotional makeup of transescents, it is important that teachers strike a balance between two broad categories of goals. One category, Learning Goals, is concerned with learning for the sake of learning. Students whose goals fall into this category want to understand and increase their competence in mastering new information or completing new tasks. A second category, Performance Goals, is concerned with normative behavior. Student activity in this category is concerned more with gaining favorable judgments (and avoiding unfavorable judgments) of significant others than it is with learning for learning's sake (Dweck, 1986). Nolen (1987) favors instruction that is learning-oriented because it energizes rather than debilitates. It fosters learning as a positive end in itself and deemphasizes the competition and social comparison associated with learning that is performance-goal-oriented.

Advocating one type of instruction over another does not dismiss the fact that both learning-goal and performance-goal activities can be found in most schools. Middle school teachers need to strike a balance between the two types of activities. Additionally, helping students attribute their successes and failures to effort rather than ability encourages them to persist in the face of challenging tasks. Focusing on achievement through effort is especially important, given the crucial need transescents have for peer recognition and acceptance and their sensitivity to criticism from adults.

Affective Dimensions

Students' affective responses toward reading and writing are contingent on their emotional development. Thus, in this section the four affective dimensions—motivation, attitudes, interest, and values—are discussed in relation to the emotional development of transescents. Throughout the discussion of these affective dimensions, it will be pointed out how teachers can maintain a balance between learning goals and performance goals as they teach reading and writing.

Motivation

Research. How do you get students to focus more on effort and less on ability? How do you influence them to make challenging and engaging choices, to develop an orientation toward learning goals rather than performance goals? These questions (Ames, 1987) form the core of the affective dimension generally referred to as motivation. Although "the literature on motivation has expanded dramatically during the past decade" (Cohen, 1986, p. 23), little of it focuses specifically on developing positive feelings toward reading and writing.

One exception in the area of reading is a survey study by Heathington (1979) that involved a sample of 254 students in grades 5 through 8, drawn from a population with a broad range of achievement levels, socioeconomic backgrounds, and geographic locations. Heathington concluded that the reading problems of this age group were clearly reflected in their responses to her questions. Briefly, the transescents in Heathington's study complained that they did not have enough time for reading, they had too many interruptions when they did read, there were not enough books on topics they wanted to read about, and (for some) they were not able to read well enough to enjoy reading. Hence, limitations in time, choices, and reading ability may affect students' motivation to read.

Research on writing indicates that one way to motivate middle school students to write is to allow them to write on topics they select, topics of personal interest (Fear et al., 1987). This study involved two upper elementary grade teachers who had different strategies for assigning writing topics to their students. The first teacher assigned topics related to the social studies or science content the students were studying. The second teacher allowed students to select topics from a list that each one had generated at the beginning of the year. The list contained ideas of things students would like to tell people about.

In interviews conducted by the experimenters, students in the first teacher's class generated significantly fewer ideas to write about than did the students in the second teacher's class. And students in the first class reported that they relied mainly on their teacher for writing topics. When students did have a choice, the topics they selected were school-related. On the other hand, students in the second teacher's class reported that frequently they relied on their own experiences for their writing and not on school-related topics. Not surprisingly, a positive relationship was found between how topics were selected and productivity. Students in the second teacher's class seemed more motivated; they generated significantly more ideas on three measures of productivity than did students in the first teacher's class.

Implications for reading instruction. Based on the Heathington study, motivating students to read is associated with one or more of these elements of instruction: (1) providing students with sufficient time to read during the school day, (2) limiting the number of interruptions during reading, (3) gathering a variety of reading materials that appeal to transescents, and (4) assessing each student's abilities for the purpose of providing instruction to help the student improve as a reader.

Providing students with sufficient time to read during the school day delivers a strong message to transescents—namely, that reading is important and deserves a place of prominence in their daily lives. A more subtle message is that reading is not a subject per se, but a tool to help students understand and enjoy a wide number of subjects. Setting aside as few as 5 minutes at the beginning or end of each class period for students to read from materials of their own choosing would amount to approximately 30 minutes of free reading per day. While not ideal in terms of allowing students to become absorbed in their reading, those 5

minutes would at least create the expectation that reading is something to be done for enjoyment, relaxation, and a break from schoolwork.

Limiting the number of interruptions during free reading at school presents a challenge. An Uninterrupted Sustained Silent Reading (USSR) period would be an alternative to the 5 minute snippets of free reading. USSR (Hunt, 1970) ensures that students can count on a special time set aside for free reading on a specified number of days each week. Besides being motivational, free reading has been shown to correlate with gains in reading achievement (Fielding, Wilson, & Anderson, 1986).

Gathering reading materials that appeal to transescents takes the cooperation of teachers, librarians, and the students themselves. Teachers face the additional task of "organizing a curriculum that will help students learn necessary skills, concepts, and ideas while they are reading books based on their individual needs, interests, and abilities" (Reed, 1985, p. 196). One simple way of coordinating these tasks is to use related readings, a strategy that encourages students to read a variety of materials (newspapers, biographies, teen magazines, book reviews, plays) on the same topic. Comparing the information learned from these varied sources can lead to improved concept development as well as to the growth of fundamental reading skills associated with content area reading instruction (Wiesendanger, 1986).

Finally, assessing students' reading abilities with appropriate follow-up instruction can be a motivating factor if students feel that their expanding skills enable them to enjoy reading more. Vocabulary development, rate adjustment, and cooperative learning methods are three areas of follow-up instruction that benefit students in middle school (Heathington, 1979; Slavin, 1984).

Implications for writing instruction. Four of the easiest and most effective ways to motivate transescents to write are (1) have students write about their own experiences, (2) provide new experiences, (3) use literature as a starting point, and (4) use a variety of media (Fisher & Terry, 1982; Hennings, 1982). If properly structured, all of these activities also promote learning over performance.

Because transescents have a need for success, what better way for them to be successful writers than to write about what they know best—their own experiences? Transescents have many experiences to write about, and they should be encouraged to use their senses in describing their experiences. Revision can be incorporated as a positive aspect of the writing process by having students revise their writing as their experiences change.

Transescents have a need for novel and challenging activities. Teachers can fill this need by providing exciting experiences for students to write about. A field trip, a science fair, or an interview with a local celebrity can serve as the basis for writing. A creative teacher can turn an ordinary activity into a novel writing project by providing the right stimulus for writing activities.

Good literature allows readers to identify with others like themselves. It also exposes students to people and places far

Teachers can work with students to instill an interest in writing.

removed from their own lives. Writing activities can revolve around literature the students choose themselves or literature the teacher reads to the students as a group.

Teenagers are quite knowledgeable about music, movies, and television. Teachers can capitalize on students' knowledge in these areas and use a variety of media to motivate them to write. For example, students might write about their favorite rock or movie stars, about a concert they recently attended, or even about their feelings as they listened to a Mozart recording. They might also design a television commercial for a popular product. Such writing activities can be used to develop a sense of the skills needed for communicating about what is relevant in young people's lives.

Attitudes

Research. A concern over the presence or absence of favorable attitudes toward reading and writing is probably the most written about dimension in the affective domain of the literature on literacy. Attitude is thought to influence students' comprehension of reading materials (Mathewson, 1985), as well as predict their love of reading.

> Since reading is the basis of most other school subjects, it seems logical to suppose that when the child finds reading a pleasurable experience, positive attitudes toward reading will rapidly become generalized to most other subjects. The expanding interest in other subjects should, in turn, lead to a deeper love of reading as a primary source of information and enjoyment (Athey, 1985, p. 542).

Middle school students' attitudes toward reading seem largely unaffected by either low achievement level or low socioeconomic level. For instance, the results of administering Estes' (1971) Reading Attitude Scale to 400 lower socioeconomic, low-achieving sixth graders showed that these students were highly positive toward reading (Dwyer & Joy, 1980).

Recent research in the area of writing indicates that students' attitudes toward writing are influenced by the frequency, amount, and type of writing assignments used in the classroom (Daly, Vangelisti, & Witte, 1988). Once formed, these writing attitudes affect students' choices of majors in college (Daly & Miller, 1975), writing performance (Selfe, 1985), and teachers' perceptions of students' writing ability (Daly, 1979). In addition, students' attitudes toward writing

are related to their satisfaction and interest in writing and to their feelings about their writing improvement (Jeroski & Conry, 1981). Research also shows that students with poor attitudes toward writing have low opinions of their writing ability (Selfe, 1985). Of primary importance to teachers is a finding from the National Assessment of Educational Progress (Applebee, Langer, & Mullis, 1986) that indicates that students' attitudes toward writing deteriorate from grades 4 through 11.

Implications for reading instruction. Teachers can control four factors that have bearing on students' attitudes toward reading: (1) curriculum factors, (2) classroom setting, (3) student perceptions, and (4) teacher characteristics (Vaughan & Estes, 1986). Although discussed separately, all of these factors are interrelated and influence school learning in general.

According to Vaughan and Estes, *how* the curriculum is taught is as important to positive attitude development as *what* is taught. For example, transescents need to feel free to express their thoughts, for only then will they be stimulated to think critically and creatively. Because choices in curriculum materials also influence students' attitudes, a variety of texts and other sources of print should be readily available in the classroom. Paperbacks are especially effective and are less intimidating than hardbound textbooks or novels. Finally, it is essential that students understand the purpose of their reading assignment and receive suggestions for efficiently completing the assignments.

Classroom setting also plays a part in

developing positive attitudes. Desks and other furniture need to be arranged in a manner that encourages peer interaction yet provides space for students to work alone with minimal distraction. Vaughan and Estes (1986, p. 243) humorously note, "Straight rows of desks are good for two things: listening to lectures and sweeping between." They also point out that classroom setting is not defined by physical surroundings alone. Atmosphere plays a significant role in attitude development. Holding classroom interruptions to a minimum does more than soothe the teacher's nerves; it also suggests to the students that what they are doing is important.

Student perceptions have a direct bearing on the development of positive attitudes about reading. We all enjoy doing the things we know well, as reflected in the old adage, "Nothing succeeds like success." Dulin (1978, p. 112), however, suggests changing that adage to " 'Nothing succeeds like *perceived* success,' that is, results perceived by the *learner* as well as the teacher." What this means to the teacher, according to Dulin, is that it is important to provide daily opportunities in which success in reading is obvious to students. When students perceive themselves to be successful, they tend to have better attitudes.

Not surprisingly, teacher characteristics have a bearing on the attitudes students develop toward reading. When students are asked to name their favorite subject and their favorite teacher, the two are frequently the same. According to Vaughan and Estes (1986), the teacher is the most potent force in the classroom in terms of affecting students' attitudes toward reading. Teacher enthusiasm for the subject matter, fair grading and discipline practices, realistic expectations, and an appropriate amount of attention to detail are but a few of the characteristics that cause students to judge a teacher as good and reading as enjoyable whatever the content area.

Implications for writing instruction. Because the classroom is a place where many students develop their attitudes toward writing, the teacher is an important factor. In order to have an effective writing program that helps transescents develop positive attitudes toward writing, teachers need to (1) create a positive environment for writing, (2) ensure that writing tasks are purposeful, and (3) provide some situations in which writing is not evaluated.

A positive environment for writing involves a free and nonthreatening atmosphere in which students have time to proceed at their own pace through the steps of the writing process (Hayes & Flower, 1980; Norton, 1985). Positive writing environments for transescents are characterized as providing room for individual choices and opportunities for sharing what is written. Because students at this age level are learning to make choices and to assume responsibility for those choices, the writing environment must provide a variety of instructional activities. These activities might include choices in topics, form, purpose, and audience. Finally, because transescents have a need for recognition and acceptance among their peers, they should have opportunities to share their writing with classmates. This can be done through school newspapers, bulletin boards, oral reading, and learning logs.

One of the challenging tasks teachers face when designing writing activities is making certain the activities are purposeful. Purposeful writing activities are characterized as having a "normal sense of an audience and of communicative intent" (Scardamalia & Bereiter, 1986, p. 794). Unfortunately, much of the writing done in classrooms is not purposeful writing, but writing that involves filling in worksheets, taking tests, and other such activities (Applebee, 1981). Granted, the number of purposeful reasons for classroom writing tasks is limited. But in order to help students develop positive attitudes toward writing, teachers need to integrate writing throughout all content area subjects. By writing purposefully in science, social studies, mathematics, and language arts, students come to understand that writing is an important and useful tool, not just a skill practiced during writing class.

When students feel they are writing in a highly evaluative situation (writing a pass or fail composition as opposed to writing in a journal that no one will read), their level of anxiety increases (Daly & Hailey, 1984). Writing anxiety affects students' attitudes toward writing and is related to lower writing performance (Daly & Miller, 1975). This is not to say that teachers should never evaluate their students' writing. But, as discussed earlier, transescents need a balance between novel, challenging activities and safe, comfortable activities. Therefore, students should have opportunities to write material that will not be evaluated as well as material that will. In situations where writing is evaluated, teachers

should make positive comments about some aspect of the writing. By doing this as often as possible, teachers will assure students that writing can be a method of learning and not just a means of demonstrating performance. (See Chapter 9, this volume, for additional suggestions on evaluating writing.)

Interests

Research. Much has been written on the importance of interests as an affective dimension of literacy. Research has established that reading involves not so much what we do with our eyes as how interested we are in what we are reading. It has been shown that low-achieving seventh grade students are able to comprehend far beyond their frustrational reading level when the material is interesting to them (Belloni & Jongsma, 1978). It also has been shown that "interesting" is the single largest categorical response that middle school students give to books they have read (Carter & Harris, 1982). Although transescents vary widely in their reading interests, they tend to be consistently interested in paperbacks rather than hardbacks, in books recommended by their peers rather than by their teachers, and in the content on the first page rather than the print size and number of illustrations (Wendelin & Zinck, 1983). The research is mixed on the importance of gender preferences, but it is quite clear that middle school students prefer stories in which the characters overcome their problems rather than succumb to them (Beyard-Tyler & Sullivan, 1980; Johnson & Greenbaum, 1982).

As mentioned previously, students are

interested in writing about topics in which they have a personal interest. But what else are they interested in writing about? What types of writing activities do they engage in on their own? The NAEP (Applebee, Langer, & Mullis, 1986) conducted a survey to answer these questions. The survey asked the students about the types of writing they do for personal/social reasons and for functional reasons. The eighth graders who were surveyed reported that the type of personal/social writing they did most was writing notes and messages; the personal/social writing they did least was writing stories or poems. The type of functional writing they did most was making lists; the functional writing they did least was writing for school newspapers, yearbooks, or magazines. Of particular interest to teachers is the additional finding that the amount of time students spent in writing stories and poetry for pleasure decreased between grades 4 and 8. Unfortunately, these findings indicate that students are not using writing as a learning tool.

Implications for reading instruction. Science and social studies texts at the middle school level often contain complex concepts that are difficult to comprehend and of little interest to students. One way of dealing with this problem and of generating interest in the subject matter is to incorporate outside reading using a technique called "Read a Book in an Hour" (Smith, 1979). In using this technique, a science teacher might assign different students different chapters (or parts of chapters) from a science fiction paperback. The students would then have the remainder of the class period to read and discuss their portions of the book as they related to the concepts presented in their science textbooks. Some postreading questions might be "Are the events in the sci-fi book possible?" "Why or why not?" "How does the textbook support or refute your thinking?"

Other ways to increase the appeal of textbooks include elaborating on the main themes of the text (Hidi & Baird, 1986) and introducing speculative thought as in the Options Guide (Bean et al., 1986). To help reluctant readers develop an interest in leisure reading, it pays to use peer-endorsed stories with action that begins on page 1, have a small cast of characters, and use dialogue to carry the action (Beckman, 1984). Also receiving a high recommendation are genres that have positive solutions and endings, such as most mysteries and adventures (Summers & Lukasevich, 1983). These genres are familiar to students and can serve as bridges to new genres. Bridging from the old and familiar to the new and unfamiliar provides the balance transescents need in their lives.

Implications for writing instruction. As the research discussed indicates, many students are not engaged in substantive writing tasks on their own. One could argue that students do not write much on their own because they lack interest in writing or because they have few opportunities to express their thoughts in classroom writing. Middle school teachers can increase their students' interest in writing by providing opportunities for them to engage in meaningful writing, such as keeping journals, contributing to school newspapers, and creating stories and poems to be bound as books and used at lower grade levels.

The results of the NEAP study cited earlier revealed that transescents were least likely to write stories and poetry or write for school newspapers, magazines, and yearbooks. The solution does not lie with increasing the number of such assignments. Rather, teachers will need to involve students gradually in the writing process, making sure that students are exposed to the various types of text structures and forms of poetry. In each instance, a balance should be maintained between learning goals and performance goals.

Values

Research. Literacy research that focuses specifically on values is limited at the middle school level. What does exist is tied inextricably to research on achievement motivation. Thus, it might be assumed that because of the high value society traditionally has placed on reading, students will be motivated to read. This assumption is not without its critics (Nicholls, 1987). As noted earlier, transescents have a strong need to be accepted by their peers, and in some classrooms students who value reading might be viewed as deviating from the norm. This would be an example of a positive goal with potential for negative consequences. Another link between the achievement motivation literature and the literature on values is the potential conflict of values between teachers and students. Teachers value students who work hard, and they reward those who succeed. In classrooms where "effort supplants ability as a source of reward

and satisfaction" (Covington, 1984, p. 16), the potential conflict between teachers' values and students' values is kept to a minimum. However, in classrooms where ability is valued over effort, students often turn to failure-avoiding strategies, such as feigning disinterest in schoolwork, as a means of maintaining their sense of self-worth (Covington).

In terms of writing research, a NAEP report (Applebee, Langer, & Mullis, 1986) suggests that middle school students generally understand that writing does have value. Students value writing for its role as a study aid, for reminding them about things, and for showing others what they know. This last finding suggests that transescents place value on performance over learning. Rated very low by students were value statements such as "helps me learn about myself," "helps me understand my own feelings," and "helps me think more clearly." An equally distressing finding from the NAEP report is that students' belief in the value of writing declines between grades 4 and 8.

Implications for reading instruction. The most important task facing teachers is to model values about reading that will discourage students from being so preoccupied with performance goals that they fail to see the value of reading for learning, relaxation, and escape. Several noncompetitive approaches to learning can help teachers with this task. For example, mastery learning enables students to acquire information through multiple test/study/retest opportunities and to make judgments about their progress based on self-comparisons, not comparisons with their peers. Other noncompetitive approaches include cooperative learning and contract learning. Cooperative learning works well in content area classes where students are divided into small groups, and individuals in each group take responsibility for learning about (and then teaching others) some part of the assignment. Contract learning helps students set realistic goals for studying their assigned materials and strengthens their perceptions of the link between effort and achievement.

Implications for writing instruction. Teachers who expect their students to value writing as a tool for learning provide opportunities for the types of writing that make explicit the link between writing and self-knowledge. For example, journal writing is an excellent means of helping students learn about themselves and their feelings. Transescents experience enormous changes, and journal writing is one means for them to express their reactions to these changes. If students are to value writing as a vehicle for self-expression, they must have opportunities to write about themselves and their feelings.

Summary

Researchers know more about *how* information is written and comprehended than they do about *why* an individual might elect to read and write in the first place. The affective dimensions of motivation, attitudes, interests, and values provide a focus for the discussion of how middle school teachers might help students choose to be skilled readers and writers. Literacy instruction that balances learning goals with performance goals helps transescents develop positive

feelings toward reading and writing based on the emotional needs of this age group.

References

Ames, Carole. (1987). *Social context and student cognitions.* Paper presented at the annual meeting of the American Educational Research Association, Washington, DC.

Applebee, Arthur N. (1981). *Writing in the secondary school.* Urbana, IL: National Council of Teachers of English.

Applebee, Arthur N., Langer, Judith A., & Mullis, Ina V. (1986). *The writing report card: Writing achievement in American schools.* Princeton, NJ: National Assessment of Educational Progress, Educational Testing Service.

Athey, Irene. (1985). Reading research in the affective domain. In Harry Singer & Robert B. Ruddell (Eds.), *Theoretical models and processes of reading* (3rd ed.). Newark, DE: International Reading Association.

Bean, Thomas W., Sorter, Jack, Singer, Harry, & Frazee, Charles. (1986). Teaching students how to make predictions about events in history with a graphic organizer plus options guide. *Journal of Reading, 23,* 739-745.

Beckman, Judith. (1984). Turning reluctant readers into lifetime readers. *English Journal, 73,* 84-86.

Belloni, Loretta F., & Jongsma, Eugene A. (1978). The effects of interest on reading comprehension of low-achieving students. *Journal of Reading, 22,* 106-109.

Beyard-Tyler, Karen C., & Sullivan, Howard J. (1980). Adolescent reading preferences for type of theme and sex of character. *Reading Research Quarterly, 16,* 104-120.

Brown, Ann L., Palincsar, Annemarie S., & Purcell, L. (1984). Poor readers: Teach don't label. In Ulric Neisser (Ed.), *The academic performance of minority children*: A new perspective. Hillsdale, NJ: Erlbaum.

Carter, Betty, & Harris, Karen. (1982). What junior high students like in books. *Journal of Reading, 26,* 42-46.

Cohen, Margaret W. (1986). Research on motivation: New content for the teacher preparation curriculum. *Journal of Teacher Education, 37*(3), 23-27.

Covington, Martin V. (1984). The self-worth theory of achievement motivation: Findings and implications. *Elementary School Journal, 85,* 5-20.

Daly, John A. (1979). Writing apprehension in the classroom: Teacher role expectancies of the apprehensive writer. *Research in the Teaching of English, 13,* 37-44.

Daly, John A., & Hailey, Joy L. (1984). Putting the situation into writing research: State and disposition as parameters of writing apprehension. In Richard Beach & Lillian S. Bridwell (Eds.), *New directions in composition research.* New York: Guilford.

Daly, John A., & Miller, Michael D. (1975). Further studies in writing apprehension: SAT scores, success expectations, willingness to take advanced courses, and sex differences. *Research in the Teaching of English, 9,* 250-256.

Daly, John A., Vangelisti, Anita, & Witte, Stephen P. (1988). Writing apprehension in the classroom context. In Bennett A. Rafoth & Donald L. Rubin (Eds.), *The social construction of written communication* (pp. 147-171). Norwood, NJ: Ablex.

Dulin, Kenneth L. (1978). Reading and the affective domain. In Susanna Pflaum-Connor (Ed.), *Aspects of reading instruction.* Berkeley, CA: McCutchan.

Dweck, Carol S. (1986). Motivational processes affecting learning. *American Psychologist, 41,* 1040-1048.

Dwyer, Edward J., & Joy, Flora. (1980). Reading attitudes across a book age spectrum. *Reading Horizons, 21,* 39-43.

Elkind, David. (1967). Egocentricism in adolescents. *Childhood Development, 38,* 1025-1034.

Estes, Thomas H. (1971). A scale to measure attitudes toward reading. *Journal of Reading, 15,* 135-138.

Fear, Kathleen L., Anderson, Linda M., Englert, Carol S., & Raphael, Taffy E. (1987). The relationship between teachers' beliefs and instruction and students' conceptions about the writing process. In John E. Readence & R. Scott Baldwin (Eds.), *Research in literacy: Merging perspectives.* Thirty-Sixth Yearbook of the National Reading Conference. Rochester, NY: National Reading Conference.

Fielding, Linda G., Wilson, Paul T., & Anderson, Richard C. (1986). The new focus on free reading: The role of tradebooks in reading instruction. In Taffy E. Raphael (Ed.), *The contexts of school-based literacy.* New York: Random House.

Fisher, Carol J., & Terry, C. Ann. (1982). *Children's language and the language arts* (2nd ed.). New York: McGraw-Hill.

Gallatin, Judith. (1975). *Adolescence and individuality.* New York: Harper & Row.

George, Paul, & Lawrence, Gordon. (1982). *Handbook for middle school teaching.* Glenview, IL: Scott, Foresman.

Harris, Theodore L., & Hodges, Richard E. (Eds.). (1981). *A dictionary of reading and related terms.* Newark, DE: International Reading Association.

Hayes, John R., & Flower, Linda S. (1980). Identifying the organization of writing processes. In Lee W. Gregg & Erwin R. Steinberg (Eds.), *Cognitive processes in writing.* Hillsdale, NJ: Erlbaum.

Heathington, Betty S. (1979). What to do about reading motivation in the middle school. *Journal of Reading, 22*(8), 709-713.

Hennings, Dorothy G. (1982). *Communication in action: Teaching the language arts* (2nd ed.). Boston, MA: Houghton Mifflin.

Hidi, Suzanne, & Baird, William. (1986). *The effect of three types of interestingness on recall from expository text.* Paper presented at the annual meeting of the American Educational Research Association, San Francisco, CA.

Hunt, Lyman C., Jr. (1970). The effect of self-selection, interest, and motivation upon independent, instructional, and frustrational levels. *The Reading Teacher, 24,* 146-151, 158.

Jeroski, Sharon F., & Conry, Robert F. (1981). *Development and field application of the Attitude Toward Writing Scale.* Paper presented at the annual meeting of the American Educational Research Association, Los Angeles, CA.

Johnson, Carol S., & Greenbaum, Gloria R. (1982). Girls' and boys' reading interests: A review of the research. In E. Marcia Sheridan (Ed.), *Sex stereotypes and reading: Research and strategies.* Newark, DE: International Reading Association.

Lipsitz, Joan. (1977). *Growing up forgotten.* Lexington, MA: D.C. Heath.

Mathewson, Grover C. (1985). Toward a comprehensive model of affect in the reading process. In Harry Singer & Robert B. Ruddell (Eds.), *Theoretical models and processes of reading* (3rd ed.). Newark, DE: International Reading Association.

Nicholls, John G. (1987). *Motivation, values, and education*. Paper presented at the annual meeting of the American Educational Research Association, Washington, DC.

Nolen, Susan B. (1987). *The influence of task involvement on the use of learning strategies*. Paper presented at the annual meeting of the American Educational Research Association, Washington, DC.

Norton, Donna E. (1985). *Through the eyes of a child: An introduction to children's literature*. Columbus, OH: Charles E. Merrill.

Reed, Arthea J.S. (1985). *Reaching adolescents: The young adult book and the school*. New York: Holt, Rinehart & Winston.

Scardamalia, Marlene, & Bereiter, Carl. (1986). Research on written composition. In Merlin C. Wittrock (Ed.), *Handbook of research on teaching* (3rd ed.). New York: Macmillan.

Selfe, Cynthia. (1985). An apprehensive writer composes. In Michael Rose (Ed.), *When a writer can't write: Studies of writer's block and other composing process problems*. New York: Guilford.

Slavin, Robert E. (1984). Students motivating students to excel: Cooperative incentives, cooperative tasks, and student achievement. *Elementary School Journal, 85*, 53-63.

Smith, Cyrus F. (1979). Read a book in an hour: Variations to develop composition and comprehension. *Journal of Reading, 23*, 25-29.

Summers, Edward G., & Lukasevich, Ann. (1983). Reading preferences of intermediate-grade children in relation to sex, community, and maturation (grade level): A Canadian perspective. *Reading Research Quarterly, 18*, 347-360.

Tonjes, Marian J., & Zintz, Miles V. (1987). *Teaching reading, thinking, study skills in content classrooms* (2nd ed.). Dubuque, IA: William C. Brown.

Vaughan, Joseph L., & Estes, Thomas H. (1986). *Reading and reasoning beyond the primary grades*. Boston, MA: Allyn & Bacon.

Wendelin, Karla H., & Zinck, R. Ann. (1983). How students make book choices. *Reading Horizons, 23*, 84-88.

Wiesendanger, Katherine. (1986). Related readings motivate students to read. *The Reading Teacher, 39*, 485-486.

Instructional Planning and Teaching in Reading and Writing

Mark W. Conley

CONFUSION PERSISTS about the middle school instruction in reading and writing, a situation caused largely by uncertainty about reading and writing goals. Although the trend away from junior highs and toward middle schools has been going on for years, only recently have educators articulated the nature and function of the middle school curriculum (Conley, 1989; Lipsitz, 1984).

The purposes of this chapter are to clarify the goals of reading and writing at the middle school level, describe effective middle school reading and writing instruction, and illustrate planning and teaching decisions consistent with effective instruction.

Goals for Reading and Writing

Approaches to middle school reading and writing traditionally have been drawn from the elementary or secondary levels rather than being uniquely developed for middle school (Conley, 1989). However, an emerging body of knowledge suggests that early adolescent learners have strengths and weaknesses that can be addressed only through effective middle school programs (Lipsitz, 1984; Preisser, Anders, & Glider, this volume).

Middle schools should emphasize three types of goals: content, process, and motivation. Content involves subject matter, the across-the-curriculum domain knowledge described in Chapter 5. Process consists of the thinking/learning processes that underlie reading and writing, much like those described in Chapter 6. Motivation is composed of desire to learn as well as ability to see connections between oneself and the school curriculum, and is similar to the description

Figure 1
Goals of Elementary, Secondary, and Middle Schools

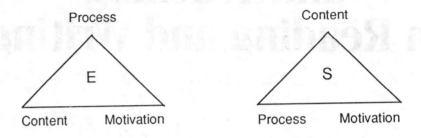

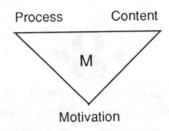

in Chapter 7.

What makes middle school teaching distinct from elementary and secondary instruction? The difference lies in the relationships among the three types of goals. Figure 1 depicts the relationships among content, process, and motivation for elementary, secondary, and middle school reading and writing instruction.

At the elementary level (*E* in Figure 1), the emphasis is on the thinking processes underlying reading and writing, on knowing how to accomplish something or the means by which it can be accomplished. Mental processes, such as planning, drafting, aligning, revising, and self-monitoring, are necessary for both reading and writing. Just as a writer engages in these activities to compose text on a page, a reader uses them to compose a model of a writer's meaning (Tierney & Pearson, 1984). A major goal at the elementary level is to create strategic readers and writers (Duffy & Roehler, 1987; Hayes & Flower, 1986). To do this, teachers focus on helping students activate knowledge they will need to make predictions about what they are reading or writing, and they stress repair strategies that can be used whenever students encounter blocks to meaning (Johnston, 1983). Instruction consistent with this emphasis involves explanations and modeling in a variety of contexts.

Responsiveness to students' thinking and a gradual shift in responsibility from teacher to student also are features of this type of instruction (Duffy & Roehler, 1987).

The emphasis at the secondary level (*S* in Figure 1) is almost entirely on content (Herber, 1978; Singer & Donlan, 1985). Specific areas such as the periodic table in science, the electoral college in social studies, algebraic equations in math, and literature in English are the focus. High school reading and writing are functional; processes are not taught for their own sake but as tools for comprehending and generating ideas about subject matter. Comprehension and writing strategies are important only insofar as they help students gain access to content. Secondary programs have been criticized for this nearly exclusive emphasis on content (Goodlad, 1984), which all too easily becomes another excuse for using dittoes and rote learning. While content is important, ignoring process and motivation goals risks turning students off to learning.

In contrast to elementary and secondary programs, instruction in middle school (*M* in Figure 1) balances content and process (as Peters suggests in Chapter 5) while relying considerably on motivation. Middle school students are faced with the demands placed on them by content area textbooks while they are still struggling to become strategic readers and writers. While the typical concept of middle school students is that they get excited only about television and friends, evidence suggests that they also can be motivated by challenging classroom experiences and attempts to link subject matter to the real world (Alvermann & Muth, this volume; (Csikszentmihalyi & Larson, 1984).

The goals of reading and writing can be summarized in a single phrase: to teach students to become lifelong learners with attention to developing their knowledge, skills, and motivation (NASSP, 1985). Reading and writing instruction that meets these goals is not easy to achieve and, in many schools, cannot be found.

We want middle school students to understand what they read and to communicate what they think in writing (Langer, 1986). However, recent research-based descriptions of reading and writing instruction suggest that we may not be reaching this goal. In a massive study on schools, Goodlad (1984) found that students spend 80 percent of the school day listening passively to teachers. In English classes, reading-related activities include answering questions based on short passages, memorizing from textbooks, and listening to teachers' interpretations. Writing often involves copying definitions or completing drills.

If reading and writing are important, why is it so difficult for Allington (this volume) and others to find good classroom examples? One reason is that the goals of the middle school and its teachers can be burdened by many constraints (Cuban, 1984). For example, confusion may exist over whether a school is functioning as a middle school or a junior high. Junior highs historically have modeled their programs after high schools. In emulating high schools, there can be an overemphasis on content at the expense of both process and motivation.

Effective middle school instruction also can be hampered by problems posed by differences in students and by gaps and changes in the curriculum.

Instruction should be a unique blend of developing subject-matter knowledge and empowering and motivating students to read and write on their own. Unfortunately, middle school reading and writing do not always live up to this potential.

Effective Reading and Writing Instruction

Instruction is what classroom teachers intentionally do to achieve desired goals. Effective instruction in reading and writing depends on a teacher's ability to actively engage students in learning within the context of a literate environment.

To become instructionally effective, middle schools must replace the passive, assignment-driven perspectives that pervade reading and writing in many classrooms with an active, cognitive view. An active view of instruction emphasizes learning in which teachers and students gradually construct meanings through a series of interactions with the content. As new information becomes integrated with old information, students develop a conscious awareness of what is being learned, when it will be useful, and how to use it effectively (Roehler & Duffy, 1989).

Active learning is supported by active instruction. For example, there are many ways for a teacher to define classroom tasks, from asking students to read the text in order to answer questions to encouraging reading centered on why the content is important. Similarly, discus-sions and the sequence of activities in a lesson can stress anything. A teacher's instructional decisions are responsible for whether students remember isolated bits of information or develop broader conceptual understandings. Depending on the instruction, students come to value memorization or restructure their understandings and integrate new experiences with old.

Consider the following lesson excerpt in which a middle school English teacher reviews students' answers to a reading guide. The reading guide is based on a short story.

Teacher: What numbers did your group get, Michelle?

Michelle: We did 1, 2, 5, 9, 10, 11, and 12.

Teacher: Okay, 1, 2, 5, 9, 10, 11, and 12. Is that right? Okay, does any group have any more or less of those numbers? What about your group, Joe?

Joe: We have 1, 5, 11, and 12.

Teacher: Okay. Can you tell us why you have those and not the other ones Michelle had?

Joe: We didn't really notice those in the story.

Teacher: But what about 9? Why didn't you choose 9? Remember in the story about the dyed hair?

In this excerpt, it is virtually impossible to determine what is being taught. The teacher's emphasis is on finding answers, but not on helping students discover meaning on their own.

Compare the above excerpt with the one below. Again, a middle school English teacher is working with a reading guide. In this segment, the teacher is discussing a theme from a short story.

Teacher: "Small things cause big problems." What does the story say about that?

Chris: Like in the story, the hen went into Gabriel's yard and laid her egg there. It was just over a stupid little egg. They started a feud which led to a fire and—

Teacher: That's a good example. What about in real life?

Jeff: Baseball. Somebody gets beaned with the ball and then they go out and argue with the pitcher.

Teacher: It starts something bigger. I'm going to start getting every group because I think it's important for you to be challenged. What happens when you get more than one person or group to contribute?

Dave: You get different ideas.

Jim: And if someone thought of an original idea, it's harder to think of more.

Teacher: Right, sometimes if we collaborate on thinking about the stories or ourselves, it can make things harder. But we also get more and better ways of looking at the world. Whenever I have a problem

understanding one of these stories—or even events in my own life—I talk it over with someone and usually I understand it better.

Notice how, in this excerpt, the teacher not only develops comprehension of the content through the questions asked, but also helps students become aware of how the group process can be used to explore meaning in the lesson and beyond. Also, to foster motivation, the teacher encourages students to think about their own lives and how they are learning. As a result, the instruction is not just an empty routine. The teacher's instruction helps students become active participants in the learning.

Active instruction in reading and writing is supported if teachers strive to create a literate environment (Atwell, 1987; Duffy & Roehler, 1987). In a literate environment, the classroom is a place where real language and real literacy are valued and promoted. Rather than an "I talk/you listen" approach to instruction, teachers and students communicate with one another in a variety of ways, both oral and written. Rather than relying solely on the textbook, they use newspapers, magazines, and pamphlets. Finally, rather than treating writing as a separate subject only for the English class, writing—like reading—is taught across the curriculum as a tool for understanding (Duffy & Roehler, 1986).

While English and social studies teachers for years have recognized the importance of making real-world connections during instruction, the notion of a literate environment can be applied to other types of classrooms as well. Consider how Mrs. Clark, a science teacher, approached the task of teaching her seventh graders how to read and report on original scientific research while including real-world connections to build motivation, balancing content and process, and shifting from more teacher to more student responsibility for what is being learned.

Clark decided she needed to model how scientists deal with research if her students were going to be able to write about it. She chose a fairly complex article comparing cells among different organs in the human body. In introducing the article, Clark asked her students to read the title and predict what it would be about. Students immediately faltered on the phrase *cell differentiation*, which Clark used as an opportunity to explain how scientists might figure out difficult vocabulary.

First, using differentiation, Clark modeled a way to unlock unfamiliar words (by thinking about what may be familiar about them). Next, she developed the meaning of cell differentiation by calling attention to the different appearance and functions of organs in the body. As the meaning of the phrase became more clear, Clark and her students asked themselves questions about what scientists might find important about cells being different. "What are the different functions of cells?" "Are all cells similar on some level?" "Are differences in cells the reason behind the difficulty of organ transplants?"

The students then read the article, paragraph by paragraph, to summarize the author's message. As they read and summarized, students noted the difficulty of the article, wondering how anyone could ever understand the technical language scientists use. Again, Clark was ready with a strategy. She showed students how to seek out any familiar words and create a single sentence summary. While developing a summary with her students, she showed them how to determine whether a summary is complete by looking at what information is covered and what is omitted. She also showed them how to raise and answer further questions about the topic of the article. As the class continued to read, Clark pointed out that they were learning to think like scientists. Not only were they learning how to unlock difficult concepts, they were developing some sophisticated scientific knowledge just like a scientist does during actual research. Subsequent lessons focused on how scientists organize information from reading and how they write scientific reports.

This episode in middle school science teaching has a successful conclusion. Through Clark's attention to creating a literate environment—emphasizing what real scientists do—students became successful and motivated. Her focus on content and process—showing students how to learn while they learn science content—empowered them to independently select and investigate their own topics based on original scientific research. Several weeks after Clark taught the lesson on thinking like a scientist, students shared and discussed a variety of well-written reports based on highly technical topics.

Active instruction in a literate environment is not restricted to the examples offered here. Teachers from across the curriculum can design lessons that actively engage students and provide real-world connections. The next sections describe how this task can be accomplished.

Planning a Lesson

The emphasis in planning an effective lesson in middle school reading and writing depends on the goal. Figure 2 presents some examples of the goals that guide planning.

A useful way to begin thinking about a lesson is to ask two questions: "What should students learn about the content?" and "Is the text poorly structured or well structured?" Answers to the first question will help focus on content goals. If the text is detailed and the content goal is to foster an in-depth understanding of facts, concepts, and principles, then planning should probably emphasize comprehension and descriptive writing. If, on the other hand, facts and concepts are self-evident but the goal is to have

Figure 2
Goals Underlying Planning Decisions for Reading and Writing

Content Goals	Understanding important facts, concepts, and principles	Understanding relationships among concepts	Understanding subject-matter principles	Understanding key concepts and technical vocabulary
Process Goals	Knowing how to construct meaning	Knowing how to construct meaning via use of expository and narrative text patterns	Knowing how to think about subject-matter content	Knowing how to develop word knowledge independently
Motivation Goals	Experiencing success with extended text	Experiencing success with using patterns to discover and generate meaning	Acquiring topic familiarity and interest	Gaining enjoyment from learning new words, success with using words to unlock and generate meaning
Reading Instruction	Comprehension	Organizational patterns	Reasoning, studying	Vocabulary development and reinforcement
Writing Instruction	Descriptive writing, records, and reports	Expository and narrative writing	Speculative or persuasive writing	Expository and narrative writing

students develop a broad understanding of principles and generalizations, then planning should stress reasoning and persuasive writing.

Having a well structured text helps determine process goals. If the text is poorly structured, students will require assistance in constructing meaning (Anderson & Armbruster, 1984). If the text contains vocabulary terms or patterns of organization that are crucial to understanding the content (cause/effect, compare/contrast, problem/solution, time order), students may require explicit modeling of ways to acquire meaning.

Last, but certainly not least, are concerns about motivation. Decisions about content and process directly affect choices about motivation. Motivation is enhanced when teachers think carefully about how instructional activities will help students achieve success. For example, vocabulary taught for its own sake is not as motivational as vocabulary taught to empower students to grasp content and learn new words on their own.

Research suggests that teacher planning is rarely as linear or as simple as the decisions implied by Figure 2. Yinger (1986) suggests that planning proceeds not as a series of decision points but as a continuous process of problem-solving, crafting, improvising, and reflecting. To illustrate, consider the task of planning a short story lesson on "The Secret Life of Walter Mitty" (Thurber, 1965).

The story is about Walter Mitty, a man who used fantasies to escape from his own miserable life. In reading the story, students often miss the relationship between the man's real life and his fantasy world, a relationship crucial for understanding the content since it offers insight into Mitty's character and, ultimately, into why fantasy is an important part of everyone's life. A content goal, therefore, is to build recognition of the relationship between fantasy and reality in the story so students can make connections to their own lives.

The text itself is well structured. It uses separate episodes to signal the real-life versus the fantasy sequences, yet the transitions from episode to episode are not always clear. If students are going to see the relationship between fantasy and reality in the story, they will need to know how to compare and contrast different episodes. A process goal, then, is to help students learn how to construct the meaning of the story through comparisons of one episode with the next.

Motivation is a little more complex. While success with understanding the story and using narrative patterns is important, many students may have difficulty sympathizing with middle-aged Mitty. Consequently, a motivation goal for the story is to help students become more familiar with and interested in Mitty's character.

Given these considerations, planning should focus on helping students identify with the main character in the story and understand how the story's structure contributes to its meaning. A combination of instructional activities emphasizing organizational patterns, reasoning, and narrative or persuasive writing would probably be most appropriate in light of the goals for this story.

This planning process also can be illustrated with an example from mathematics. Story problems are a recurring part of the math curriculum. Students often are introduced to new concepts and formulas, and story problems are used to clarify and reinforce their understanding of new concepts. When story problems contain new concepts, attention to vocabulary is required. When the underlying structure of story problems calls for comparisons among different numerical concepts (a base price versus a discounted price), attention to patterns is required. Having students write story problems for one another is one way for students to apply their understanding of how story problems are organized and solved.

Once decisions are made about what to emphasize during reading and writing instruction, teachers can provide students with guides to direct them during reading and writing. Guided reading activities, such as the use of three-level and prediction/reaction guides, can be designed for comprehension and reasoning (Herber, 1978; Readence, Bean, & Baldwin, 1985). Guided writing activities, such as the use of process writing guides noted by Raphael, Kirschner, & Englert (1986), can be created for expository and narrative writing. Vocabulary activities, such as semantic mapping, can be employed to guide comprehension as well as expository and narrative writing (Duin, 1986; Johnson, Toms-Bronowski, & Pittleman, 1982).

Guided reading activities can be an important part of a teacher's thinking about a lesson. The act of creating a reading guide focuses a teacher's decisions about content. The completed guide serves as a record of the content to be emphasized. A danger with reading guides, however, is

that they can become another way to stress answer-giving rather than meaning-getting. In effect, the guides can replace, rather than support, the careful thinking necessary to balance all the goals underlying middle school reading and writing.

Avoiding this problem requires careful attention to teachers' verbal strategies during the classroom discussions that accompany guided reading. One example is reciprocal teaching, a method that focuses specifically on process goals: students learn how to summarize, generate their own questions, clarify meaning, and make predictions (Brown & Palincsar, 1985). Teaching students how to participate in reciprocal teaching often is referred to as a "scaffolding process" in which the teacher thinks aloud and models the desired strategies until students are able to apply them on their own (Palincsar, 1984). However, teachers must avoid falling into the trap of teaching strategies for their own sake (Brown & Palincsar, 1985). When this happens, students may learn strategies in a rote way, but they will be unable to apply them (Chapters 5 & 6, this volume).

Planning lessons for reading and writing requires attention not only to goals and instruction but also to the pitfalls inherent in virtually any type of instruction. Compensating for these problems involves careful adaptations in planning that balance content, process, and motivation.

Teaching a Middle School Lesson

Students learn best when teachers exercise control and structure at the beginning of a lesson while offering more opportunity for student responsibility as the lesson progresses (Pearson &

Gallagher, 1983). A common way to do this is to begin instruction with whole-class discussion, modeling, and demonstration, and gradually move into guided practice, assessment, and (sometimes) reteaching. This section describes specific teaching strategies that support this cycle.

In many ways, lesson planning represents a teacher's "best guess." Early in a lesson, the teacher should gather data about the appropriateness of the plan, asking questions that tap into students' interest in and knowledge about the topic at hand as well as their abilities in using reading and writing to gain meaning. This strategy allows refinement of the original plan and encourages ongoing attention to achieving lesson goals.

The following verbal strategies serve two purposes early in a lesson: they allow for data gathering and they facilitate active meaning-getting during reading and writing (Conley, 1988).

Verifying content. Teachers verify students' familiarity with content by asking questions about the topic of a lesson. Followups or probes following a response encourage students to make several observations before forming a conclusion about what they are learning.

Verifying process. Teachers verify students' understanding of process by asking them to explain how they would go about learning or how they learned some aspect of content. Often, this involves encouraging students to describe how they learned what they learned.

Hooks. Hooks are vocabulary words critical for comprehending the content of a lesson or a series of lessons. More than just difficult or technical words, hooks are terms that illuminate the meaning of a story (*chain reaction*) or that are keys to lessons in a particular content area (*respiration*). By focusing attention on these critical terms, teachers pave the way for broader understandings.

Bridging. Bridging involves making connections between students and the content. It can take the form of eliciting or providing background knowledge. It also can involve modeling for students the thinking necessary for successfully completing the lesson.

Generalizing beyond the immediate lesson. Like bridging, generalizing relies on students' knowledge. Unlike bridging, which focuses on background knowledge, generalizing involves asking students to speculate about hypothetical situations, to use their knowledge about a topic to make predictions, and to think ahead.

Responsive elaboration. Responsive elaboration occurs when teachers recognize a problem in students' understanding and then provide or encourage elaborations or explanations to help students resolve the problem. Elaborations can focus on any of the strategies mentioned above, but they usually involve explanation and modeling directed at resolving the problem.

These verbal strategies are especially useful when applied in conjunction with guided reading (Conley, 1988). They can help teachers avoid the trap of emphasizing content alone, keep in touch with process and motivation goals, and watch out for and resolve breakdowns in meaning. Using these strategies throughout a lesson and listening to feedback from students will help ensure that learning

Group discussion is a key component of cooperative learning.

results from instruction.

Cooperative learning can help teachers shift control to students during reading and writing lessons. In cooperative learning, students work together in small discussion groups to accomplish shared goals (Johnson et al., 1984). For reading instruction, this involves students helping one another construct meaning from text (Conley, 1987). For writing instruction, students work together to compose and refine a common message (Atwell, 1987). The key to cooperative learning is to have students perceive that they can reach their learning goals only if the other students in their learning group reach their goals as well. Students need to discuss the goals with others, help one another understand the tasks required, and encourage one another to work hard. Strategies used specifically for cooperative learning include explanation and modeling of group processes, and monitoring (Cohen, 1986; Conley, 1987).

Explanation and modeling of group processes. Students need to be aware of their roles and responsibilities during group work. Explanations should center on establishing rules or norms for group work: everyone should play a role in the group (leader, recorder), anyone can ask anyone else for help, everyone has a duty to help anyone in need, and everybody helps. Modeling takes the form of role-playing to illustrate these responsibilities.

Monitoring. Frequent monitoring of students' progress promotes discussion and helps students become responsible for their own learning. Monitoring is necessary to stimulate students to think on higher levels and help them resolve conflicts. Monitoring should not take the form of answer-giving or directing students to an answer that is in the teacher's head. Careful monitoring consists of questions that direct students to consider different types of information or ways of thinking while they have discussions in their groups.

These activities are especially supportive to a literate environment. Cooperative discussions encourage many types of communication. Teachers can see visible signs that students are applying the content and processes taught early in the lesson. Motivation is enhanced because students' ideas are at the forefront and a premium is placed on using everyone's thoughts to construct meaning.

Teaching strategies do not work without attention to continual refinement. Students who are secure in listening to the teacher and having concepts formed for them will not be secure with a type of instruction that places greater responsibility in their hands. Similarly, teachers who are accustomed to lecturing and telling students what they should know will not be comfortable teaching students to learn on their own. Reflection about the goals underlying these strategies, as well as the extent to which the goals and strategies are already in place, is necessary for determining the best ways to incorporate them in the classroom.

Summary

Instruction in reading and writing should be guided by goals for content, process, and motivation. The appropriate emphasis at the middle school level is on content and process, with attention to motivation as support for what students are learning. This emphasis is dictated by both the particular needs of the early adolescent and the role of the middle school as a transition between the emphasis on process at the elementary level and the emphasis on content at the secondary level.

It is hard to find instruction that balances content, process, and motivation. Educators do not always have a clear sense of the mission of middle schools, and the complexity of the classroom can override goal-directed decisions about instruction. Effective planning and instruction at this level are based on active and responsive teaching as well as on a concern for using reading and writing within a literate environment. This kind of instruction starts with teachers showing students what and how to learn, while gradually involving them in taking responsibility for their own learning. Implementing these suggestions can result in fundamental changes in middle school reading and writing instruction. These changes stand a greater chance of succeeding if they can be incorporated thoughtfully over time.

References

Anderson, Thomas, & Armbruster, Bonnie. (1984). Content area textbooks. In Richard C. Anderson, Jean Osborn, & Robert Tierney (Eds.), *Learning to read in American schools: Basal readers and content texts*. Hillsdale, NJ: Erlbaum.

Atwell, Nancie. (1987). *In the middle: Writing, reading, and learning with adolescents*. Upper Montclair, NJ: Boynton/Cook.

Brown, Ann, & Palincsar, Annemarie. (1985). *Reciprocal teaching of comprehension strategies: A natural history of one program for enhancing learning* (Technical Report No. 334). Urbana, IL: University of Illinois, Center for the Study of Reading.

Cohen, Elizabeth. (1986). *Designing group-*

work. New York: Teachers College Press. (1987).

Conley, Mark. (1988). The development of teacher explanations during content reading lessons. In John Readence & Scott Baldwin (Eds.), *Dialogues in literacy research*. Chicago, IL: National Reading Conference.

Conley, Mark. (1987). Grouping. In Donna Alvermann, David Moore, & Mark Conley (Eds.), *Research within reach: Secondary school reading*. Newark, DE: International Reading Association.

Conley Mark. (1989). Middle school and junior high reading programs. In Shirley Wepner, Joan Feeley, & Dorothy Strickland (Eds.), *Administration and supervision of reading programs*. New York: Teachers College Press.

Csikszentmihalyi, Mihaly, & Larson, R. (1984). *Being adolescent: Conflict and growth in the teenage years*. New York: Basic Books.

Cuban, Lawrence. (1984). *How teachers taught*. New York: Longman.

Duffy, Gerald, & Roehler, Laura. (1986). *Improving classroom reading instruction: A decision-making approach*. New York: Random House.

Duffy, Gerald, & Roehler, Laura. (1987, January). Teaching reading skills as strategies. *The Reading Teacher, 40*, 414-421.

Duin, Ann. (1986). *The effects of intensive vocabulary instruction on expository writing*. Paper presented at the annual meeting of the National Reading Conference, Austin, TX.

Goodlad, John. (1984). *A place called school*. New York: McGraw-Hill.

Hayes, John, & Flower, Linda. (1986). Writing research and the writer. *American Psychologist, 41*, 1106-1113.

Herber, Harold. (1978). *Teaching reading in content areas*. Englewood Cliffs, NJ: Prentice Hall.

Johnson, Dale, Toms-Bronowski, Samuel, & Pittelman, S. David. (1982). *An investigation of the effectiveness of semantic mapping and semantic feature analysis with intermediate grade level children*. (Program Report No. 83-3). Madison, WI: Wisconsin Center for Education Research.

Johnson, David, Johnson, Roger, Holubec, Edythe, & Roy, Patricia. (1984). *Circles of learning: Cooperation in the classroom*. Alexandria, VA: Association for Supervision and Curriculum Development.

Johnston, Peter. (1983). *Reading comprehension assessment: A cognitive basis*. Newark, DE: International Reading Association.

Langer, Judith. (1986). *Children reading and writing*. Norwood, NJ: Ablex.

Lipsitz, Joan. (1984). *Successful schools for young adolescents*. New Brunswick, NJ: Transaction Books.

National Association of Secondary School Principals. (1985). *An agenda for excellence at the middle level*. Reston, VA: National Association of Secondary School Principals.

Palincsar, Annemarie. (1984). *Reciprocal teaching: Working within the zone of proximal development*. Paper presented at the annual meeting of the American Educational Research Association, New Orleans, LA.

Pearson, P. David, & Gallagher, Margaret. (1983). The instruction of reading comprehension. *Contemporary Educational Psychology, 8*, 317-344.

Raphael, Taffy, Kirschner, Becky, & Englert, Carol S. (1986). *Text structure instruction within process-writing classrooms: A manual for instruction*. (Occasional Paper No. 104). East Lansing, MI: Michigan State University Institute for Research on Teaching.

Readence, John, Bean, Thomas, & Baldwin, Scott. (1985). *Content area reading: An integrated approach*. Dubuque, IA: Kendall-Hunt.

Roehler, Laura, & Duffy, Gerald. (1989). The content area teacher's instructional role: A cognitive mediational view. In James Flood & Diane Lapp (Eds.), *Instructional theory and practice for content area reading and learning*. Englewood Cliffs, NJ: Prentice Hall.

Singer, Harry, & Donlan, Daniel. (1985). *Reading and learning from text*. Boston, MA: Little, Brown.

Thurber, James. (1965). The secret life of Walter Mitty. In Robert Pooley, Andrew Grommon, Virginia Lowers, & Olive Niles (Eds.), *Accent: U.S.A.* Glenview, IL: Scott, Foresman.

Tierney, Robert, & Pearson, P. David. (1984). Toward a composing model of reading. In Julie M. Jenson (Ed.), *Composing and comprehending*. Urbana, IL: National Conference on Research in English and the ERIC Clearinghouse on Reading and Communication Skills.

Yinger, Robert. (1986). Examining thought in action: A theoretical and methodological critique of research on interactive teaching. *Teaching and Teacher Education, 2*, 263-282.

Assessing Reading and Writing

Sheila W. Valencia

William McGinley

P. David Pearson

THIS CHAPTER IS A plea for putting middle school literacy assessment back into the hands of those whose lives are most affected by it—students and teachers. It is organized into five parts. We begin with a rhetorical justification for our position on assessment. Then we introduce the attributes that characterize good classroom assessment and present an overall framework for examining various aspects of the reading and writing processes. The heart of the paper is a rationale for using a portfolio construct for both reading and writing assessment and a discussion of the types of activities that might become part of a portfolio. Finally, we illustrate our perspective with a set of examples of middle school teachers gathering data for student portfolios.

Background

The middle school years represent a period of transition in students' view of reading and writing. While fluent reading and writing continue to be major goals of literacy instruction, students also learn how to use reading and writing as ways of learning and communicating in all subject areas and in daily life. Anderson et al. (1985, p. 61) aptly describe the role of reading in subject-matter learning:

> As proficiency develops, reading should be thought of not so much as a separate subject in school but as integral to learning literature, social studies, and science.

Researchers describe a similar role for writing in literature, social studies, and science (Applebee, 1981, 1984; Gage, 1986; Langer & Applebee, 1987; Martin et al., 1975).

If the middle school years are to be a time when reading and writing become the primary means of learning or accomplishing other goals, then assessment in the school literacy curriculum must reflect these functions. Teachers and researchers must explore assessment procedures that allow them to examine students' ability to use reading and writing as tools for learning, insight, understanding, communication, enjoyment, survival, and participation in their world.

Historically, both the general public and professional educators have come to regard assessment as a series of paper and pencil tests imposed on teachers and students by those in positions of authority—those concerned with accountability. Too often, assessment is something we do for the authorities, rather than something we do for ourselves and our students. However, assessment ought to be what we do to help ourselves and our students evaluate progress. Through daily interactions we gather evidence to guide decision-making about student learning, instruction, and curriculum. Assessment should be a natural part of the teaching/learning process and not something added on or imposed as an afterthought.

Teachers and administrators need to learn to rely on their own expertise to develop and use a wide variety of assessment tools to evaluate student progress. At this stage of knowledge about reading and writing processes, we no longer need to rely solely on formal and indirect performance measures, such as those found on most commercially available tests—the norm-referenced standardized tests or criterion-referenced tests so often associated with assessment. Instead, we can return to measures grounded more

directly in classroom instruction. We do not advocate that educators discontinue using commercially available tests. Instead, we argue for a more realistic perspective on the value of commercially available tests, one that admits that it is dangerous to rely on any single test score as a measure of learning, no matter how scientific it may appear to be.

We know from what Shulman (1975) has called the practical wisdom of teaching, that we can learn much about students by keeping track of their learning during classroom interactions. With these strategies, which some call "situated" (Collins, Brown, & Newman, in press) or contextualized assessment strategies (Lucas, 1988a, 1988b), information is gathered as an integral part of the teaching/learning process.

We must add to our assessment repertoire assessments of situated performance—ongoing analyses of students completing a variety of literacy tasks that have been initiated at the prerogative of the school, the teacher, or the student. However, performance measures alone are not sufficient, even when they are personally initiated and functionally motivated. Equally important is information we can gather only by observing students during literacy events or by holding conversations with them to determine what they think about their own skills in, strategies for, and dispositions toward literacy.

Classroom and Individual Assessment

By moving to contextualized assessments of reading and writing, we expand the pool of assessment opportunities. Daily in every classroom, teachers can, do, and should use many different assessment strategies. These should be guided by the attributes of sound contextualized assessment. These principles can serve as important criteria for teachers as they evaluate, design, and characterize their own assessment strategies to reflect their students, their classrooms, their curricula, and themselves.

1. *Assessment is continuous*. Because learning is a continuous, dynamic process, so too, is assessment. Not only does learning take place over time, but the learner and task change with every new instructional situation. Although we frequently acknowledge this idea conceptually, we rarely apply it to classroom assessment. Instead, most evaluation is based on end-of-unit or end-or-year tests. As such, we have come to regard assessment as a static entity, as a test or set of tests. Failing to account for continuity, we may forget (1) that learners' growth needs a closer look, (2) that knowledge is cumulative and transferable, and (3) that the basis for future learning comes from the growth and integration of knowledge over time.

Ongoing measures need not be staged or formal, nor must they result in a grade. In fact, their beauty lies in their simplicity and ubiquity; they allow us to take advantage of what happens daily in most classrooms without necessarily assigning grades. The objective is to guide instruction and to provide continuous feedback and support to students. We would be wise to heed Diederich (1974, p. 2) as he discusses his impressions of assessment in writing classes:

> Students are graded on everything they do every time they turn around. Grades gener-

ate anxiety and hard feeling between [everyone]. Common sense suggests that [grades] ought to be reduced to the smallest possible number necessary to find out how students are getting along toward the four or five main objectives of the program, but teachers keep piling them up like squirrels gathering nuts.

2. *Assessment is multidimensional*. In the interest of efficiency, we tend to look for single indices of effectiveness. We must resist this temptation and insist on multiple measures. The more measures we have, the more we can trust any given conclusion about student or group performance. In a sense, repeated measures help teachers establish something akin to a test developer's criteria of reliability. Also, by using different measures, we may get new perspectives and new insights. Each assessment examines different learning areas or looks at learning in a new context. Because learning varies across time and situation, assessments must be multidimensional.

3. *Assessment should be collaborative*. Many constituencies have a stake in school assessment—students, teachers, parents, administrators, school board members, the community, and the larger society. Each requires somewhat different information, and each should be involved in shaping the assessment agenda. At the administrative level, for example, school board members are interested in how well children read and write compared with students across the county, state, school, or classroom. Teachers want to know how well their students are progressing to meet the goals of the school or classroom curriculum so they can plan new instructional

steps. Students need to know what is expected of them, how achieving those expectations will help them satisfy personal goals, and what progress they are making in meeting those expectations. Teachers should take advantage of these perspectives and pool available information.

The essense of such collaboration lies in working with students. We communicate our support of students' learning process when we work with them in developing assessments. In traditional assessment situations, we act as passive examiners and detached observers of the "truth" rather than as advocates for our students. Collaborative assessments strengthen the bond between teachers and students and allow students to learn about evaluation processes and criteria.

Involving students in assessment helps them move from relying on others to making independent judgments about their own literacy abilities. Students observe the teacher as an evaluator and examine the criteria and the processes the "expert" uses in evaluation, a modeling strategy similar to that used in apprenticeship training (Collins, Brown, & Newman, in press). As students engage in self-evaluation, they reexamine and refine their own criteria for reading and writing. In contrast, students who spend their entire school careers subjected to the evaluation criteria of others are unlikely to blossom suddenly into self-evaluators.

4. *Assessment must be grounded in knowledge.* Those who accept the responsibility of being assessors must be knowledgeable about the content and processes they are assessing. In the case of literacy, assessors should be familiar with both basic and instructional processes in reading, writing, and language. At times, we enter into an assessment situation with prespecified criteria and tasks. At other times, we simply observe students in their natural learning environment; look for patterns to enlighten understanding; and interact with students—prompting, guiding, questioning, and listening with the skills of a knowledgeable educator. If we want to capitalize on all available assessment possibilities, there is no substitute for knowledge; and the further away we move from someone else's tests, the greater our need for knowledge of both reading and writing processes and assessment strategies.

5. *Assessment must be authentic.* Assessment must be functional and ecologically valid. Just as instruction should focus on genuine objectives, assessment should be anchored in genuine tasks and purposes (Edelsky & Harman, 1988) because application changes as purposes change. For example, it would be appropriate to assess students' ability to read for details when reading directions, but less appropriate when reading a novel. The mechanics of writing would be of little (if any) concern in journal writing but would be a high priority in writing a letter to a public official.

Authenticity of assessment supports an assessment-learning relationship. Assessment tasks should be similar to learning tasks so students will not be surprised by them, but they also should offer students an opportunity to apply, rather than simply regurgitate, knowledge they have acquired. For example, the best index of spelling competence might be a student's ability to spell a set of words correctly in a daily assignment rather than on Friday's test. When assessment tasks reflect learning objectives, students come to understand that how they use reading and writing is more important than getting a high score on an isolated test. Authenticity requires that teachers assess students only on what has been, or could be, a part of a regular learning activity; the assessment activity should have intrinsic value.

The above principles support a portfolio approach to assessment (Burnham, 1986; Camp, 1985; Carter & Tierney, 1988; Lucas, 1988a, 1988b). We use the term *portfolio* in both its physical and its philosophical senses. In its physical sense, it is a container in which we can store the artifacts of our literacy—the examples, documents, and observations that serve as evidence of growth and development—so that they are available for visitation and reflection. As a concept, the idea of a portfolio forces us to expand the range of things we would consider as data for instructional decision making. It also reflects the attitude that assessment is a dynamic rather than a static process, captured most accurately in multiple snapshots taken over time. All who have a stake in contributing to the portfolio (students, teachers, parents) have a right to "visit" it whenever they wish to reflect on and analyze its contents.

A Framework for Conceptualizing Literacy

Reading and writing can be conceptualized as holistic processes that are enabled by underlying skills. Enabling skills in reading could be specific decoding, vocabulary, or comprehension skills; in writing, they could be spelling, punctuation, grammar, usage, rhetorical, or organizational skills. But reading and writing also are processes that serve certain functions in the life of any individual. Individuals can read and write to learn information, to demonstrate understanding, to gain insight, to communicate with others, to satisfy personal needs, to participate in a culture, or to demonstrate to authorities the trappings of literacy.

The relationships among reading and writing processes, the functional contexts in which these processes exist, and the subskill infrastructure of each can be represented as a set of concentric circles. The outer circle represents functional context—the purposes literacy serves in our lives. The middle circle represents the holistic reading and writing processes themselves. In the innermost circle are all those skills that constitute the infrastructure, or component subskills, of each process.

Infrastructure

Our assessment focus in the past 20 years has been on the inner circle, those skills constituting the infrastructure of reading and writing. For example, most basal reading programs assess between 15 and 30 specific skills per year in the middle school years (Foertsch & Pearson, 1987). These skills range from knowing the meanings of specific words in a reading unit to knowing root words or affixes, from finding main ideas for brief passages to determining the literal meaning of figurative expressions. Stu-

Figure 1
Dimensions of Reading and Writing

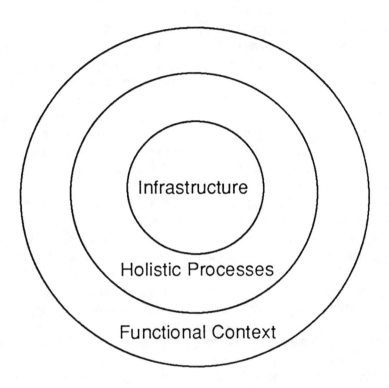

dents often are asked to take tests in which their writing ability is indexed by their ability to find and correct errors in spelling, grammar, usage, or punctuation. Even students who participate in process writing approaches are sometimes evaluated primarily on strict adherence to the conventions of writing or to some very specific notion of theme organization.

We do not argue that these skills are unimportant or that they should not be taught or assessed. However, we believe there are dangers in making such skills a major instructional goal, and that assessing them in isolation leads to highly problematic or misleading conclusions about student performance (Valencia & Pearson, 1988). These enabling skills or strategies are important only in that they provide a way to build a meaning for a text. Even strategies such as notetaking, summarizing, self-questioning, predicting, semantic mapping, outlining, and more extended forms of writing are essential only because they provide students with the means to learn from texts (Moore & Murphy, 1987; Tierney, 1982). It is a student's ability to orchestrate and apply these skills in a meaningful context that merits our evaluation. Assessment of reading and writing should focus on "developing the expertise needed to apply and adapt strategies and knowledge to many situations" (Valencia & Pearson, 1988, p. 30). That is, skills are best evaluated when they are serving the processes or functions depicted in the two outer layers of the circles in Figure 1.

Holistic Processes

Recent curricular refocusing has moved the assessment focus from subskills to the holistic processes of reading and writing, where the emphasis is on comprehending and composing larger pieces of text in a more global way. This shift first became apparent in 1986, when the National Assessment of Educational Progress (NAEP) implemented holistic scoring of writing samples, attempting to concentrate attention on the attributes of the piece as a whole communicative package rather than on the smaller independent components. The comparable starting point for a holistic perspective in reading probably is the popularization of miscue analysis of oral reading errors (Goodman, 1969; Goodman & Burke, 1972), which has been bolstered by the growing use of retellings as a measure of comprehension (Goodman & Burke, 1972; Morrow et al., 1986). More recently, the statewide reading assessment efforts in Illinois and Michigan focused on reading comprehension as a holistic understanding of the major ideas and concepts in a text (Valencia & Pearson, 1987; Wixson et al., 1987). Other holistic assessment efforts can examine students' ability to monitor their reading and writing as well as their disposition to revise, envision an audience for their writing, or seek help when problems arise (Baker & Brown, 1984; Garner, 1987; Tierney & Pearson, 1984; Tierney et al., 1989).

Functional Context

Holistic assessment perspectives represent a concern for the global processes and are an important shift away from isolated skills. However, they neglect to view reading and writing as processes in communicative contexts (Freeman & Sanders, 1987; Halliday, 1975; Heath, 1983; O'Flahavan & Tierney, in press). We have yet to devise many assessment techniques that emphasize the different purposes and functions of reading and writing (Applebee, 1984; Freeman & Sanders, 1987; Martin et al., 1975; McGinley & Tierney, 1988). For example, the summaries students write about a novel in school testing situations are very different from those they create in informal conversation with friends; yet we tend to assess summaries per se, without accounting for audience and purpose.

Interrelationships among the Circles

We have rarely looked at the interactions among the three constructs in the concentric circles in Figure 1. For example, how might we assess grammar or usage differently when students write to satisfy personal needs versus when they write to request information from someone in a position of authority? This is the essence of what we referred to earlier as "situated" assessment.

Interestingly, some recent approaches to literacy reconceptualize the enabling skills depicted in our innermost circle to include the processes of reading and writing themselves (our middle circle). They view the processes as the means by which one can achieve specific goals both in school and in daily life (Freeman & Sanders, 1987; McGinley & Tierney, 1988; Walters, Daniell, & Trachsel, 1987). Mackie (1981, p.1) points out that "to be literate is not to have arrived at some predetermined destination, but to utilize reading, writing, and speaking so that our world is progressively enlarged." This view extends the traditional notion of enabling from the generic processes of reading and writing to more contextually defined goals of reading and writing.

If we construe literacy in this way, then reading and writing become the means or skills with which students can achieve such goals as personal expression, enjoyment, learning, understanding, insight, communication, survival, and cultural participation. Accepting reading and writing as enabling skills suggests that our outermost circle must be considered the most important in developing assessment strategies. In the best of situations, we would assess the processes and their infrastructures as they serve these important literacy functions. When we learn how to account for these functions in our assessment schemes, we will have achieved authentic, situated assessment.

Building an Assessment Portfolio

Most teachers have access to norm-referenced test scores, criterion-referenced test results, and assessments based on reading and writing activities occurring in the classroom. These are valuable pieces in the assessment puzzle. Norm-referenced tests help us understand students' performance in comparison with other groups of students in the nation. As such, they permit schools and our society to perform important gatekeeping and monitoring functions. Criterion-referenced tests measure students against some prespecified standard (e.g. 80 percent correct), usually set by the school, the district, or a publisher. These forms of assessments offer one type of systematic information to add to a portfolio, but they represent a narrowly defined concept of reading and writing.

Too often teacher-constructed assessments, which have the potential to move beyond this narrow concept, seem to be shaped by the standards of commercially produced tests. Studies that examine textbook and teacher-made tests indicate that many are frighteningly similar to the ubiquitous norm-referenced test (Armbruster et al., 1984; Armbruster, Stevens, & Rosenshine, 1977; Foertsch & Pearson, 1987). Even when students are encouraged to write their own answers, usually they are asked to provide only brief, fill-in-the-blank responses to lower level questions (Applebee, 1984). Teacher-initiated assessments that deviate from the paper-and-pencil tradition have been denigrated as unreliable, subjective, and unfair. Unfortunately, this tight definition of assessment undermines the potential for classroom teachers to act as instructional decision makers (Pearson & Valencia, 1987; Calfee & Hiebert, 1988) and leaves no room for creative approaches or professional judgment. We cannot afford to adopt such a narrow approach to assessment.

As Stanley and Hopkins (1972, p. 5) remind us:

> Let us not fall into the trap of asking whether we should use teacher judgments or test scores. Faced by the complex problems of measurement and evaluation of pupil growth and influences affecting it, we cannot reject any promising resource. Various sorts of information supplement each other.

We have arrived at a theoretical crossroads in our attempt to develop a viable assessment system. Fortunately, the choice about which road to follow is clear; we must align and integrate assessment with sound instruction in order to prevent the kind of split professional life teachers are forced to lead when they switch back and forth from open and flexible instructional practices to closed and rigid assessment systems (Tierney & McGinley, 1987). We must admit that teacher judgment is an inevitable and important source of evaluative information.

However, the road to more enlightened assessment practices is neither well paved nor well marked. Some trailblazing is clearly called for to enhance our repertoire of assessment strategies and, in the process, improve students' disposition toward learning.

Describing Portfolio Assessment Strategies

A portfolio approach to assessment is neither laissez-faire nor structureless. When teachers leave the security of commercially produced assessments that are conceptualized, monitored, and controlled by others, they need criteria for classifying, monitoring, and evaluating their own assessment strategies. We conceptualize these criteria as a set of five continua on which any approach to assessment can be classified. We have chosen the continuum metaphor in the belief that shifts in our criteria are more a matter of degree than of kind. These continua will encourage us to explore the range of possibilities and to strive for variety and balance in our approaches to literacy assessment. The five continua are focus, structure, mode, locus of control, and intrusiveness.

Focus. The first step in the assessment process is to identify the questions to be addressed—in other words, to determine what we hope to learn about the student, group, or class as a result of engaging in the assessment task. It is helpful to think of a range of questions we might want to ask that spans the layers of the concentric circles in Figure 1—functional context, holistic processes, and infrastructure. These questions help focus assessment efforts.

infrastructure	processes	context

We begin with questions related to the functional context, which determines the first line of assessment criteria as well as how far into the processes and infrastructure one needs to go. Functional context questions place reading and writing tasks in meaningful contexts where the focus is on how well the intended purpose of the literacy activity is achieved. While these questions are posed from the perspective of the teacher, they are equally useful to students who wish to become skilled in self-evaluation. For example:

- How do students use reading and writing
    - for personal expression?
    - for gaining new insights?
    - for demonstrating knowledge?
    - for learning new information?
    - for getting along in society?
    - for participating in the culture?
    - for demonstrating literacy competence?
    - for thinking critically?
- How well are students able to determine and use appropriate forms of reading and writing for a variety of different purposes?

Other questions might focus more on holistic processes of reading and writing. The focus is on overall meaning and processes rather than on the acquisition of expertise in any specific skills. For example:

- How well are students able to use composing strategies such as planning, drafting, revising, and editing?
- What strategies do students use for sharing writing and getting feedback?
- How well are students able to communicate ideas through their writing?
- What strategies do students use for getting help with their reading and writing?
- How well are students able to guide and monitor their own learning?
- How well do students understand the important ideas of a piece of writing?

- How well are students able to use reading strategies such as preparing, monitoring, adapting, and responding?

Infrastructure questions focus on the skills that enable reading and writing. Although they are not usually a primary concern in the middle school, they still occupy an important place in the curriculum and in the minds of teachers and administrators. They continue to form the foundation for the development of more sophisticated literacy skills, and as such merit assessment. The key, however, is to ensure that these skills are assessed in meaningful functional contexts, not in isolation. For example:

- How well are students able to use the mechanics of writing (punctuation, capitalization, usage, spelling) to construct meaning?
- How well do students organize and sequence ideas in their writing?
- How well are students able to use word identification, vocabulary, and comprehension skills to gain meaning from texts?
- How well are students able to apply study skills to understand content area material?

We may want to focus on one or several questions during any assessment opportunity. However, this continuum reminds us that it is neither necessary nor desirable to hold students accountable for all possible skills and strategies every time we assess. In some cases, we might be concerned with evaluating writing for an appropriate audience rather than editing for punctuation. In other cases, we might want to evaluate how well students are able to use context to determine the meanings of several new conceptually important words presented in a science chapter. At other times, we might emphasize the effectiveness of a piece of persuasive writing and how well it is organized. Our aim should be to provide cross sections of assessment foci—a well-balanced assessment portfolio.

Structure. The structure of the assessment indicates how standardized and prespecified the assessment strategy is. Assessments run the gamut from highly structured to semistructured to completely unstructured and spontaneous.

---

structured semistructured unstructured

The most structured assessments specify everything: the desired outcomes/goals, the correct responses, the method of collecting and scoring the data, and any special required time limits or directions. Standardized tests, uniform writing sample assessments, basal reader tests, and informal reading inventories are examples of these types of measures. They call for limited input and judgment from the classroom teacher and the student. Essentially, any trained proctor could administer, score, and report results on any of these measures. A slightly less formal measure might be a teacher-constructed multiple-choice test where the teacher designs the content but leaves other aspects of the assessment to external control.

Somewhere in the middle of the continuum are semistructured, or informal, assessments that require more input and interpretation from the teacher and/or provide greater latitude in students' responses. Asking students to retell a passage just read or to submit an example of a persuasive piece of writing are examples of informal assessment strategies. In the former, the passage is specified but student responses are more open, as are the criteria for evaluating response quality. With persuasive writing, the assessment is imposed, but the topic choice is open to the student and the scoring criteria can be quite flexible.

At the unstructured end of the continuum are those spontaneous observations, interactions, or examples of student work that provide important insights into how the student is progressing. Inclusion in the portfolio is all that distinguishes these assessment activities from the daily, on-the-spot assessments teachers continually make during instruction. Whether they are or are not included in a portfolio, spontaneous assessments are important sources of information for instructional decision making. Documenting them in the portfolio provides reminders and allows us to examine patterns of behavior over time.

Mode. The modes of assessment refer to the processes used to collect information about students' progress. They range from the most durable samples of student work to interviews to the less concrete, but no less important, observations.

---

samples interviews observations

We typically think of assessment as

pencil-and-paper tasks or samples of students' work through which students demonstrate knowledge. These are direct measures of durable products (Cooper, 1981) or artifacts of learning. These indices are usually easy to administer or collect, and they provide us with concrete evidence to share with others. They may be initiated by the teacher or by the student, and may be planned or spontaneous. They may represent a wide range of foci, from literacy functions to subskills. Although many perceive samples of student work as objective, easily evaluated measures, this is not necessarily the case. This misconception probably derives from our naive association of assessment with the term *test*. In reality, the range of possibilities is far greater than we usually imagine.

For example, traditional thinking would suggest that this mode of assessment is simply some type of teacher-constructed written test (multiple-choice, short answer, essay). A somewhat different sample might be collected for the portfolio by asking students to review several pieces in their writing folders and to select one they feel is a good example of their writing ability. Another sample might be an audiotape of a student's oral reading or a videotape of a class debate or dramatization. Each is a durable record of an actual sample of student work that can be examined and reexamined over time by teachers, students, and parents.

While this mode has some attractive advantages, it is not flawless. By definition, samples of work are products; as such, they rarely capture the energy and process that went into creating them. Al-though they possess the lure of objectivity, they are as prone to subjectivity as more judgmental forms of assessment. For example, emphasis on outcome-based learning in the late 1970s led many teachers and school districts to develop their own criterion-referenced assessments. Criterion-referenced assessments usually require a mastery cutoff score, such as 80 percent correct. Teachers soon found that as they wrote their own tests, they had to adjust both text and item difficulty on an ad hoc basis in order to keep close to their 80 percent cutoff score. Since there is no clear conception of task or text difficulty (the knowledge base required for meaningful assessment), objectivity is a misnomer. The point is not that subjectivity or teacher judgment is undesirable, but rather that in paper-and-pencil tests subjectivity may simply be moved back one level from public inspection so it is not quite so obvious. Evaluations of work samples are not inherently more objective than any other assessment; their value rests in their durability over time, not in their objectivity.

At the other end of the mode continuum, observations offer several advantages. They permit the evaluator to view learning without intruding on the learning experience. Because they occur more naturally (Moore, 1983), they can contribute a more valid picture of a student's abilities. At the least, they afford an opportunity to assess processes and strategies while students actually are learning (Clay, 1985; Taylor, Harris, & Pearson, 1988).

Observations often arise out of continuous, less structured approaches to assessment. For example, the teacher might observe Henry as he asks his neighbor to help him answer the questions at the end of the social studies chapter, or Susan as she struggles at the writing center for 30 minutes attempting to begin a first draft, or Marcus as he talks to a friend about a book he is reading.

Observations have been criticized for their unreliability, and certainly judgments based on a single observation merit such criticism. But this problem can be counteracted in several ways. The first important deterrent to unreliability is knowledge. We evaluate more consistently when we know what we are to evaluate. This knowledge base can be strengthened and supported by providing teachers with guidelines, checklists, and characteristics to look for. Second, reliability improves with repeated observations, which have the added advantage of reminding us to look for patterns rather than for single indicators of performance.

Observations also have been criticized for being subjective. In response to such criticism, many professionals advocate tightly planned, structured, systematic observations (Cunningham, 1982). But, as argued earlier, subjectivity (in the sense of teacher judgment) is an inescapable characteristic of all assessments.

Using interviews at the midpoint of the mode continuum enables teachers and students to interact in collaborative settings, share responsibility in shaping the focus of the assessment, and alter the assessment situation through negotiation. Interviews guided by clear purposes but open to questions allow students to share their own views about

school, about reading and writing as personal activities, and about how they solve (or fail to solve) their literacy problems. Interviews—be they formal, with a preplanned set of questions, or informal, such as a conversation about a book a student has finished—often are overlooked as a mode of assessment.

Locus of control. Responsibility for evaluation usually rests with the teacher, but, as we suggested in the discussion of collaboration, students can, and should, evaluate their own progress. The points on the locus of control continuum range from traditional teacher evaluation to collaboration between student and teacher (or between student and peer) to student self-evaluation.

teacher	collaboration	student

Intrusiveness. The intrusiveness continuum is not independent of other continua. Logically, one would expect it to be related to structure, mode, and locus of control, although the relationship is not linear. An observation checklist used as part of the school report card may be quite formal and teacher controlled; however, it would be fairly unintrusive from the student's perspective. A 2-page book report to be completed anytime during the semester might be more informal and offer more shared control and yet be quite intrusive.

intrusive	unintrusive

The rationale for this continuum is to illustrate the value of assessing students, whenever possible, in their natural learning environments. As with the other continua, it serves as a way for teachers to monitor the techniques used to collect information for the assessment portfolio.

Illustrative Assessment Scenarios

It is impossible for us to recommend an exhaustive set of assessment strategies for classroom use. We have described our principles and criteria (our continua) carefully because we believe teachers must tailor assessment practices to their classroom situations. Guidelines, not tests, serve teachers better in this endeavor. To illustrate how assessments can be tailored, we provide five illustrative assessment scenarios. For each scenario, we depict the specific assessment questions and procedures used by a middle school teacher to evaluate some aspects of reading and writing performance, classify each according to the five continua, and elaborate on ways in which the strategy might be adapted to answer different questions or to fulfill different assessment needs.

Scenario 1

The question. How well are students able to guide and monitor their own learning?

The situation. A seventh grade English teacher wants to help his students improve their ability to monitor their own reading to ensure that it makes sense. He has his students use paper bookmarks (or stick-on notes) to record problem spots (difficult concepts, unknown words, questions they would like to discuss) they encounter while reading an assigned chapter in a novel. After they discuss the chapter in class, he holds individual conferences with several students (different students are scheduled for conferences each week). First, he has each student retell the chapter to check on comprehension (see Appendix A). If the student reads with good understanding and no problem areas are evident, the teacher decides against assessing self-monitoring. If, on the other hand, the student exhibits some comprehension difficulty or the teacher identifies possible problems, the two discuss the trouble

Rating the assessment activity (self-monitoring)

Focus		X	
	infrastructure	processes	context
Structure		X	
	structured	semistructured	unstructured
Mode	X	X	
	samples	interviews	observations
Locus of Control		X	
	student	collaboration	teacher
Intrusiveness	X		
	intrusive		unintrusive

spots. They examine the notes on the bookmarks, review the chapter for other potential problem spots that were not noted, and then discuss strategies for coping with the difficulties. The teacher jots down some anecdotal notes and sometimes even attaches the student's bookmark to the notes for later placement in the student's portfolio.

What can we learn? This task amounts to asking students to edit their own reading. The bookmark technique is a good one, since most students do not have the luxury of writing in their texts while they read. By observing their notes, interviewing, or even collecting these bookmarks, teachers may gain insight into each student's ability to process a piece of text. Collaboratively, student and teacher identify possible problems and design instructional strategies.

To adapt this technique to writing, teachers might ask students to proofread or edit their drafts with one or two specific purposes in mind. These purposes may be as detailed as proofreading for spelling or punctuation errors or as broad as revising the presentation of a line of reasoning or an argument. The student then may confer with the teacher (or submit papers), using both first and second drafts to collaboratively evaluate progress.

This particular type of activity can be framed in a variety of ways. The focus may be on specific vocabulary skills, the author's craft, prewriting strategies, or organization; the mode can be observation, interview, or sample; the activity may be teacher initiated (intrusive) or student initiated (unintrusive). Thus, it has the potential to fall virtually any-

where along each of the five continua. Furthermore, this assessment activity can be repeated using different materials and focusing on many different aspects of reading or writing.

There are many other strategies for gathering information about students' ability to monitor their own learning. Another way to assess self-monitoring is simply to ask students to annotate each work sample as they file it in their portfolio. They might rate the quality of each on a general 1-10 scale, they might rate it on specific criteria, or they might write a short statement about difficulties encountered or their degree of satisfaction with the product.

Scenario 2

The question. How do students respond to a piece of literature?

The situation. An eighth grade English class has just finished reading *The Diary of Anne Frank,* and the teacher has asked them to write an essay of no more than 3 pages detailing their reaction and response to the book in a way that provides a helpful overview to another group of eighth grade students who are beginning to read the book. As she finishes her directions for the assignment, the teacher reminds the students to focus on the content of the responses and not to worry about mechanics and grammar on this draft. There will be plenty of time for that when they complete the version they will actually send to students in her other eighth grade English class.

What can we learn? For the first draft, the teacher is clearly interested in evaluating students' responses to a piece of literature rather than their ability to

Rating the assessment activity (informational essay in drafts)

Focus			X
	infrastructure	processes	context
Structure		X	
	structured	semistructured	unstructured
Mode	X		
	samples	interviews	observations
Locus of Control			X
	student	collaboration	teacher
Intrusiveness		X	
	intrusive		unintrusive

control the mechanical features of the writing process. She could use a holistic scale (see appendix B) for evaluating the writing activity. A holistic scale places the focus on the quality of the communication to the potential audience. Alternatively, she could use an analytic scale (see appendix C) in which separate subscales rate traits such as fidelity to the themes of the book, sense of audience, organization, and style. When the students complete the final version, the teacher may want to incorporate subscales dealing with the conventions of written language or the impact of the message. Notice that the motivation for adhering to conventions is inherently greater when students have a real audience in mind rather than an audience consisting of the teacher or some vague, hypothetical group (pretend you are writing to …).

Although this is primarily a writing activity, the teacher also can learn something about her students' reading performance. For example, what the students consider important to relate to an-other student is a good index of what they attended to when reading the text.

As with our other illustrative scenarios, this scenario could be slightly modified to take on many different values on most of the five continua. For example, if the teacher tells students that correct mechanics are absolutely essential, she can immediately shift the focus of the activity from the context to the infrastructure. If she specifies the exact form of the response (e.g., a 5-paragraph theme), the task becomes structured and even more intrusive.

Scenario 3

The question. How well are students able to compose an informational text?

The situation. A sixth grade language arts teacher requests that students keep a portfolio of all the writing they do throughout the year. As a result, each student's portfolio contains several samples of narrative, personal, and informational writing. At various points throughout the year, she asks her students to select a piece they feel represents their best effort at composing in a particular genre. Prior to submitting their papers, students are given the opportunity to make any final revisions they think necessary.

Before submission, the teacher informs students that the piece must be accompanied by a letter to her explaining and justifying its selection. She also tells them that she will evaluate the letters on the basis of the three aspects of writing they have been studying in the past month—quality of content, organization, and voice. In addition, she will evaluate each letter on the basis of how persuasive it is in convincing her that the piece really includes these critical qualities of good informational writing.

What can we learn? In this scenario, the teacher is interested in learning a number of things about her students' ability to compose informational texts. The pieces themselves are a source of information about students' knowledge of the specific content they are reporting, as well as about their ability to organize and synthesize information in their own language. Most important, by asking students to write a letter justifying the quality of their selection, the teacher has asked that they begin to take steps toward becoming evaluators of their own writing. In so doing, she has created a situation with equal potential for instruction and assessment. In writing about their own work, students evaluate and rethink the standards they associate with good informational writing. By examining similar self-evaluations over time, the teacher can determine what features of writing students are focusing on and how their focus changes as a result of instruction over the course of the year. Are they concerned with features related to the infrastructure of the piece, with the piece as a whole, or with the functions or purposes the piece serves?

This activity may be framed in other ways. For example, in asking students to write about their writing, the teacher may choose to tighten the structure by specifying criteria for evaluation or to open the structure by asking students to select their criteria for evaluation.

Rating the assessment activity (informational writing and justification letter)

Focus		X	
	infrastructure	processes	context
Structure		X	
	structured	semistructured	unstructured
Mode	X		
	samples	interviews	observations
Locus of Control	X		
	student	collaboration	teacher
Intrusiveness			X
	intrusive		unintrusive

Scenario 4

The question. How well are students able to use their prior knowledge and reading skills to learn new information from a textbook?

The situation. In his sixth grade social studies class, a teacher has decided to use a prereading mapping activity followed by a postreading group semantic mapping activity as a way of preparing for and then following up the reading of a chapter on the development of Greek civilization. To do the prereading mapping activity, he begins with a blank chart and writes Ancient Greece in the middle, asking students to share ideas that come to mind when they think of Ancient Greece. Once 25 to 30 ideas have been added to the chart (within categories), he asks the students to read the chapter and look for new ideas to add to the chart or think of ways they may wish to revise the chart. Once the reading is finished, he meets with the whole class to revise the chart, adding another 30 ideas to it, putting in labels for some of the new categories, and switching a few ideas from one category to another. As a culminating activity, he asks that each student develop a written summary of the information included in the class map.

What can we learn? This activity is interesting because other than the summary at the end of the activity, there is no provision for any artifacts representing individual performance; the map itself is a group effort. During the mapping activity, the teacher observes the contributions of individual students and draws conclusions about their knowledge before reading the chapter and about what they learned while reading it. He also can make anecdotal notes to add to the portfolio. The summary activity provides the teacher with a chance to learn a great deal about students' ability to organize and present ideas.

With some modification, mapping can provide more insight into individual performance. For example, some teachers ask students to complete pre- and postreading maps on their own; in such cases, maps become individual rather than group artifacts. The disadvantage of

Rating the assessment activity (map and summary)

Focus		X (summary)	X (map)
	infrastructure	processes	context
Structure		X	
	structured	semistructured	unstructured
Mode	X (summary)		X (map)
	samples	interviews	observations
Locus of Control		X	
	student	collaboration	teacher
Intrusiveness		X	
	intrusive		unintrusive

individual mapping is that students do not get a chance to learn from one another during the group mapping sessions. As a more intrusive measure (but perhaps more informative with respect to assessing growth for particular concepts presented in the text), maps also can be much more structured. The teacher can provide all the categories for the association task, in which case it may look more like a study guide or an incomplete outline.

Scenario 5

The question. How well are students able to use reading and writing to create a research report?

The situation. A ninth grade language arts teacher has just completed a month long instructional unit on report writing. Initially, she met with the science teacher to discuss which topics the students would be studying in November. Together they outlined possibilities for a related language arts writing unit. Students were required to select a topic of personal interest related to the solar system, planets, or space exploration; state a hypothesis; gather information from at least three sources; and develop a complete report to be shared with their peers as well as their language arts and science teachers.

Over the past several weeks, the students were introduced to several different strategies for selecting and narrowing topics of study. In addition, the teacher introduced the students to many possible sources of information in the library (encyclopedia, books, magazines, films) and in the community (interviews with experts, museums).

Since the teacher had been using a process approach to teach writing, students composed their reports using the strategies they had acquired. Additionally, the teacher set aside time over several weeks to work with students on two new skills: synthesizing information from several sources and using footnotes and bibliographic information. Students shared their final reports during two combined language arts and science class periods. Students with common interests formed groups in which they discussed their reports and provided feedback. The papers were submitted to both teachers for grading.

Rating the assessment activity (checklist)

Focus		X	
	infrastructure	processes	context
Structure		X	
	structured	semistructured	unstructured
Mode			X
	samples	interviews	observations
Locus of Control			X
	student	collaboration	teacher
Intrusiveness			X
	intrusive		unintrusive

Rating the assessment activity (learning logs)

Focus		student determined	
	infrastructure	processes	context
Structure			X
	structured	semistructured	unstructured
Mode	X		
	samples	interviews	observations
Locus of Control	X - - - →		
	student	collaboration	teacher
Intrusiveness			X
	intrusive		unintrusive

As students moved through their drafts and revisions, the teacher observed their strategies for getting started and for getting help with revision. Using a checklist several times during the month as a guideline (see Appendix D), she kept track of each student's progress and used the data to form short term instructional groups on several of the goals and strategies explicit in the unit.

During the month, the teacher also suggested that students write in their learning logs at least twice a week (Kirby & Liner, 1981). They were encouraged to write about their learning experiences as they gathered information and composed their reports: their problems, need for additional guidance, new insights, and feelings about their efforts. The logs were shared with the teacher at the students' discretion.

The final report was evaluated using information from four sources: the language arts teacher, the science teacher, the student, and the special interest group with whom the report was shared. Each evaluator considered the paper from a different perspective. The language arts teacher used three main criteria: the overall quality of the paper

Rating the assessment activity (report)

Focus	X	X	X
	infrastructure	processes	context
Structure	X		
	structured	semistructured	unstructured
Mode		X	X
	samples	interviews	observations
Locus of Control	X - - - →	X	X
	student	collaboration	teacher
Intrusiveness		X	
	intrusive		unintrusive

(measured by a holistic scoring technique), the ability to synthesize several sources of information into a coherent original piece, and use of the appropriate form for footnotes and bibliographic information (a primary instructional goal for this unit). Students were provided with a self-evaluation questionnaire (Appendix E) to guide their reflections on the process of writing the report and on the quality of the final product. The science teacher evaluated both the quality of the information presented and students' ability to use a scientific report to state a hypothesis, present information, and draw appropriate conclusions. The interest group evaluated each report on how well the student presented the information to the group and on the author's ability to react to questions about the report. All these assessments were used to arrive at a final grade for the project.

What can we learn? This rich instructional context provides the teacher with unlimited opportunities to assess students during the entire monthlong process of reading and writing to create their reports. The instructional unit also results in a concrete artifact—the report—and the added experience of presenting the work to peers and to experts. Notice that for many of our continua, we have marked several points rather than a single point. This is because in situations such as these, assessment opportunities tend to be flexible and dynamic; that is, a single strategy can relate to more than one structure, mode, or level of focus, and it can change over time.

Concluding Statement

In this chapter, we have build a case for portfolio assessment for reading and writing during the middle school years. A portfolio is both a physical collection of the artifacts of students' reading and writing and a disposition toward assessment. This disposition is characterized by the belief that assessment must be continuous, multidimensional, collaborative, knowledge-based, and authentic. Our recommendation for portfolios is based on the conviction that records gathered while students are engaged in functional and contextualized literacy tasks ultimately will prove more useful to both teachers and students than will any set of numbers derived from tests that have little relevance to the purposes and needs of either group.

The scenarios and assessment tools we have provided are illustrative rather than exhaustive, descriptive rather than prescriptive. The principles and continua put forward in this chapter should be regarded as a conceptual framework to use in developing and evaluating assessment strategies. The array of assessment opportunities available to us as teachers is limited only by our creativity, our knowledge of reading and writing processes, and our grasp of sound assessment criteria. It is our responsibility to avail ourselves of these opportunities.

References

Anderson, Richard C., Heibert, Elfrieda H., Scott, Judith A., & Wilkinson, Ian A. (1985). *Becoming a nation of readers*. Urbana, IL: University of Illinois, Center for the Study of Reading.

Applebee, Arthur N. (1984). *Contexts for learning to write*. Norwood, NJ: Ablex.

Applebee, Arthur N. (1981). *Writing in the secondary school*: *English and the content areas*.

Urbana, IL: National Council of Teachers of English.

Armbruster, Bonnie B., Anderson, Thomas H., Bruning, Roger H., & Meyer, Linda A. (1984). *What did you mean by that question? A taxonomy of American history questions* (Technical Report No. 308). Urbana, IL: University of Illinois, Center for the Study of Reading.

Armbruster, Bonnie B., Stevens, Robert J., & Rosenshine, Barak. (1977). *Analyzing content coverage and emphasis: A study of three curricula and two tests* (Technical Report No. 26). Urbana, IL: University of Illinois, Center for the Study of Reading.

Baker, Linda, & Brown, Ann L. (1984). Metacognitive skills and reading. In P. David Pearson (Ed.), *Handbook of reading research*. New York: Longman.

Burnham, C.C. (1986). Portfolio evaluation: Room to breathe and grow. In Charles Bridges (Ed.), *Training the teacher of college composition*. Urbana, IL: National Council of Teachers of English.

Calfee, Robert, & Hiebert, Elfrieda. (1988). *The teacher's role in using assessment to improve learning*. Unpublished manuscript.

Camp, Roberta. (1985). The writing folder in postsecondary assessment. In Peter J. Evans (Ed.), *Directions and misdirections in English evaluation*. Ottawa, Canada: Canadian Council of Teachers of English.

Carter, Mark A., & Tierney, Robert J. (1988). *Reading and writing growth using portfolios in assessment*. Paper presented at the National Reading Conference, Tucson, AZ.

Clay, Marie M. (1985). *The early detection of reading difficulties* (3rd ed.). Portsmouth, NH: Heinemann.

Collins, Allan, Brown, John S., & Newman, Susan E. (in press). Cognitive apprenticeship: Teaching the craft of reading, writing, and mathematics. In Lauren B. Resnick (Ed.), *Cognition and instruction: Issues and agendas*. Hillsdale, NJ: Erlbaum.

Cooper, John O. (1981). *Measuring behavior*. Columbus, OH: Charles E. Merrill.

Cunningham, Patricia M. (1982). Diagnosis by observation. In John J. Pikulski & Timothy Shanahan (Eds.), *Approaches to the informal evaluation of reading*. Newark, DE: International Reading Association.

Diederich, Paul. (1974). *Measuring growth in English*. Urbana, IL: National Council of Teachers of English.

Edelsky, Carole, & Harman, Susan. (1988). One more critique of reading tests—with two differences. *English Education, 20*(3), 157-171.

Foertsch, Mary, & Pearson, P. David. (1987). *Reading assessment in basal reading series and standardized tests*. Paper presented at the National Reading Conference, St. Petersburg, FL.

Freeman, Evelyn B., & Sanders, Tobie. (1987). The social meaning of literacy: Writing instruction and the community. *Language Arts, 64*, 641-645.

Gage, John. (1986). Why write? In David Bartholomea & Anthony Petrosky (Eds.), *The teaching of writing* (pp. 8-29). Chicago, IL: National Society for the Study of Education.

Garner, Ruth. (1987). *Metacognition and reading comprehension*. Norwood, NJ: Ablex.

Goodman, Kenneth S. (1969). Analysis of oral reading miscues: Applied psycholinguistics. *Reading Research Quarterly, 5*, 9-30.

Goodman, Yetta M., & Burke, Carolyn L. (1972). *Reading miscue inventory manual: Procedures for diagnosis and evaluation*. New York: Macmillan.

Halliday, Michael. (1975). *Explorations in the functions of language*. London: Edward Arnold.

Heath, Shirley B. (1983). *Ways with words*. Cambridge, MA: Cambridge University Press.

Kirby, Dan, & Liner, Tom. (1981). *Inside out: Developmental strategies for teaching writing*. Portsmouth, NH: Boynton/Cook.

Langer, Judith A., & Applebee, Arthur N. (1987). *Writing and learning in the secondary school* (National Institute of Education Grant No. NIE-G-82-0027). Stanford, CA: Stanford University School of Education.

Lucas, Catherine K. (1988a). Toward ecological evaluation. *The Quarterly of the National Writing Project and the Center for the Study of Writing, 10*(1), 1-17.

Lucas, Catherine K. (1988b). Toward ecological evaluation, part 2. *The Quarterly of the National Writing Project and the Center for the Study of Writing, 10*(2), 4-10.

Mackie, Robert (Ed.). (1981). *Literacy and revolution: The pedagogy of Paulo Freire*. New York: Continuum Publishing.

Martin, Nancy, Meday, Peter, Smith, Harold, & D'Arcy, Pat. (1975). Why Write? In Nancy Martin (Ed.), *Writing across the curriculum*. Portsmouth, NH: Boynton/Cook, 34-59.

McGinley, William, & Tierney, Robert J. (1988). *Reading and writing as ways of knowing and learning* (Technical Report No. 423). Urbana, IL: University of Illinois, Center for the Study of Reading.

Moore, David W., & Murphy, Ann G. (1987). Reading programs. In Donna E. Alvermann, David W. Moore, & Mark W. Conley (Eds.), *Research within reach: Secondary school reading*. Newark, DE: International Reading Association.

Morrow, Lesley M., Gambrell, Linda, Kapinus, Barbara, Marshall, Nancy, & Mitchell, Judith. (1986). Retelling: A strategy for reading instruction and assessment. In Jerome Niles (Ed.), *Solving problems in literacy: Learners, teachers, and researchers*. Thirty-Fifth Yearbook of the National Reading Conference. Rochester, NY: National Reading Conference.

O'Flahavan, John F., & Tierney, Robert J. (in press). Reading, writing, and critical thinking. In Beau F. Jones & Lorna Idol (Eds.), *Dimensions of thinking and cognitive instruction* (vol. 2). Hillsdale, NJ: Erlbaum.

Pearson, P. David, & Valencia, Sheila W. (1987). Assessment, accountability, and professional prerogative. In John E. Readence & R. Scott Baldwin (Eds.), *Research in literacy: Merging perspectives* (pp. 3-16). Thirty-Sixth Yearbook of the National Reading Conference. Rochester, NY: National Reading Conference.

Shulman, Lee S. (1975). Teaching as clinical information processing. In Nate L. Gage (Ed.), *National conference on studies in teaching*. Washington, DC: National Institute of Education.

Stanley, Julian C., & Hopkins, Kenneth D. (1972). *Educational and psychological measurement and evaluation*. Englewood Cliffs, NJ: Prentice Hall.

Taylor, Barbara, Harris, Larry A., & Pearson, P. David. (1988). *Reading difficulties: Instruction and assessment*. New York: Random House.

Tierney, Robert J. (1982). Learning from text. In Allen Berger & H. Alan Robinson (Eds.), *Secondary school reading: What research reveals for classroom practice* (pp. 97-110). Urbana, IL: ERIC Clearinghouse on Reading and Communication Skills and the National Council on Research in English.

Tierney, Robert J., & McGinley, William. (1987). *Serious flaws in written literacy assessment*. Paper presented at the American Educational Research Association Annual Meeting.

Tierney, Robert J., & Pearson, P. David. (1984). Toward a composing model of reading. In Julie M. Jensen (Ed.), *Composing and comprehending*. Urbana, IL: National Council of Teachers of English.

Tierney, Robert J., Soter, Anna, O'Flahavan, John F., & McGinley, William. (1989). The effects of reading and writing upon thinking critically. *Reading Research Quarterly, 24*(2), 134-173.

Valencia, Sheila W., & Pearson, P. David. (1988). Principles for classroom comprehension assessment. *Remedial and Special Education, 9*, 26-35.

Valencia, Sheila W., & Pearson, P. David. (1987). Reading assessment: Time for a change. *Reading Teacher, 40*, 726-732.

Walters, Keith, Daniell, Beth, & Trachsel, Mary. (1987). Formal and functional approaches to literacy. *Language Arts, 64*, 855-868.

Wixson, Karen K., Peters, Charles W., Weber, Elaine M., & Roeber, Edward. (1987). New directions in statewide reading assessment. *Reading Teacher, 40*, 749-755.

Appendix A
A Schema for Scoring Retellings:
The Retelling Profile*

Directions: Indicate with a checkmark the extent to which the reader's retelling includes or provides evidence of the following information.

	none	low degree	moderate degree	high degree
1. Retelling includes information directly stated in text.				
2. Retelling includes information inferred directly or indirectly from text.				
3. Retelling includes what is important to remember from the text.				
4. Retelling provides relevant content and concepts.				
5. Retelling indicates reader's attempt to connect background knowledge to text information.				
6. Retelling indicates reader's attempt to make summary statements or generalizations based on text that can be applied to the real world.				
7. Retelling indicates highly individualistic and creative impressions of or reactions to the text.				
8. Retelling indicates the reader's affective involvement with the text.				
9. Retelling demonstrates appropriate use of language (vocabulary, sentence structure, language conventions).				
10. Retelling indicates reader's ability to organize or compose the retelling.				
11. Retelling demonstrates the reader's sense of audience or purpose.				
12. Retelling indicates the reader's control of the mechanics of speaking or writing.				

Interpretation: Items 1-4 indicate the reader's comprehension of textual information; items 5-8 indicate metacognitive awareness, strategy use, and involvement with text; items 9-12 indicate facility with language and language development.

*From J.N. Mitchell & P.A. Irwin (1989). *The reading retelling profile: Using retellings to make instructional decisions*. Unpublished paper.

Appendix B
A Holistic Scoring Scale*

Level 1. Not competent

Either the content is inadequate for the topic selected or deficiencies in the conventions of written expression are so gross that they interfere with communication.

Level 2. Not competent

The student can express a message which can be readily understood, which contains adequate content for the selected topic, and which demonstrates at least marginal command of sentence sense.

The writing, however, is grossly deficient in one or more of these skills, judged by standards appropriate for high school:

Spelling
Usage
Punctuation and capitalization

Level 3. Marginally competent

The student can compose a complete series of ideas about a topic with a minimum of gross deficiencies in spelling, usage, or punctuation, judged by standards appropriate for high school.

The writing, however, does not contain at least one competent paragraph or is not competent in one or more of these skills, judged by standards appropriate for high school:

Sentence sense
Spelling

Usage
Punctuation and capitalization

Level 4. Competent

The student can compose a complete series of ideas about a topic with basic skills at a level appropriate for high school and with at least one competent paragraph.

The writing, however, does not demonstrate all the characteristics of highly competent writing:

Good overall organization
Competent paragraphing
Regular use of transitions
Interpretive meaning (as
opposed to literal writing)

Good sentence structure
Good vocabulary
Appropriate use of subordination

Level 5. Highly competent

The student can compose a complete series of ideas about a topic with basic skills at a level appropriate for high school and with these characteristics of highly competent writing:

Good overall organization
Competent paragraphing
Regular use of transitions
Interpretive meaning (as
opposed to literal writing)

Good sentence structure
Good vocabulary
Appropriate use of subordination

The writing however, does not demonstrate thesis development and does not contain critical or creative thinking.

Level 6. Superior

The student can compose a complete series of ideas about a topic with excellent basic skills, with the characteristics of highly competent writing, with adequate thesis development, and with at least one passage demonstrating critical or creative thinking.

The passage of superior writing, however, tends to be an isolated example.

Level 7. Superior

The student can compose a complete series of ideas about a topic with excellent basic skills, with critical or creative thinking, and with a sustained vitality and richness of expression.

*From R.A. McCaig. A districtwide plan for the evaluation of student writing. In S. Haley-James (Ed.), *Perspectives on writing in grades 1-8.* Copyright 1981 by the National Council of Teachers of English. Reprinted by permission.

Appendix C
An Analytic Scoring Scale
Showing Code Number of Ongoing Revisions*

A. Quality and Scope of Intent

5 Clear perception of topic, problems, and issues is outlined in the introduction; seriousness may not be explicit, but is implied; use of detail is specific to issues raised

3 Reader can discern point of view of writer, but not as clearly as 5; no development issues before launching into pros and cons; detail is minimal, glossy

1 Superficial addressing of the issue; "I think" stance; broad, general statements; little or no detail

B. Organization and Presentation of Content

5 Focus of topic is clear; digressions are relevant and usually signaled; all or most of essay is clearly elaborative, supports arguments fully through logical development

3 Lacks clear focus, but remains on topic; some evidence of faulty reasoning, but adequate development of reasoning; sense of beginning, middle, end

1 Has not given reader sense of which aspect is most important or is incomprehensible; scant or no paragraph development; scant or no elaboration of main points through use of examples

C. Style and Tone

5 Language generally consistent with rhetorical task and within itself; no gaps in information; generally, content links smoothly through logical development; variety of sentence types

3 Appeals more to reader's emotions than to intellect; no slang, no jargon; little or no use of subordination; reader can follow flow of thought, but less so than 5

1 Language detracts from persuasive task; may be flippant; lack of connectivity or less so than 3; some gaps in content; little or no flow between ideas

D. Mechanics

5 One or no errors in usage; generally very few or no spelling or punctuation errors

3 Errors in usage, but text remains comprehensible; errors in spelling and punctuation, but text comprehensibility is not affected

1 Text comprehensibility greatly affected by errors; frequent, flagrant errors where text is difficult to process

E. Affective Response of the Raters

5 Essay was interesting; a sense of connection with the writer

3 Moderately interesting; a sense of moderate connection with the writer

1 Not really interesting; no sense of connection with the writer

F. Overall Impression Score

7 Off task

5 Exceptional or near exceptional essay; persuasive argument; use of accepted, mechanical conventions, logically developed, connected prose, rich detail, elaboration; generally, good flow of thought

3 An acceptable piece; few mechanical errors; more gaps in information than in 5; development of ideas is there, but must be flushed out by reader; an occasional appeal to reader's emotions rather than intellect

1 A poor effort; many errors in mechanics, consistency of tone, logical development, flow of thought, connectedness; comprehensibility of the piece is adversely affected

*Adapted from A. Purves. (1982). *International evaluation of assessment of written composition.* Unpublished paper.

Appendix D
A Writing Analysis Checklist*

The Writing Process

1. How often does the writer get ideas for writing

___ from the imagination?
___ from discussion with others?
___ by imitating a book, story, poem, TV show?
___ from the teacher's assignments?
___ from some other source? Which?

2. When the writer means to rehearse what will be written, and narrow down the topic, does the writer

___ talk to classmates?
___ talk to the teacher?
___ draw a picture first?
___ start writing right away?

3. In drafting a paper, does the writer

___ write one draft only?
___ invent spellings, use a dictionary, or limit vocabulary to the words he or she can spell?
___ scratch out words and lines, and cut and paste?
___ seek comments from others about the way the drafting is going?

4. Does the writer revise a paper before it is considered finished? Do the drafts

___ all look like different papers, new beginnings?
___ look like mechanical refinements of earlier drafts?
___ interact with and build on the ideas of early drafts?

The Functions of Writing

5. What forms of writing has the writer produced?

___ stories?
___ poems?
___ expressive writing (personal experiences and opinions)?
___ persuasive writing?
___ descriptive writing?
___ expository writing (that which explains or gives directions)?

6. What kinds of topics has the writer written about?

___ topics about which the writer was an expert?
___ topics about which the writer had to learn more before writing?
___ topics about things that were present?
___ topics about things that were past or absent?
___ topics about abstract ideas?

7. What audiences has the writer written for?

___ the teacher?
___ classmates?
___ people known to the child? Whom?
___ people unknown to the child? Whom?

8. In trying to stick to the topic, did the writer

___ limit the focus of the topic before starting to write?
___ stick to one thing or ramble?
___ focus more on the object of the writing or on the writer?

9. In trying to stick with the purpose of writing, does the writer

___ keep expressing personal feelings, although the topic and purpose suggest doing otherwise?
___ declare one purpose but pursue another (such as "The story about..." which is expository, not narrative)?
___ shift from one purpose to another?

10. In trying to meet the audience's need for information

___ does the writer appear to assume the audience knows and is interested in the author?
___ is he or she careful to tell the audience things they will need to know in order to understand what is talked about?
___ does the writer address the same audience throughout?

Qualities of Writing Styles

11. ___ Does the writer use exact, well-chosen words?

12. ___ Does the writer "paint pictures with words" (make the reader see what the writer saw)? Does the writer focus on immediate "here-and-now" images?

13. In regard to the organization of the papers

    ___ does the writer keep the focus on one aspect of the topic at a time?
    ___ do the papers have identifiable openings?
    ___ are the details arranged in a reasonable order and do they relate reasonably to one another?
    ___ is there an identifiable ending to the papers?

Fluency of Writing

14. How long are the papers (in words or lines per paper)?

15. What is the average number of words per sentence?

16. What is the average number of words per T-unit?

Mechanics of Writing

17. In handwriting, does the writer

    ___ have problems forming letters? Which ones?
    ___ have problems spacing between letters? Keeping vertical lines parallel? Keeping the writing even on the baseline?
    ___ write with uniform pressure? In smooth or in jerky lines?

18. In regard to spelling,

    ___ does the writer misspell words in the first draft?
    ___ does the writer correct the spellings of many words between the first and later drafts?
    ___ what does the writer do when uncertain of how to spell a word?

19. Does the writer have trouble with standard English usage?

    ___ Does the writer write in complete sentences? If not, what are the units of writing like?
    ___ Does the writer have problems with punctuation and capitalization? With which elements? In what circumstances?
    ___ Are errors made in standard English grammar? If so, describe the errors.

Enjoying Writing

20. ___ Does the writer take pleasure in writing? How do you know?

Appendix E
A Self-Evaluation Questionnaire*

1. List the successful things you did in writing this paper.

2. List the things that a reader will think are successful.

3. List the things you were unable to do in this paper that would have made it more successful.

4. In the process of writing this paper, what aspects were easier than when you have written previous papers?

5. In the process of writing this paper, what aspects were more difficult than when you have written previous papers?

*From L. Faigley, R.D. Cherry, D.A. Jolliffe, & A.M. Skinner. *Assessing writers' knowledge and processes of composing*. Copyright 1985 by Ablex Publishing. Reprinted by permission.

PART THREE

Implementing Reading Programs

PRELUDE

The following chapters are designed to provide a hands-on perspective for middle school reading. Each chapter tells a story about one school district's attempt to implement reading programs. Each story results in unique insights about how to implement improvements, ranging from the impediments to change reported by Anders and Levine in Chapter 10 to the utility of employing collaborative models as reported by Conley and Tripp-Opple in Chapter 14. Together, the five chapters provide five tangible examples other educators can use as a basis for implementing their own middle school literacy programs.

Accomplishing Change in Reading Programs

Patricia L. Anders
Ned S. Levine

THIS IS A STORY about a large urban district where 15 junior high schools tried to make the transition to the middle school philosophy and format. Embedded in the story are two messages. One focuses on what makes change difficult; the other on authentic literacy experiences and strategy instruction as critical features of effective middle school reading programs.

Background

The initial stages of change in our schools were fairly predictable. A research group took time to learn from authorities and "the literature" what the difference was between the middle school construct and the existing junior high format. Two years later, a report was published that served as a guide for what middle schools should be. Included in this publication were statements concerning instructional priorities and a method for organizing. Principals were brought in during the first summer of the transition year to receive theoretical training on the philosophy and format of middle schools. The charge was for the principals to engage a planning team to implement these changes despite the fact that, due to resource constraints, only two days of inservice a year were provided at each site.

Reading, of course, was a main focus. Conceptually, the emphasis was on reading throughout the content areas. This emphasis required changes in attitudes and skills. Reading could no longer be thought of solely as a class or core subject, but as a process to be applied and taught in each area (see Chapter 5, this volume). The outcome of the first year's efforts was predictable. The similarity to the myth about the blind men and the elephant was striking. People possessing varying perspectives on the elephant all tried to build their own. As one English teacher said, "All this middle school stuff is okay. I still will only have to see a student for one period and then I'll be through with him or her for the day."

The second year we began again. We revised our training programs. Summer training with school teams of administrators and staff focused on planning and implementing the intended program as well as on the content of the middle school. This experience with staff development programs emphasized the difficulty of change. Vonnegut (1987) gives his own assessment of the possibility of achieving a given change in a satirical, whimsical novel, *Bluebeard*. A fictional character offers his views through the publication of a nonfiction tome, *The Only Way to Have a Successful Revolution in Any Field of Human Activity*.

> Most people, we are told (and I might add, I heartily agree) cannot open their minds to new ideas unless a mind-opening team with a peculiar membership goes to work on them. Otherwise, life will go on as before, no matter how painful, unrealistic, ludicrous, or downright dumb that life may be.
>
> The team must consist of three kinds of specialists. The rarest of these specialists is an authentic genius—a person capable of having good ideas not in general circulation. The trick is to convince people then that the ideas are good and should be discovered and shared. "A genius working alone is invariably ignored as a lunatic." The second sort of specialist is a lot easier to find. What you need here is a highly intelligent citizen in good standing in his or her community, who admires the freshness and pertinence of the genius and testifies that the genius is far from mad. The validation, in Human Development Training

called "sponsorship," is essential to create an audience. A person like that, however, can only "yearn out loud for changes" because they usually lack the wherewithal to make those changes.

> The third type of specialist is a person who can explain anything, no matter how complicated, to the satisfaction of most people, no matter how pigheaded or stupid they may be. This type of person will say almost anything to gain attention or to be interesting or exciting. This is the venerable talk show host. However, working alone, this person may strike his/her constituents as, shall we say, suffering from eternal constipation.
>
> If you can't get a cast like that together, you can forget about changing anything (p. 191).

Like Vonnegut, we have learned that change is difficult. Consequently, the first part of this chapter deals specifically with the process of change in middle schools; the second part elaborates on practices emphasized in our reading efforts.

The Dynamics of Change

A survey of the literature on change suggests several barriers to change. The first is that research-based definitions of good teaching (Brophy & Good, 1986) drive many policymakers to invent lists and inventories of observable classroom behavior and adopt them as an evaluation tool for judging the effectiveness of teaching. Translated into checklists for the site administrator, these "research implications" become expectations to be observed in classroom instruction. The evaluator focuses on the presence of a particular practice; its use is rewarded, its absence penalized. Whether the observed behavior is appropriate to the content of the lesson or to the needs and interests of the students does not enter into the evaluation system.

A second barrier to change in reading (closely related to the first) is the perception of administrative commitment. Specifically, Dawson (1984) found the following variables to interfere with teacher change: (1) receiving mixed messages from the administration as to what is important, (2) viewing change as something being implemented in response to "central office pressure," and (3) the administrator's reputation of failing to follow through.

A third barrier to change, for adults and adolescents alike, is requiring public performance of an unmastered skill (Hord et al., 1987). Teachers and students must receive support during the early, premastery stages of learning. The focus should be on the conditions for a successful response rather than on the response as a measure of personal competence. Consequently, the instructional leader needs to have skill and tolerance in order to reduce both negative labeling of individuals and the potential for resistance, and to encourage people to see themselves as resources for changing negative conditions to positive ones in practical and specific ways. Situations must be created in which every person's perspective is important so that all can become allies working toward mutual goals, reducing the sense of polarity in a group or classroom.

A fourth barrier is the fact that the act of teaching is continually oversimplified. Teachers are asked to assimilate new behaviors more rapidly than is possible. Even teaching skills that appear simple require much training, while skills embedded in complex models require as many as 25 practice episodes to master (Good, 1981; Showers, Joyce, & Bennett, 1987). Further, current reviews of the effects of staff development and inservice programs show varying results with teachers, depending on their years of experience (Levine, 1983; Showers, Joyce, & Bennett). Findings suggest that first year teachers are overwhelmed, usually lacking the ability to do long term planning and considering themselves successful if they are prepared for the short term. They feel particularly inadequate when it comes to classroom management and use of time, and have difficulty planning and running multiengagement lessons. It is difficult for these teachers to master all of the critical practices necessary for an excellent reading program. Their own learning experiences need to be simple, limited in scope, and couched in the most basic behaviors to provide content validity—yet highly engaging and entertaining. Extensive practice needs to be provided in the staff development program design.

In contrast, experienced teachers who are relatively sophisticated participants in staff development programs require higher potency in their training to ensure transference of the skill to practice. For this level of expertise, the staff development program may be less entertaining than with the less experienced teacher, but it must provide more intense and realistic training to ensure transfer.

A fifth barrier to change is the lack of a clear expectation for change to occur. In confronting the entrenchment of past practices, change agents first must prepare the environment for change. Developing teacher commitment to explore possible changes begins with clear, direct leadership from building and central office administrators. It includes training by a credible person identified as both an adequate practitioner and an excellent presenter (Crandall, 1982).

We also found that how changes are presented to teachers is important. An appropriate presentation takes into account the context in which the practitioners work and provides opportunities for teachers to experience the practice, apply it, critique it, and modify it for personal use. The training itself must be followed by continuous support and assistance from trainers or from others perceived as adequate practitioners of the innovation and must account for what we know about teachers as adult learners. The presentation must engage teachers in continuous, concrete talk about teaching and effective teaching practices, not the social issues of the school or its clients.

Teachers should be observed frequently and provided with accurate, honest critiques of their teaching (Little, 1982). They should plan, design, prepare, and evaluate their own teaching activities and materials and should instruct one another in the practice of teaching within structured settings, often using peers from the same institution to conduct training (Glatthorn, 1982; Little, 1982). Attention to basic needs such as work conditions and safety is a prerequisite for the effectiveness of change and for a successful staff development program (Herzberg, Mausner, & Snyder-

Staff development programs are an important part of accomplishing change.

man 1959; Maslow, 1954; Sergiovanni, 1967). Trust must be established through administrative decisions that treat mistakes as opportunities for learning (Levine, 1983; Showers, Joyce, & Bennett, 1987), and training must vary according to the background of the participating teachers (McLagan, 1983).

We have learned that students of teachers who have the opportunity to participate in these sorts of staff development programs reap the benefits of openness and exploration. Teachers who are willing to be risk-takers are more likely to promote risk-taking among their students. Teachers who recognize and value learning from mistakes will more likely accept mistakes from their students. Teachers who have control over their own behavior and decisions are more likely to encourage their students to develop similar types of self-control.

Change is never easy and is never without tension. Environments typified by change are often relatively chaotic and unpredictable. Thus, administrators and teachers who are looking for controlled environments with a high degree of order and discipline often resist change. For example, middle schools in which administrators evaluate teachers on the amount of control and discipline imposed on the students send a message to teachers and students alike that the uncertainty accompanying change is not welcome. In such a school, the "law and order" tenet prevents many teachers from making changes in their teaching and signals to students that risk-taking and authentic involvement in ideas or activities are not the goals of the school's academic leaders.

Changes We Made

Assuming that an environment conducive to change is achieved, what change should be made? This section describes two changes we tried to implement. The first focused on instructional activities that promote authentic literacy experiences; the second focused on strategies.

Promotion of Authentic Literacy Experiences

May Powell was one of our seventh grade students. She did little reading or writing; she was belligerent, negative, and difficult. The reading specialist placed her in the lowest reading group. One day May's teacher for the low reading class happened to lay *I Always Wanted to Read* by Mary McLeod Bethune in the middle of her desk. As was May's habit, she handled everything on the teacher's desk, picking things up and laying them down at random (a behavior designed to drive the teacher crazy), until she came to that book. She picked it up and started to walk away. The teacher said, "Hey, May! You can't have that. It's my book, I'm reading it!" May's response was "Aw, c'mon. I just wanna look at it." She sat down and read for the rest of the period. On her way out of class, the teacher again asked for the book. May pleaded to take it home, promising to bring it back the next day. She did, too, and thereafter she read whatever was placed on the teacher's desk.

Similarly, Fader (1973), in *Naked Children*, writes of Wentworth, a young man observed in an English class for low readers. Wentworth was reading a sophisticated automotive magazine during school. Afterwards, Fader asked him why he was in such a low English class since certainly he could read. Wentworth's reply was that he didn't want teachers to know what he could do because then he would have to read what they wanted instead of what he wanted. Estes and Vaughan (1978, 1985) cited students like Wentworth as evidence of the "Wentworth Syndrome"—kids who can read, but who choose not to let their teachers know. They do not let their teachers know for many reasons; one is that they want control over their own activities.

Such reluctance is not unusual in middle school reading programs. How can we change reading programs to help such students? The reading and writing activities that follow (all of which have been well accepted by our teachers) take advantage of the strengths and characteristics of literacy processes while building on the energetic, social nature of the student who is struggling to know, to build, and to understand. Together they promote authentic literacy experiences, a critical instructional feature.

Reading aloud. We read aloud to our students daily. Reading should consist of a rich diet of literature, poetry, and exposition, and should represent a wide range of topics and interests. Reading aloud can have a number of uses. Students can respond to it critically either during oral discussions or in personal journals. Students can use information from reading aloud in projects or can follow up on what is shared by silently reading similar works. The teacher's modeling of oral reading also can help students when they read aloud their own writing.

Books and other materials selected to be read aloud should be on students' intellectual and social levels, but it is not necessary that they be readable by students. Students need only to listen to and engage in ideas, problems, emotions, and information. Listening can be done with more difficult text than they would read independently. The selected materials should be something the teacher likes and can read aloud well. Lists of suggested read-aloud material are available from local librarians, the National Council of Teachers of English, *Journal of Reading*, *The Reading Teacher*, and commercial publications such as *The New Read-Aloud Handbook* by Jim Trelease (1989).

There are many good reasons for reading aloud. First, students cooperate while listening to the teacher and share emotional responses to the story. Second, such reading provides a common experience and a common knowledge base for a class to share. Third, while being read to, students hear the flow of language that helps them construct meaning and develop interpretive techniques. Fourth, reading aloud is an effective way to settle a class. Many teachers read aloud at the beginning of class periods, and their students are rarely late to class. Finally, reading aloud introduces students to the teacher's interests and invites them to see a teacher in a different light. Atwell (1987) relates that some students were so convinced of her interest in certain relevant topics that they would write their journals to her because "only she could understand," something that could not have happened if it had not been for her compelling and interesting read-aloud sessions.

Independent reading. Our middle schoolers also have time every day for independent reading. They select their own reading material, which may or may not relate to their content-area studies or projects. This practice requires only that an abundance of materials be available from which students may choose. Again, lists for stocking the library and reading rooms are readily available from professional and commercial sources, and students themselves are a wonderful resource for needed materials.

Various methods can be used to encourage independent reading. For example, an in-school "Young Readers" program might be sponsored on a yearly basis. Young Readers is a popular event in many states and regions. The children nominate about 20 books as "the best book I ever read." During the next year, students read a certain number of books on the recommended list and at the end of the year vote for their favorite book. The author of that book is then brought to the region for a Young Readers Conference. A similar program could be run just as effectively on a schoolwide basis.

Another idea is to display a Top Ten reading list for the school. A librarian and perhaps a student committee can keep track of the titles most often checked out and maybe even have the students fill out a reaction form. Students thus can learn what their peers think are "the best books."

Independent reading is important for several reasons. First, it is a good way to gather assessment information (see Chapter 9, this book). Second, interdisciplinary projects, common in the middle school curriculum, stimulate reading interests. Third, students often become interested in a particular author, and independent reading time gives them the opportunity to follow up on those interests. Fourth, students can use their independent reading for information they may use later in their own writing efforts.

Our teachers make students responsible for keeping records of their independent reading activities. Students use folders, checklists, and notebooks to make a public record of how they spend their time. Teachers and students confer to set goals and assess progress. Practices such as independent reading are opportunities for students to control much of their own activity. Successful teachers think about what is involved in the independent activity and provide modeling and explanation for students who might have difficulty with the responsibility.

Writing groups. This practice has recently received much attention from teachers. The idea is that students write what they choose to write and share it with their peers for feedback, evaluation, recommendations for rewrite, and possible publication. Atwell (1987) calls these groups Writing Workshops, and Harste, Woodward, and Burke (1984) call them Authoring Cycles; other labels probably exist for basically the same process. While each might differ slightly in format or design, the purpose in all of them is to have students write what they care about, know about, and want to know about by having them engage in real or authentic writing.

A program that emphasizes student writing and the writing process is compatible with middle school youngsters. It suits their social and psychological needs to know and explore. It bridges the processes of reading and writing because all language processes are employed as students read and rewrite their work.

Students can write in the genre of the content area being studied. Research reported by Langer and Applebee (Applebee, 1981; Langer & Applebee, 1987) suggests that students have little opportunity to write in their content area classrooms and that when students do write, the quality and quantity of knowledge acquired and understood improves dramatically. All kinds of writing are important because as readers write they must construct meaning, and construction of meaning is the key to reading comprehension.

Strategy Instruction

A second focus of change was strategies. Our middle schoolers benefit from strategy instruction when reading and writing. This instruction can make the difference between successful risk-takers who make great strides in accomplishing the goals of the school curriculum and students who are frustrated because they lack the strategies to try. In the following sections, we describe the criteria used to select strategies for such instruction, suggest one strategy, and explain the rationale behind it (see Chapters 5 and 6 as well as the next two chapters, this volume).

First, a word of caution. We need to recognize that some students will develop their own strategies and that those strategies might be more effective and efficient than what reading/literacy educators might generate. We also need to realize that sometimes our recommended strategies get in the way of what some students do naturally.

A recommended plan. Teachers can make good decisions when planning for strategy instruction by following guiding questions suggested by Anders and Pearson (1984, p. 314):

1. *What?* Students need to know what it is you want them to do. They must, in effect, develop a concept of the strategy. And to know what something is, they will have to know what it is not. For example, if they are to learn main ideas, they need an operational definition of a main idea and they need to know how a main idea differs from a detail or an irrelevant statement. They need to be able to recognize one when it "hits them in the face."

2. *How?* What all students need desperately is a set of procedures to use when they are asked to apply a strategy. Where do I start? What do I try first? Second? What do I do when I don't succeed the first time?

3. *Why?* We would argue that if you cannot generate a legitimate, understandable reason for asking students to perform a task—a reason you can share with them—then perhaps you should not teach the task. We believe the answer to *why* should relate to the purposes for the reading. The purposes for the reading should be for certain types of information, for a literary experience, or for pleasure and escape. The strategy is taught and practiced because it may help the reader accomplish that functional goal.

4. *When*? We assume that not all strategies were meant to be applied to all texts or to all tasks. Part of the effective use of a strategy is knowing when to ignore it. For example, in teaching about main ideas, we would likely want students to reserve it for informational texts and to forget it when they were reading stories.

By answering these questions, we limit strategies to those that are most helpful to students. We believe certain strategies are particularly suited to middle school students because of the characteristics these strategies share with characteristics of the middle school student (Bos & Anders, in progress). Eight characteristics of such strategies follow.

The first characteristic is that these strategies help students activate prior knowledge. Sometimes students are not aware that what they know from the real world can be related to school learning. The strategies themselves do not provide answers for students; rather, students must rely on what they have experienced or known in the past.

Second, such strategies help students see the organized and hierarchical nature of knowledge. Through the use of interactive strategies, students will organize their prior knowledge to connect it with new knowledge.

Third, strategies help students predict relationships between and among higher and lower ideas in a hierarchy. Knowledge is categorical; it relates to other ideas; it has connectedness. Strategies should make explicit the interrelatedness as well as the hierarchical nature of knowledge. As students engage in the strategies, you can almost see them move up and down, inside and out, and all around the ideas and their connections.

Fourth, strategies encourage cooperative learning among students. Students are asked to justify their thinking and to compare their thinking with that of those around them. Students work to achieve a consensus through discussion, data gathering and logic. This characteristic is particularly appealing to the social nature of the middle school student.

Fifth, strategies promote the setting of purposes before reading. Reading experts long have known the importance of purpose setting for reading comprehension (Stauffer, 1969), and strategies promote such thinking and planning.

Sixth, strategies encourage students to read to see if their predictions are borne out by the author in the content area text reading assignment. Using a prereading interactive strategy as a during- and after-reading aid helps students read and think to confirm the predicted relationships between and among ideas.

Seventh, as students elaborate on their strategies after reading, the processes of prediction, confirmation, and integration are enhanced. Students return to the text (and, in some cases, to other sources) to gather enough information to satisfactorily categorize and relate information.

Eighth, strategies help students distinguish between and among distinctive features of ideas. The details that make one idea relate to another become apparent.

Thus, strategies help students connect with authentic ideas, ideas that help them make sense of their world. These strategies have been demonstrated to be successful with mildly handicapped students

Figure 1
Relationship Chart
Fossils

KEY	
Relationship	+
No Relationship	0
Uncertain	?

Important Ideas

Important Words	Type of Life		Location			Extinct?	
	Plant	Animal	Sea	Land	Lakes	Extinct	Not Extinct
Trilobites							
Crinoids							
Giant cats							
Coral							
Bryozoans							
Guide fossils							
Dinosaurs							
Fresh water fish							
Brachiopods							
Small horses							
Ferns							
Enormous winged bugs							
Trees							

from ages 9 through 18 (Anders, Bos, & Filip, 1984; Bos et al., 1985), as well as with nonhandicapped eighth graders (Anders, Bos, & Wilde, 1986).

A sample strategy. The Semantic-Syntactic Feature Analysis (SSFA) is one of the strategies we use. It employs both a matrix chart and modified cloze-type sentences. Thus, when talking about the SSFA strategy, we often refer to it as the relationship chart and sentences.

The original idea for SSFA came from the work of Johnson, Toms-Bronowski, and Pittelman (1981), who investigated the efficacy of the relationship chart for vocabulary learning. Students using the relationship chart demonstrated success in learning meanings and remembering

Figure 2
Relationship Sentences
Fossils

1. Trilobites were animals that lived in the _____ and that are now _____ .

2. _____ and _____ are extinct land animals.

3. A sea animal that is now extinct is a _____ .

4. Fern fossils are fossils of _____ that lived on the land and that are _____ .

5. _____ , _____ , and _____ are animals that live on land or in lakes and are not extinct.

new words. Anders and Bos (1986) suggested that the relationship chart should be adapted for vocabulary and comprehension instruction in the content areas.

To develop a relationship chart (Figure 1), we first read an assignment to determine the main concepts, as represented by a word or a phrase in the text. Second, we list those concepts. Third, we study the list to determine the idea representing the superordinate concept, or the idea that includes all the others and becomes the name for the relationship chart. Sometimes we have found that the superordinate concept is implied but not listed, in which case we simply add the concept to the list. Fourth, we organize the list by categorizing ideas that seem to go together. In the passage on fossils, we found three categories of important ideas: type of life, location, and whether the fossil represents an extinct form of life. Fifth, we list the headings for each of the categories across the top of the page. These may be thought of as coordinate-level concepts, or concepts that tie together ideas. If an author does not use

words that should be category headings, add those terms to the vocabulary concept list. Notice that these are labeled Important Ideas on the student's relationship chart. Finally, we list the words and phrases down the side of the chart, where they are identified as Important Words.

Before asking students to read the assignment, give each one a copy of the relationship chart. Using a model chart at the front of the room, explain its purpose and how it is to be used to discuss ideas in preparation for a reading assignment. Explain that we are looking for connections between ideas. When an important idea and an important word are connected, we will put a + in the box; when they are not connected, we will put a 0 in the box; and when we cannot decide, we will put a *?* in the box.

Introduce the superordinate concept and the important ideas. This is an opportune time to ask students what they already know about these ideas. We have found that some students almost always have background knowledge to offer the class. Once meanings for the superordinate concept and the important ideas have been established, introduce the first important word. Encourage students to share their current knowledge. With more technical vocabulary, students often possess less background knowledge. In most instances, we provide the conceptual meaning for the word. In other instances, we ask students to read to discover the meaning. For example, in the case of the relationship chart for fossils, none of our students knew the technical meaning of *trilobites, crinoids, bryozoans,* or *brachiopods.* However, they did predict that these were types of fossils. Students filled out the relationship chart with this broad level of understanding and, when they began reading, they discovered the more technical definitions.

After introducing the first important word, ask students to predict the relationship between the word and each important idea listed along the top of the chart. In determining each relationship, it is important to ask students for justifications and explanations for the predicted relationship. In this way, students analyze the critical features of the meaning and contribute their background knowledge to the discussion. Use the symbol system to record their predictions on the model relationship chart, and have students record them on their inidividual charts. Through discussion, attempt to reach a consensus. When consensus within the group is not possible, place a question mark in the appropriate box. Later, when the students read, encourage them to read to resolve the lack of consensus.

Complete this procedure for each word (this discussion generally takes about 30 minutes for 20 to 25 concepts).

Next, ask students to use the information from the chart to predict the appropriate words to fill in the blanks in the relationship sentences (Figure 2). The sentences ask students to further connect ideas. We have found them to be particularly effective for enhancing long-term memory (Anders & Bos, 1988). In some cases, the class will not agree on the word or words to go in a sentence, and students are instructed to read to find out which word(s) would be more appropriate. Sometimes, the text is not adequate to confirm students' predictions, and we must refer to other sources.

Next, students read the passage to verify or reject their predictions and to search for information that may help to predict the relationship between ideas for which no consensus could be found. After reading, students compare their chart and sentences with the information from the text. We try to reach a consensus, either by using the information provided in the text or by finding other resources that may address our concerns.

The relationship chart might be adapted in a couple of ways. One way would be to change the symbol system used to signify the predicted relationships. When relationships are varied rather than absolute, numbers could be used, with a *1* signifying a very low relationship, a *2* meaning that ideas were somewhat related, and a *3* meaning that ideas were highly related. Another change in the chart might be to make the chart open ended at both the coordinate and detail levels. These blanks would be used if new categories or details emerged during discussion or reading. Students also could begin to generate their own sentences. Such changes make the strategy even more interactive and give students more responsibility for determining important ideas, details, and relationships. As students become adept at creating such relationship charts, they become more independent learners.

Conclusion

Our work suggests that even the least skilled students improve when given the opportunity to participate in authentic literacy experiences and when they know how to use certain strategies. Thus, we believe that authentic literacy experiences and strategy use are critical features of the middle school reading program.

Achieving such change, however, is hindered by several realities. Supervisors and administrators often have contradictory agendas; change is threatening; many veteran teachers are content with their present methods; and newer teachers are not in a position to institute new programs. Consequently, leadership and staff development is critical for educational change.

When thinking of change and the growth that accompanies any change process, we are reminded of a seed. When a seed is planted in the ground it changes. If the environment is right and if the seed is nurtured and fed, it destroys its "seed self" and becomes a seedling, and eventually a fruit-bearing plant. The paradox here is that in order to grow, the seed has to self-destruct. In many ways, this is analogous to what happens as a child becomes an early adolescent and as teachers learn to change. Because children and teachers are more complicated than seeds, they need considerable nurturing. It is up to those who are responsible for the organization and maintenance of the middle school to provide the conditions and environment for such nurturing.

References

Anders, Patricia L., & Bos, Candace S. (1988). *Comparison of semantic features analysis and direct instruction of word meanings for improving reading comprehension*. Paper presented at the American Educational Research Association, New Orleans, LA.

Anders, Patricia L., & Bos, Candace S. (1986). Semantic feature analysis: An interactive strategy for vocabulary development and text comprehension. *Journal of Reading*, *29*, 610-616.

Anders, Patricia L., & Pearson, P. David. (1984). Instructional research on literacy and reading: Parameters, perspectives, and predictions. In Robert J. Tierney, Patricia L. Anders, & Judy Nichols Mitchell (Eds.), *Understanding readers' understanding: Theory and practice* (pp. 307-321). Hillsdale, NJ: Erlbaum.

Anders, Patricia L., Bos, Candace S., & Filip, Dorothy. (1984). The effect of semantic feature analysis on the reading comprehension of learning disabled students. In Jerome R. Niles (Ed.), *Changing perspectives on research in reading, language processing, and instruction* (pp. 162-166). Thirty-Third Yearbook of the National Reading Conference. Rochester, NY: National Reading Conference.

Anders, Patricia L., Bos, Candace S., & Wilde, Sandra. (1986). *The effect of semantic feature analysis on eighth graders' vocabulary and reading comprehension*. Paper presented at the National Reading Conference, Austin, TX.

Applebee, Arthur. (1981). *Writing in the secondary school*. Urbana, IL: National Council of Teachers of English.

Atwell, Nancie. (1987). *In the middle: Writing, reading, and learning with adolescents*. Portsmouth, NH: Boynton/Cook.

Bos, Candace S., & Anders, Patricia L. (In progress). *Interactive teaching: An instructional methodology for teaching concepts*. University of Arizona, Tucson, AZ.

Bos, Candace S., Anders, Patricia L., Filip, Dorothy, & Jaffe, Lynne. (1985). Semantic feature analysis and long term learning. In Jerome Nile & Rosary V. Lalik (Eds.), *Issues in literacy: A research perspective*. Thirty-Fourth Yearbook of the National Reading Conference. Rochester, NY: National Reading Conference.

Brophy, Jere, & Good, Thomas. (1986). Teacher behavior and student achievement. In M.C. Wittrock (Ed.), *Handbook of research on teaching* (3rd ed., pp. 328-375). New York: Macmillan.

Crandall, David P. (1982). *Models of the school improvement process: Factors contributing to success*. Andover, MA: Network of Innovative Schools.

Dawson, Judith. (1984). *The principal's role in facilitating teacher participation: Mediating the influence of school context*. Philadelphia, PA: Research for Better Teaching.

Estes, Thomas, & Vaughan, Joseph L. (1978, 1985). *Reading and learning in the content classroom*. Boston, MA: Allyn & Bacon.

Fader, Daniel. (1973). *Naked children*. New York: Macmillan.

Glatthorn, Allen. (1982). Cooperative professional development: Peer centered options for future growth. *Educational Leadership*, *45*(3), 77-99.

Good, Thomas. (1981). Teacher expectations and student perceptions: A decade of research. *Educational Leadership*, 415-422.

Harste, Jerome, Woodward, Virginia, & Burke, Carolyn. (1984). *Language stories and literary lessons*. Portsmouth, NH: Heinemann.

Herzberg, Frederick, Mausner, Bernard, & Snyderman, Barbra. (1959). *The motivation to work*. New York: John Wiley & Sons.

Hord, Shirley, Rutherford, William, Huling-Austin, Leslie, & Hall, Gene. (1987). *Taking charge of change*. Alexandria, VA: ASCD.

Johnson, Dale, Toms-Bronowski, Susan, & Pittelman, Susan. (1981). An investigation of the trends in vocabulary research and the effects of prior knowledge on instructional strategies for vocabulary acquisition (Theoretical paper No. 95). Madison, WI: University of Wisconsin, Center for Educational Research.

Langer, Judith, & Applebee, Arthur. (1987). *How writing shapes thinking*. Urbana, IL: National Council of Teachers of English.

Levine, Sarah L. (1983). A developmental perspective on school leadership. *Principal*, 23-28.

Little, Judith W. (1982). Norms of collegiality and experimentation: Workplace conditions of school success. *American Educational Research Journal*, *19*(3), 325-340.

Maslow, Abraham. (1954). *Motivation and personality*. New York: Harper.

McLagan, Patrick. (1983). *Models for excellence*. Washington, DC: American Society for Training and Development.

Sergiovanni, Thomas J. (1967). Factors which affect satisfaction and dissatisfaction. *Journal of School Administration*, *5*, 66-82.

Showers, Beverly, Joyce, Bruce, & Bennett, Barrie. (1987). Synthesis of research on staff development: A framework for future study and state of the art analysis. *Educational Leadership*, *45*(3), 77-88.

Stauffer, Russell G. (1969). *Directing reading maturity as a cognitive process*. New York: Harper & Row.

Trelease, Jim. (1989). *The new read-aloud handbook*. New York: Penguin Books.

Vonnegut, Kurt. (1987). *Bluebeard*. New York: Delacorte.

Developing a Strategic Reading Program

Joy N. Monahan

THIS IS THE STORY OF a program used in grades 6-8 in the Orange County &a **11** &a Public Schools in Orlando, Florida. It is illustrative of the recent reconceptualization of reading as a strategic process (see Chapter 6, this volume) and of the movement away from teaching discrete skills in a basal reader. In this program students are involved in practical reading and writing activities using the assigned content area texts, with an emphasis on strategies good readers use (Paris, Lipson, & Wixson, 1983).

What Should Be in a Strategic Reading Program

As our reading curriculum was formulated, five areas of focus emerged: students' needs, teachers' role, move to expository text, gradual progression, and learning environment.

Students' Needs

Students' needs provide the basis for strategic reading. Middle school students are searching for self. They want independence. Physically they need to be active (George, 1983; Irvin, 1990; Lounsbury, 1984). When middle schoolers use strategies that include discussing and accepting others' ideas, social and emotional needs are being met simultaneously. Peer interactions facilitated by using thinking strategies in cooperative learning groups make powerful incentives to participate in the classroom. Positive self-concept is reinforced through learning strategies that can help students improve their grades and develop an understanding of the subject area. By building on students' prior knowledge before lessons and teaching metacognitive strategies, teachers increase interest and motivation, changing students' passive reactions into active learning goals.

Teachers' Role

Middle school teachers provide explanations about how, why, when, and where to use learning and thinking strategies. They provide instruction, modeling, and practice in using strategies. For instance, modeling a think aloud strategy for understanding a passage of text assures the student that even teachers must interact with the text for comprehension while reading. This is similar to what was recommended by psychologist Vygotsky (Vygotsky, 1978; Wertsch, 1985), who saw adults as instructors, supporters, and helpers in the learning process. He described a potential zone of development (or range of success) from a learning, or beginning, level to a much higher level if the student is encouraged and assisted by a supportive teacher. The teacher is a mediator between the student and the challenging content, providing the student with scaffolding that is gradually removed as the learner becomes more successful at the task.

Moving to Expository Text

Teachers must demonstrate strategy instruction using expository as well as narrative text, encouraging students to accumulate a repertoire of strategies that work for them when they are studying by themselves and have trouble with an expository text assignment in, say, geography or earth science. Learning to read content or information texts takes time and practice. The middle school years provide the time for this transition from narrative stories of elementary instruction to expository texts where the focus is on learning content.

Interest and familiarity with a text is fostered by activities that have students identify table of contents, glossary, in-dex, maps, charts, and chapter headings. Teachers need to be aware of sections of text that are inconsiderate—written in a language or style not easy to understand. Armbruster and Anderson (1984) list some questions to help teachers identify inconsiderateness in a textbook to help determine when students need extra help.

- Are the arrangement of ideas or building blocks of the specific subject area and the relationships connecting those ideas presented in a way students can grasp?

- Are the relationships among ideas clear enough for logical connections? Is there ambiguity, obscurity of expression, or wordiness? Does one idea flow to the next?

- Is one point at a time addressed, with no irrelevant or distracting information?

- Does the text fit the knowledge base of the reader?

To help students organize textbook information so they can link it to prior knowledge or show logical relationships, interaction frames modeled after the organization patterns of the text are helpful. For example, a compare and contrast matrix frame or a problem and solution frame, recommended by Jones and colleagues (1987), increases students' motivation, participation, and learning by logically organizing the text information.

Gradual Progression

The fourth aspect of a strategic reading program is the transition from full support during the initial learning of a

Figure 1
Modeling Teaching Strategies

Stages	Asks Questions	Answers Questions	Finds Evidence	Line of Reasoning
1. Modeling	T	T	T	T
2. Guided Practice	T	T	S	S
3. Guided Practice	T	S	T	S
4. Practice/Application	T	S	S	S
5. Student Control	S	S	S	S

T: Teacher   S: Student

strategy to student independence in comprehending text (Paris, 1985; Pearson, 1985). Stages for teaching strategies, shown in Figure 1, illustrate this progression. (Information in Figure 1 is adapted from an article by Gordon, 1985.)

Note that in the first stage the teacher demonstrates all the steps with detailed modeling and explanations. As the stages progress, students learn through practice steps. Each of the stages may have to be repeated until students have thorough understanding and control of the strategy. By Stage 5, the teacher has

released the learning responsibility to the student, who is an independent learner with that strategy.

Learning Environment

The final focus was the environment, particularly the interaction of students with other students, students with the teacher, and students with instructional materials. Creating a climate for thinking and trying out new ideas helps satisfy transescents' need to explore, particularly with their peers. For example, arranging desks in groups of four facilitates interaction during a multimode discussion cycle such as Think-Pair-Share, in which students listen to a question or presentation, have time to think individually, talk with one another in pairs or groups of four, and finally share responses with the larger group (McTighe & Lyman, 1988). Selecting content that explores and encourages creative thinking and appreciation for the opinions of others increases interaction between student and teacher. Organizing the class for large group or cooperative learning group discussions increases students' opportunities to comprehend what they read in content area texts (Alvermann, Dillon, & O'Brien, 1987).

Students need to realize that learning and remembering requires them to use what is in their heads (background experience) plus what the author has said to build a more lasting understanding. Think-aloud demonstrations by teachers, describing what is going on in their heads while reading, give students an idea of how to interact with the text to get meaning (Davey, 1983; Chapter 6, this volume). Activities such as these help build a classroom climate in which it is all right for students to be creative in thinking of solutions as long as they produce evidence for their conclusions.

The Change Process

Where We Were When We Started

For the 15 years before starting the change process, the reading program in Orange County consisted of a single basal reader with an accompanying management system. The result was fragmented skill instruction, reinforced by the criterion-referenced State Student Assessment Tests of Minimal Skills (given in grades 3, 6, 8, and 11). Secondary reading programs consisted of diagnostic-prescriptive labs, at least one per school (some schools had three).

In the late seventies, the district moved to the University of Florida's P.K. Yonge model, in which a content area teacher brought the entire class to the lab three days a week for nine weeks. A developmental, individualized, diagnostic-prescriptive approach was used as the reading teacher and the content area teacher worked together managing prescriptions with kits, workbooks, and reading machines. This team effort provided content area teachers with inservice reading experience. Students thought reading lab was a neat place to go because everyone in the class participated and was successful. Although the reading lab files were full of success stories, these same students were not comprehending their reading assignments in content area classrooms.

Deciding the Next Step

In trying to decide how to improve our program, we read articles in *The Reading Teacher* and *Journal of Reading,* attended presentations at the International Reading Association (IRA) Convention and the National Reading Conference (NRC), and held discussions at the Conference on Reading Research (CORR). These experiences guided us in taking new directions in reading instruction. In addition, research at the Institute for Research on Teaching (IRT), Michigan State University, pointed out the need for much more active, constructive, discussion-filled teaching than was permitted in our diagnostic-prescriptive lab setting.

Initiating Change

In creating change, the Orange County School District identified key people — consultants, principals, teachers, administrators — to envision a strategic reading program for middle schools and to help convert the program into practice. As these people spent time together studying and discussing the research, they recognized that we needed a new definition of reading. More than decoding and word-by-word plodding, reading is an active, constructive thinking process that goes on before, during, and after reading text. Reading is the interaction of the reader, the text, and the context (Duffy, Roehler, & Mason, 1984; Palincsar & Brown, 1985). We also needed to change the way we (1) asked questions, (2) practiced and taught vocabulary, (3) provided comprehension instruction, (4) related comprehension and composition, and (5) viewed the teacher's role (Cook, 1986; Pearson, 1985; Wixson & Peters, 1984).

Changes in the reading program were initiated with selection in 1982 of the College Board's Degrees of Reading Power (DRP) program for assessing reading. The DRP was selected because it seemed to make testing more educational (Haney, 1983), and was a pragmatic effort to move away from discrete skill testing toward the measurement of the process of reading. The DRP emphasizes three components: (1) a comprehension test with a cloze-type format that measures the most difficult prose a student can process, (2) a readability measure for the student's textbook, and (3) a staff development effort to assist the teachers in developing strategic readers (Paris, Lipson, & Wixson, 1983). The DRP assesses students and instructional materials so teachers can know how wide a gap exists between the two.

Teachers set classroom goals by comparing students' DRP comprehension ability with the DRP readability analysis of instructional materials. Discrepancies in DRP measures indicated instructional needs. Additionally, the DRP information helped teachers establish compatible classroom learning groups, analyze instructional materials and texts for readability, purchase classroom textbooks, and gather data that show student or class achievement growth.

Classroom action research also proved to be a valuable ally in helping teachers prove to themselves that they were making a difference. For example, by using a strategy such as graphic organizers with the second period class only, but giving the same pre- and posttest to all classes, a teacher received solid verification that using graphic organizers improves learning and remembering (Monahan, 1985).

Developing the Curriculum

A committee of elementary, middle, and secondary school teachers, principals, reading resource teachers, and consultants collaborated for several months to design a middle school reading program. Their objectives for a middle school reading program were to:

- Teach students that reading is an interactive process of getting meaning from print.

- Help make a transition from learning-to-read to reading-to-learn.

- Provide instruction in the acquisition of basic reading skills through an integrated reading process.

- Help students develop a basic sight vocabulary and expand their concepts to enable them to read material with comprehension and at a rate appropriate to the purpose of the reading task and the material's level of difficulty.

- Help students internalize the reading-learning process across the curriculum so they would value and use reading as a process of obtaining meaning for lifelong learning.

Districtwide writing teams of teachers used these objectives in building a reading curriculum. They produced a handbook, *Middle School Curriculum Planning Guide for Reading* (OCPS, 1986), which was given to every middle school reading teacher. This handbook identified key strategies from the research that would produce strategic teachers and strategic readers. A series of 32 folders was developed, one for each of the identified strategies. Each strategy folder contained five components: (1) a description of the strategy, (2) the procedure for using the strategy, (3) a bibliography of where more information could be located about the strategy, (4) some handouts and transparency blackline masters to use when presenting the strategy to the staff, and (5) articles from research about the strategy.

Each reading teacher uses the *Curriculum Planning Guide* as well as the *Reading Resource Specialist Handbook* (OCPS, 1985). Although basal reader texts are available, the major focus is to teach content area reading-learning

strategies to help students become strategic readers across the curriculum.

Training the Teachers

There is always resistance to change, so our shift to teaching strategic reading in Orange County was gradual, even with many inservice sessions on the reconceptualization of reading and what it meant for our reading program. Reading teachers needed to expand their thinking to include reading as a process that can be applied across the curriculum. Content teachers needed to recognize that they must help students bridge the gap between what they already know and the new subject knowledge being studied.

Teachers who were experimenting with new methods reported in sharing sessions that teaching learning strategies with content textbooks created interest and motivation for students. These sessions proved helpful to content area teachers and their classroom teaching (Monahan, 1985) as well as to reading teachers.

In the sixth grade, reading teachers, one for each team of math, science, social studies, and language arts, now have two full days of staff development during the school year. These teachers become reading resource "specialists," showing their team how to use strategies in their classes. When students hear about graphic organizers in math, in science, in social studies, and in language arts class, they begin to recognize the value of graphic organizers and use them in all learning settings.

In the seventh and eighth grades, a reading resource specialist (RRS) serves each middle school. The RRS is not assigned students, but works with the content area teachers in organizing and managing reading strategies. The RRS also participates in team teaching efforts with classroom teachers, provides inservice training for the school staff in the area of reading, and interprets the reading program for parents and the community. Monthly inservice sessions for all 18 reading resource specialists in the district help ensure networking and encourage them to generate new ideas as they study the research.

Resources and District Support

In addition to the materials available for each sixth grade teacher and each RRS, each school has the following materials:

- DRP tests and MiCRA-DRP software (College Board) to measure students' comprehension ability and textbook difficulty.
- *Becoming a Nation of Readers* (Anderson et al., 1985), the Report of the Commission on Reading.
- *Content Reading Including Study Systems* (Santa et al., 1988), which focuses on teaching students how to learn through reading, studying, and writing strategies incorporated as part of content instruction.
- *Guide to Curriculum Planning in Reading* (Cook, 1986), developed to assist in the implementation of current views about reading, also serves as a valuable resource and reference.
- *New Directions in Reading Instruction* (Monahan & Hinson, 1988), an attractive flip chart that classroom

teachers can use to obtain a handy overview of current research plus summaries of several powerful strategies.
- A list of research-based articles from current journals and professional books on reading, which reflects the new view of reading instruction and is used during inservice sessions.

A program consultant and a resource teacher provide additional support. Two days of districtwide staff development are provided, one in preplanning and one at midterm. Each spring, the middle and secondary reading departments sponsor a two-day statewide invitational reading seminar to provide time for reading teachers and content area teachers to learn, share, and grow. Nationally known researchers participate at these seminars and other special professional days. Teachers themselves present in breakout sessions. For example, a high school physics teacher might relate that her students rely so much on graphic organizers that they will not begin an assignment until they have prepared one with their teacher. Next door might be a sixth grade reading teacher describing the steps of applying reciprocal teaching to a social studies assignment, while in yet another session down the hall three middle school principals describe and compare strengths of their reading programs.

These professional growth and development opportunities focus on how to teach reading as an interactive, constructive, strategic process. Emphasis is placed on background knowledge activation, purpose setting, prediction, direct explanation, modeling, self-monitoring, question-answer relationships, guided-to-independent practice with reinforcement, and feedback. Ways are stressed to promote extensive team planning between the content area teachers and the reading teachers. This results in having both enthusiastic reading teachers and content area teachers dedicated to developing strategic readers.

At these monthly training sessions, a teacher might demonstrate how a semantic mapping strategy (Johnson & Pearson, 1984) was used in his or her classroom and then invite anyone to come visit and see it in action. Visitation is encouraged both within schools and to other schools. The reading resource teacher or curriculum facilitator covers the class of the visiting teacher.

Research-Based Strategies

As Herrmann (Chapter 6) described, strategic readers can analyze their reading tasks by setting the purpose for reading and then selecting the right strategy or strategies for getting it done. The strategic reader is described more fully in Figure 2.

The strategies described in this section are a sample of those we use in our middle schools. All of them combine reading and writing. Some become almost instant favorites with both teachers and students.

Semantic Mapping actively involves students in a visual method of expanding and extending vocabulary knowledge by displaying in a relationship pattern words related to other words or concepts. Assign students to work in groups

and ask them to jot down in categories as many words as they can think of that are related to the concept being explored. Write the selected concept on the chalkboard with spokes extending outward, each waiting for a category list to be attached. Using the groups' results, compile a class semantic map on the chalkboard while conducting a discussion focusing on key categories. The individual or group map makes a great springboard for a writing activity (Johnson & Pearson, 1984).

Reciprocal Teaching helps produce active readers. Teacher and students work together in small groups with the teacher initially modeling a strategy and then leading students to become the "teacher" and teach the strategy. Four strategies taught in this way to help students monitor their understanding and learning of textbook selections are (1) devising questions about the text (self-questioning), (2) summarizing, (3) predicting what is going to happen next in the text, and (4) clarifying or resolving inconsistencies. Research has established that reciprocal teaching with seventh and eighth grade learning disabled students results in significant gains across content areas (Palincsar & Brown, 1986).

Graphic Organizers assist teachers and students in identifying and classifying the major relationships between concepts, objectives, and key vocabulary of the lesson through visual representations. For example, for a prereading activity the teacher analyzes the key vocabulary words and arranges them diagrammatically in ways that highlight the text meaning. For postreading, students can arrange key vocabulary terms pro-

Figure 2
Profile of a Strategic Reader*

The Strategic Reader

- Understands how different reading goals and various kinds of texts require particular strategies (analyzes)
- Identifies task and sets purpose (discriminates between reading to study for a test and reading for pleasure)
- Chooses appropriate strategies for the reading situation (plans)
    Reading, skimming, summarizing
    Paraphrasing
    Looking for important ideas
    Testing understanding
    Identifying pattern of text
    Sequencing the events
    Looking for relationships
    Reading ahead for clarification
    Mentally executing the directions
    Relating new knowledge to prior knowledge
    Summarizing
    Questioning
    Clarifying
    Predicting
- Monitors comprehension, which involves
    Knowing that comprehension is occurring (monitors)
    Knowing what is being comprehended
    Knowing how to repair comprehension (regulates)
- Develops a positive attitude toward reading

*Adapted from Paris, Lipson, & Wixson, 1983, & Cook, 1986

vided in a list according to relationships they understood by creating a graphic organizer of their own. Or, working in cooperative learning groups with the vocabulary words, students can arrange various relationship patterns or organizers on $3'' \times 5''$ cards. Sharing with the large group the rationales for their list brings out positive interaction and discussion (Moore, Readence, & Rickelman, 1988; Vaughan & Estes, 1986).

The Frayer Model helps analyze and test concept attainment and can be used as a word categorization activity. It is essential to present concepts in a relational manner because it helps understanding and remembering. Teachers should present relevant and irrelevant information about the concept, examples and nonexamples of the concept, and subordinate and coordinate relationships of the concept. Figure 3 provides an example of the Frayer Model that works as a large group effort, in cooperative learning group activities, or individually (Frayer, Frederick, & Klausmeier, 1969; Thelen, 1982).

Figure 3
Frayer Model*

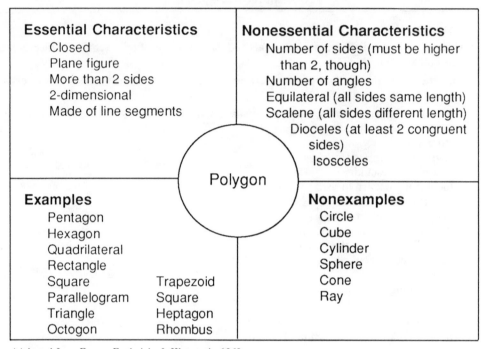

Essential Characteristics
Closed
Plane figure
More than 2 sides
2-dimensional
Made of line segments

Nonessential Characteristics
Number of sides (must be higher
than 2, though)
Number of angles
Equilateral (all sides same length)
Scalene (all sides different length)
Dioceles (at least 2 congruent
sides)
Isosceles

Polygon

Examples
Pentagon
Hexagon
Quadrilateral
Rectangle
Square   Trapezoid
Parallelogram Square
Triangle   Heptagon
Octogon   Rhombus

Nonexamples
Circle
Cube
Cylinder
Sphere
Cone
Ray

*Adapted from Frayer, Frederick, & Klausmeir, 1969

Informed Strategies for Learning explicitly instruct students in strategic behavior tasks and motivate them to become independent learners. Teachers inform students about the strategy they are going to learn by discussing the strategy, how it works, when and why it should be used, and when it is not effective. Then they model effective use of the strategy by demonstrating how it works in all parts of the curriculum. Students then practice on relevant materials, with teachers providing feedback and praise during discussions and after practices. The students gradually build their repertoire of strategies as teachers withdraw explicit support (Paris, 1985).

Semantic Feature Analysis shows how words differ. It requires minimal teacher preparation time because it capitalizes on a student's prior knowledge. List on the left border of a matrix some words within a chosen category. List across the top border some features shared by some of the words. Students decide which words share which features. Class discussion provides further reinforcement and clarification (Johnson & Pearson, 1984).

Think Alouds feature teachers verbalizing their thoughts while reading aloud—modeling the kinds of strategies skilled readers use during reading and pointing out specifically what they are doing to cope with a particular comprehension problem. Points to make during think alouds (Davey, 1983) include: (1) make predictions; (2) describe the picture you're forming in your head; (3) share an analogy that links new knowledge with prior knowledge; (4) verbalize a confusing point to show how you monitor your continuing comprehension; and (5) demonstrate fix-up strategies by rereading, reading ahead, changing the picture in your head, and checking the context to figure out a word.

K-W-L *Plus Variation* helps students activate prior knowledge and experience through a prediction chart. Completing the chart helps set purposes for reading and connects students' backgrounds to the concept at hand. Students read a few paragraphs to confirm, reject, or add to prior knowledge on the chart of predictions. This process continues until the assignment is completed. Students develop their ability to use their own experiences as they attempt to reconstruct an author's ideas during content area learning. The chart also provides a quick assessment of what students know about the topic to be studied. K-W-L Plus improves comprehension and summarizing abilities and enhances middle school students' self concepts (Ogle & Carr, 1987).

Summarizing is a difficult strategy to learn. Teachers can make it easier by providing direct explanation of how to write summaries, modeling the process, giving guided practice in group summary work, and allowing students to write individually (Brown, Campione, & Day, 1981). Taylor (1986) discusses how to teach this strategy with a variety of innovations, such as using a hierarchy, cooperative grouping, or mapping technique. Marshall (1989) suggests first creating a semantic map, turning it into a formal outline, and then using the major headings of the outline to write a summary.

A One-Sentence Summary provides an overview of the main idea by having students state the idea or text being summarized, telling how it begins, what is in the middle, and how it ends.

Story or Chapter Mapping uses the concept of semantic mapping to visually represent main ideas and supporting details from stories or the key concepts in content area assignments. Using lesson objectives provided by the teacher, students map to organize ideas, receive information, and think critically. Students are creating a product of their own, and since it is a student's personal interpretation of the relationships of the major and supporting ideas presented, there is no right or wrong way (Anderson, 1978; Hanf, 1971).

Question Answer Relationships (Raphael, 1984) teaches students that there is a three-way relationship between the question, the text to which it refers, and the knowledge the reader already has. This strategy helps students find information in the text.

The ReQuest Procedure, an acronym for reciprocal questioning, helps readers cope with text material. Teacher and students take turns asking one another questions about common portions of an assignment they have read together. This helps students think and develop questioning techniques and fosters an active search for meaning (Manzo, 1969, 1985).

Summary

Strategic reading can be taught and learned in school. To match the philosophy of the middle school, there could be no better goal for the reading program. However, development of such a program requires much planning and careful implementation.

References

Alvermann, Donna E., Dillon, Deborah R., & O'Brien, David G. (1987). *Using discussion to promote reading comprehension*. Newark, DE: International Reading Association.

Anderson, Richard C., Hiebert, Elfrieda H., Scott, Judith A., & Wilkinson, Ian. (1985). *Becoming a nation of readers: The report of the commission on reading*. Washington, DC: National Institute of Education.

Anderson, Thomas H. (1978). *Study skills and learning strategies* (Technical Report No. 104). Urbana, IL: University of Illinois, Center for the Study of Reading.

Armbruster, Bonnie B., & Anderson, Thomas H. (1984) *Content area textbooks*. In Richard C. Anderson, Jean Osborn, & Robert J. Tierney (Eds.), *Learning to read in American schools: Basal readers and context texts* (pp. 193-226). Hillsdale, NJ: Erlbaum.

Brown, Ann L., Campione, Joseph C., & Day, John D. (1981). Learning to learn: On training students to learn from texts. *Educational Researcher*, *10*, 14-21.

College Board. (1982). *Understanding the DRP: Charts and tables*. New York: College Entrance Examination Board.

Cook, Doris M. (Ed.). (1986). *A guide to curriculum planning in reading*. Madison, WI: Wisconsin Department of Public Instruction.

Davey, Beth. (1983). Think aloud: Modeling the cognitive processes of reading comprehension. *Journal of Reading*, *26*, 44-47.

Duffy, Gerald G., Roehler, Laura R., & Mason, Jana. (1984). *Comprehension instruction: Perspectives and suggestions*. New York: Longman.

Frayer, Dorothy A., Frederick, William G., & Klausmeier, Herbert J. (1969). *A scheme for testing the level of concept mastery* (Working Paper No. 16). Madison, WI: Wisconsin R&D Center for Cognitive Learning.

George, Paul S. (1983). *The theory z school*. Columbus, OH: National Middle School Association.

Gordon, Christine. (1985). Modeling inference awareness across the curriculum. *Journal of Reading*, *28*, 444-447.

Haney, Walt. (1983). Making testing more educational. *Educational Leadership*, *43*(2), 4-13.

Hanf, Marilyn B. (1971). Mapping: A technique for translating reading into thinking. *Journal of Reading*, *14*, 225-230, 270.

Irvin, Judith. (1990). *Reading and the middle school student: Strategies to enhance literacy*. Boston, MA: Allyn & Bacon.

Johnson, Dale D., & Pearson, P. David. (1984). *Teaching reading vocabulary* (2nd ed.). New York: Holt, Rinehart & Winston.

Jones, Beau F., Palincsar, Annemarie, Ogle, Donna S., & Carr, Eileen G. *Strategic teaching and learning*. Alexandria, VA: Association for Supervision and Curriculum Development.

Lounsbury, John H. (Ed.). (1984). *Perspectives: Middle school education, 1964-1984*. Columbus, OH: National Middle School Association.

Manzo, Anthony V. (1985). Expansion modules for the ReQuest, CAT, GRP, and REAP reading/study procedures. *Journal of Reading*, *28*, 498-502.

Manzo, Anthony V. (1969). The ReQuest procedure. *Journal of Reading*, *13*, 123-126.

Marshall, Nancy. (1989). The students: Who are they and how do I teach them? In James Flood and Diane Lapp (Eds.), *Instructional strategies for content area reading and learning*. Englewood Cliffs, NJ: Prentice Hall.

McTighe, Jay, & Lyman, Frank, Jr. (1988). Cueing thinking in the classroom: The promise of theory-embedded tools. *Educational Leadership*, *45*(7), 18-24.

Monahan, Joy N. (1985). Action research: Teachers working together. *Greater Washington Reading Journal*, *10*, 15-16, 22.

Monahan, Joy N., & Hinson, Bess. (1988). *New directions in reading instruction*. Newark, DE: International Reading Association.

Moore, David W., Readence, John E., & Rickelman, Robert J. (1988). *Prereading activities for content area reading and learning* (2nd ed.). Newark, DE: International Reading Association.

Ogle, Donna, & Carr, Eileen. (1987). K-W-L Plus: A strategy for comprehension and summarization. *Journal of Reading, 30,* 626-631.

Orange County Public Schools. (1986). *Middle school curriculum planning guide for reading.* Orlando, FL: Orange County Public Schools.

Orange County Public Schools. (1985). *Reading resource specialist handbook.* Orlando, FL: Orange County Public Schools.

Palincsar, Annemarie S., & Brown, Ann L. (1986). Interactive teaching to promote independent learning from text. *The Reading Teacher, 39,* 771-777.

Palincsar, Annemarie S., & Brown, Ann L. (1985). Reciprocal teaching: Activities to promote "reading with your mind." In Theodore L. Harris & Eric J. Cooper (Eds.), *Reading, thinking, and concept development.* New York: College Board Publications.

Paris, Scott G. (1985). Using classroom dialogues and guided practice to teach comprehension strategies. In Theodore L. Harris & Eric J. Cooper (Eds.), *Reading, thinking, and concept development.* New York: College Board Publications.

Paris, Scott G., Lipson, Marge Y., & Wixson, Karen K. (1983). Becoming a strategic reader. *Comtemporary Educational Psychology, 8,* 293-316.

Pearson, P. David. (1985). Changing the face of reading comprehension instruction. *The Reading Teacher, 38,* 724-738.

Raphael, Taffy E. (1984). Teaching learners about sources of information for answering comprehension questions. *Journal of Reading, 27*(4), 303-311.

Santa, Carol M., Danner, Maureen, Nelson, Marylin, Havens, Lynn, Scalf, Jim, & Scalf, Lynn. (1988). *Content reading including study systems: Reading, writing, and studying across the curriculum.* Dubuque, IA: Kendall/Hunt.

Taylor, Barbara M. (1986). Teaching middle grade students to summarize content textbook material. In James F. Bauman (Ed.), *Teaching main idea comprehension.* Newark, DE: International Reading Association.

Thelen, Judith. (1982). Preparing students for content reading assignments. *Journal of Reading, 25,* 544-549.

Vaughan, Joseph L., & Estes, Thomas H. (1986). *Reading and reasoning beyond the primary grades.* Boston, MA: Allyn & Bacon.

Vygotsky, Lev S. (1978). *Mind in society: The development of higher psychological processes.* (M. Cole, V. John-Steiner, S. Scribner, & E. Sauberman, Eds. and Trans.) Cambridge, MA: Harvard University Press.

Wertsch, J.V. (1985). *Vygotsky and the social formation of mind.* Cambridge, MA: Harvard University Press.

Wixson, Karen K., & Peters, Charles W. (1984). *Reading redefined* (Michigan Reading Association position paper). Grand Rapids, MI: Michigan Reading Association.

Developing Integrated Programs

Laura R. Roehler
Kathryn U. Foley
Mara T. Lud
Carol A. Power

THE FOLLOWING COMMENTS were made by middle school teachers as they began a longitudinal staff development project designed to improve literacy instruction. They reflect teachers' continuing concerns about limited time, content coverage, and student motivation. Integration of subject matter can help alleviate these concerns.

> "If you want to really help, help me find more time."

> "I can't get through all the curriculum I have to teach now, yet every school year brings new curriculum for me to teach, and now you're adding literacy."

> "I feel like I'm going in a dozen directions at once. Nothing makes sense anymore. If I'm confused, think how the kids must feel."

> "We never have time to get into anything in depth."

> "Now they want me to teach reading, and I'm a science teacher."

> "Where does motivation fit into all of this?"

12

Integration means combining concepts and strategies from different areas. For instance, classification strategies can be developed in mathematics, in science, and in reading; cause and effect, sequencing, and compare-contrast strategies can be developed in social studies; and oral language can be developed in literature class and in the fine arts. In short, reading and language can be integrated with content areas. This chapter is the story of what one group of middle school teachers accomplished in this regard.

Background

A group of middle school teachers and teacher educators in Michigan met to create and implement a program to improve students' reading and language usage across all subject areas. As we grappled with the issues of time, content coverage, and student motivation, an inservice goal emerged. We decided to create, share, and implement units that successfully integrated reading and language usage with content areas through the use of concrete, meaningful experiences that made usefulness explicit.

As we created integrated units, we confronted two prevalent problems. The first was time. Teachers are bombarded regularly with demands to add to their already bulging daily teaching schedules. The second problem was public concern about accountability. Aroused citizens are demanding greater evidence of developing literacy. In short, teachers are being asked to do more with existing time and to do it better.

Students face similar problems. Their school experience continues to consist of largely isolated bits of content knowledge separated from realities that exist beyond classroom walls. Language learning continues to be disconnected fragments that have no apparent usefulness.

We decided that one way to solve these problems was to consciously build bridges between language and subject areas so that students could experience and understand the interconnectedness of various school experiences. Integration of subject matter, in which usefulness of language is highlighted, became the bridge.

Information Shared about Integration

In order to develop understandings about subject matter integration, we shared current views of integration, elements that constitute integration, interrelationships important to integration, and research about subject matter integration.

Current Views of Integration

Today's educators promote subject matter integration. Examination of most language arts textbooks reveals support for subject matter integration, and review of national conferences shows that integration is being emphasized. In 1983, the National Council of Teachers of English (NCTE) published *Integrating the Language Arts in the Elementary School* (Busching & Schwartz, 1983), which summarizes current knowledge about subject matter integration. The book emphasizes the integration of reading, writing, speaking, and listening into all subject areas. Its use in classrooms is advocated, particularly in terms of integrating language usage into all curricular areas.

Subject matter integration assumes that language must be learned and used in the context of some content. Students do not learn to read or write without reading or writing about something. In short, language strategies are used in the context of subject areas (see Chapter 5, this volume).

Many students are not aware that language is being used in social studies or science or math. Likewise, many students are unaware that content is being used in language arts, English, or reading class when language strategies and skills are being learned and used. Because many teachers talk only about their subject areas, students come to believe that math class is only for math and science class is only for science. Students have been heard to say, "This is English class. We don't do science in here." or, "This is social studies class. Why are you asking me to use complete sentences?" Simply making students aware of the natural integration of language with content is the first step in successfully integrating subject matter.

Elements of Integration

Two elements can be used when integrating: (1) the knowledge base of our culture, and (2) the language strategies used when giving and receiving information in that knowledge base. The knowledge base incorporates the ideas, thoughts, and feelings that our culture has deemed useful and worthy to pass from one generation to the next. It is called world knowledge. The bulk of world knowledge is divided into various content areas or subjects taught in schools and is contained in printed materials such as textbooks. In middle schools, world knowledge is generally found in the content areas of social studies, science, literature, music, art, and mathematics.

Language strategies associated with speaking, listening, reading, writing, doing, and observing are the fundamental tools for sharing the knowledge base. Language strategies provide ways for world knowledge to be communicated (Herrmann, this volume). Instruction of language strategy knowledge generally occurs in the areas of reading, English, or language arts, but language strategy usage is applied in all subject areas.

In summary, the subject matter of middle schools consists of world knowledge drawn from the knowledge base and language strategy knowledge that provides the means for communicating thoughts and feelings.

Interrelationships Important to Integration

Various types of interrelationships are important to integration. First, for subject matter integration to occur, teachers need to understand interrelationships among the various kinds of language strategies, such as predicting, decoding, and composing. Second, the interrelationships among language strategies and content areas such as science, social studies, and mathematics need to be understood. Finally, the interrelationships between subject matter and initial learning or subsequent use need to be understood. Each interrelationship is discussed in the following sections.

Interrelationships among language strategies. Language strategies are rarely used alone. Multiple strategies are used as a story is written, as a story is read, and when someone speaks and another person listens. Understanding this interrelatedness is necessary if teachers are to integrate effectively and efficiently.

Language strategies are found within the language modes of listening, reading, speaking, and writing (Roehler, 1979). Reading and listening, including observing, are broad modes of language strategies concerned with receiving or obtaining meaning; writing and speaking, including doing, are broad modes concerned with expressing or providing meaning. To put it another way, language is a two-way classification of language modes. Listening is oral receptive mode, and reading is written receptive mode;

Figure 1
Relationships among Language Modes and Various Language Strategies

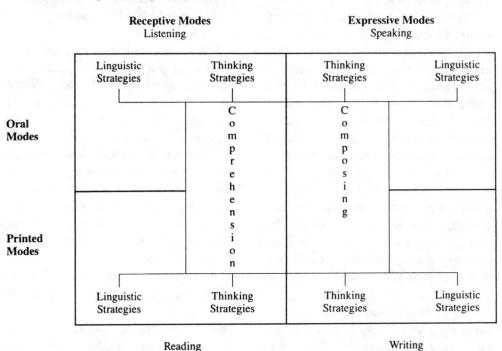

speaking is oral expressive mode, and writing is written expressive mode. Each mode is subdivided into two types of language strategies that students must understand and use: linguistic strategies and thinking strategies.

Linguistic strategies convey the meaning of the communication. For receptive modes, it is decoding; for expressive modes, it is mechanics. These strategies provide the means for receiving thoughts, feelings, and ideas (linguistic conventions, word recognition) and the means to express thoughts, feelings, and ideas (punctuation, spelling, intonation).

Linguistic strategies, however, are only half the necessary language strategies. It is not enough to spell or use grammar rules or say all the words. Students also need to know how to think or reason as they compose or comprehend. Thinking strategies provide the means for developing and interpreting thoughts. For the receptive mode, the goal is comprehension; for the expressive mode, it is composing. Comprehension occurs when thinking strategies are used to understand messages; composing occurs when thinking strategies are used to create messages. Figure 1 illustrates the relationships among the modes of language and the relationships of linguistic and thinking strategies.

Interrelationships among language strategies and content areas. By themselves, strategies have no useful function. They exist only as a means of understanding, creating, and communicating information, ideas, and feelings from the knowledge base. This natural combination of the knowledge base and language strategies must be captitalized on in a conscious way in all middle school classrooms to help students become aware of the interrelatedness of language and world knowledge. Purposeful integration cannot occur unless teachers understand the relationships among content and strategies. All teachers need to understand that language strategies support and assist in understanding a given subject area's knowledge base. In turn, knowledge base concepts are communicated through language strategies. A knowledge base is useless unless it can be communicated from one individual to another; likewise, strategies are useless unless there is a knowledge base to be communicated. Consequently, the integration of world knowledge and language strategies benefits all content areas.

Interrelationships among subject matter and types of learning. Once teachers understand how language strategies are developed and how they are naturally integrated into subject areas, understandings need to be developed about the relationship between initial learning and subsequent use. Students cannot be expected to use knowledge without first learning about it. Similarly,

initially learned knowledge is of little value unless it is used. Consequently, there is an interrelationship between initially learned knowledge and subsequent use of knowledge.

While language strategies and world knowledge are naturally integrated, initial learning of knowledge and ultimate use of that knowledge are not naturally integrated. They are not easily learned together. Most students cannot learn something new and apply it immediately. They cannot simultaneously remember and maneuver large amounts of new information because of short term memory limitations. Combining initial learning with its application is not always effective or efficient.

While the two levels of learning cannot be integrated easily, they can be integrated with world knowledge and language strategies. Natural integration can occur when teachers consciously combine initially learned language strategies or concepts from world knowledge with previously learned strategies or concepts, and help students become aware of that integration. Such combinations result in several types of subject matter integration. Initial learning of language strategies can be integrated with either previously learned strategies or previously learned concepts; the initial learning of concepts from world knowledge can be integrated with either previously learned concepts or previously learned language strategies.

Teachers who understand how language strategies relate to one another, how they relate to subject areas, and how language strategies and world knowledge relate to levels of learning have the basic information needed to successfully develop and implement integrated units. However, before we could begin our unit development, we felt we needed to explore the research on subject matter integration.

Research on Subject Matter Integration

Once we understood the components of integration and the interrelationships among language strategies, content areas, and level of learning, we turned logically to what the research had to say about integration. Rigorous research on subject matter integration was sparse. While many studies are reported, few reflect high standards of research and almost none include classroom observation of teaching. Consequently, few research data are available for use when making decisions about integration.

One study, however, did include classroom observation as well as subject matter integration across the curriculum (Schmidt et al., 1985). The study found that teachers generally favored integrating language into all subject matter areas. However, only minimal amounts of integration could be documented in the teachers' classrooms.

In fact, less than 10 percent of instructional time in the classrooms was spent in integrated subject matter activities. While some teachers integrated one language strategy with another, rarely were initially learned language strategies integrated with learned world knowledge or vice versa. Similarly, initially learned world knowledge from one subject area was not integrated with previous knowledge from another subject area. This lack of integration occurred even though the teachers' knowledge was adequate, their attitudes were positive, and their planning of integrated lessons was complete. Apparently, while teachers knew about subject matter integration and supported it, they did not use it in classroom instruction. Teachers' interviews showed that constraints within classrooms and schools kept them from using subject matter integration in their ongoing instructional activities. These constraints included use of teaching materials that discouraged integration, basic skills mandates that discouraged integration, and lack of time and support for developing integrated units.

After sharing knowledge and developing understandings about subject matter integration, we agreed that it is a worthwhile goal and that students need to be made aware of the naturally occurring integration of language and content knowledge. When we examined our own instruction, however, we found that we faced the same constraints as the teachers in the study. These constraints and what we did to neutralize them are discussed in the next section.

Constraints on Integration

As we began to consider our own use of subject matter integration, we found that we all supported integration in theory but were using very little of it in our lessons.

As we discussed why we were not using integration, five constraints began to emerge. Over the course of the school year, as each constraint was discussed, decisions were made and implemented about how to neutralize it.

First, we felt that integration was not occurring because our classroom instructional materials discouraged it. If the materials were about world knowledge, language strategies were virtually ignored; if the instructional materials were for English or reading class, the content of the other subject areas was virtually ignored. We decided that one solution was to draw students' attention to the interrelatedness of language strategies and world knowledge within the instructional materials. We found that this solution worked when the materials emphasized language strategy and world knowledge but not when they didn't.

The second constraint was the isolated, fragmented content that students are exposed to in middle schools. This constraint was caused primarily by the division of subject matter into separate classes taught by different teachers with little time or encouragement to discuss with one another how to effectively integrate their subject matter. We partially solved this problem by developing integrated units that explicitly illustrated how subject matter could be integrated during ongoing lessons. Rather than take instructional time to reteach in one subject area what had already been taught in another, we decided to use one another's prior instruction as the base for upcoming units. For instance, if the language strategy of classifying had been taught in reading class, the science teacher could quickly activate the students' background knowledge about classifying and move directly into the science content where the students would use their classifying strategies. Likewise, if a cause and effect strategy already had been taught in social

studies class, the English teacher could review the strategy with the students and spend most of the instructional time on understanding the literature selections.

Once one of us had taught students how to organize material for a written report, all of us could eliminate the initial learning of those strategies and spend our time on subsequent use or application. We could all benefit by keeping one another informed about the content of lessons, which increased the usefulness of language strategies and the effectiveness of instruction.

Our solution seemed reasonable except in situations where none of the teachers had taught the strategy. This led to the third type of constraint, determining which teachers were responsible for which language strategies. We decided that selected language strategies used frequently in content areas would be taught by all teachers, but most of the language strategies should be taught initially by English or reading teachers. These teachers reciprocally agreed that, whenever possible, they would include world knowledge that already had been taught in other subject areas as the content for assigned reading and writing.

As we discussed subject matter integration across the curriculum, a fourth constraint emerged — inadequate support from colleagues and administrators. This support affects the degree of subject matter integration that one teacher can accomplish. Subject matter integration is most effective when it occurs in all the students' classes. However, if some teachers are unwilling to incorporate it into their classes, the usefulness of integration is curtailed and instructional time and effort increases. The more collegial support there is, the broader the students' understanding of integration.

The role of the administrator also is crucial. The most effective type of subject matter integration occurs when administrative support allows for flexible curricula that lead to deeper understandings for students. The required content can be placed in subject areas where it is most appropriate, content and strategies can be developed simultaneously, and duplication can be eliminated.

We solved the constraint of inadequate support from colleagues and administrators by creating ways for all participants to develop ownership for subject matter integration across the curriculum. Those feelings of ownership helped teachers generate the energy needed to implement integration.

The last problem we discussed was the time needed to create integrated units. We understood that integration saves time for student learning, but the time needed to develop the units was overwhelming. To solve this problem, we decided to create "unit banks" that could be exchanged and used by other teachers.

Integrated Units Created by the Teachers

The following units are examples of subject matter integration developed by the teachers in this project. Each unit incorporates language strategies and world knowledge within lessons that highlight usefulness.

All units contain warm-up, focusing, and expressing activities. Warm-up activities are designed to help students activate their background knowledge and develop interest in the topic; focusing activities provide students with information about the topic or the language strategies needed for the lesson; and expressing activities provide opportunities for the students to use the information about the topic or language strategies as the teacher monitors, responds, and interacts. Within each unit, it is noted where language strategies either should be taught initially or reviewed briefly if they have been taught previously.

These units represent a beginning for subject matter integration. They must be adapted to fit the needs of the students in any given classroom.

First Sample Unit
Developing Problem Solving While Integrating Mathematics and Language Strategies

Overview This unit develops conceptual understandings about problem solving, money usage, and calculations, which are all critical components of mathematics. Relevant language strategies are noted and should be consciously used throughout the unit. The unit highlights usefulness because middle school students enjoy the types of activities involved (honoring a victorious team, planning and implementing celebrations).

Overall Goal To develop useful understandings of the problem-solving model by planning a celebration for a victorious school team.

Objective One To learn the problem-solving model.

Warm-up activity. Generate enthusiasm about the idea that the class is going to sponsor a celebration for a victorious football (basketball, baseball, track) season, although the class currently has a small amount of money ($20) available and needs more for the celebration. This situation becomes the basis for a unit on problem solving. Have students brainstorm about how to solve the problem of not having enough money for the celebration. As students offer suggestions, list them on the board. Group the suggestions according to categories of solutions such as in-school sources, community sources, or class sources.

Focusing activity. Using the results of the categorized suggestions, introduce and explain the problem-solving model. Use one solution, such as having local merchants contribute money, as the model is explained. Adjust the lesson to the students' current understandings. If the students already know the problem-solving model, quickly move through this activity. If they don't, take time to help them develop initial understanding. Step One, understand the problem. The class wants to honor the victorious team but doesn't have enough money. Step Two, devise a plan. How can we get more money? (Solution: Have local merchants who support the team contribute money or use money from game admissions.) Step Three, solve the problem. Each of five sponsoring merchants donates $20. $20 x 5 = $100; $100 + $20 (from class) = $120. Step Four, look back and evaluate. $120 will be adequate for sponsoring a victory celebration.

Expressing activity.

1. Have students brainstorm additional ways to gain needed money that might have emerged during the focusing activity. Using all the ideas, have students go through the problem-solving steps in pairs. One students thinks through the problem; the other student monitors the coherence of the thinking. Pairs alternate roles with different solutions for gaining money. Have students use previously learned language strategies of thinking aloud and looking back for evaluation, or teach these strategies prior to this activity.

2. Using a class discussion format, have students decide how best to get money. (A guiding factor for the discussion is the feasibility of the proposed solutions.) The choice of the best solution determines the total amount of money available, which, in turn, regulates the type of celebration.

Objective Two To apply problem-solving abilities.

Warm-up activity. Have students brainstorm ways to celebrate the victorious season (assembly, after-school reception, party during class time) and what to include in the celebration (food, speakers, mementos for team members).

Focusing activity. Using the brainstorming ideas, have students categorize them under possible ways to have a celebration.

Expressing activity.

1. Recalling the amount of money available for the celebration, the students, in pairs, apply the problem-solving model to the categorized ideas. Students take turns thinking aloud or monitoring. The goals is to have feasible ways to celebrate.

2. Using a class discussion format, students decide the best way to celebrate

the victorious season of the honored team.

Objective Three To apply the problem-solving model to the team's statistics.

Warm-up activity. Students brainstorm the places to find the team's statistics (school newspaper, coach, local newspaper).

Focusing activity. After brainstorming the various types of statistics to gather, students collect team statistics.

Expressing activity. Using the problem-solving model as a guide, students create team statistics for a celebration. Students work individually, in pairs, or in small groups.

Objective Four To apply the problem-solving model to the celebration plans.

Warm-up activity. Have students brainstorm various components of the celebration.

Focusing activity. Have students review plans to date in order to assign responsibilities. In groups, students assume responsibility for the celebration by obtaining the principal's approval, sending out invitations, choosing a location, ordering supplies, and organizing the program.

Expressing activity. Students conduct their celebration for the victorious team.

Summary of First Sample Unit

This unit provides opportunities for students to develop conceptual understandings about problem solving, money usage, and planning while using language strategies that have been previously learned. Students should be motivated because of their interest in victorious teams and celebrations.

Second Sample Unit
Developing Understandings of the Economic/Social Structures of Societies While Integrating Social Studies and Language Knowledge

Overview This unit develops conceptual understandings about the economic and social structures of societies. It contains lessons that build on knowledge of past societies, compares that knowledge to current societies, and concludes with knowledge about future societies. Use of language strategies is noted so that students can be made aware of their presence. Usefulness is stressed by highlighting students' current understandings of their economic and social lives. This usefulness should help students generate and sustain interest.

Overall Goal To help students understand through the study of the Middle Ages that all societies have economic/social structures and that these structures can be used to predict outcomes of future events.

Objective One To develop understandings of the economic/social structure of the Middle Ages.

Warm-up activity. Have students brainstorm about the economic and social structures of their society, using their own background experiences. Ask questions about how we get money, food, clothing, education, entertainment, and housing. Ask questions about the structures we use in order to live together (schools, communities). Create a semantic map of the students' responses. If students have not previously learned about semantic maps, teach them how to make one.

Focusing activity. Students read chapters of the textbook, supplementary texts, or trade books that contain information about the economic/social structure of the Middle Ages. The poem *Beowulf* can be used to help students gain a sense of what medieval life was like if *Beowulf* has been taught in literature class. Other literature about the Middle Ages that has been taught in other subject areas also can be used.

Expressing activity.

1. Have students compile a Middle Ages dictionary in which they define vocabulary and supply illustrations for each term. Have them use dictionary skills learned in English class or teach them dictionary skills before compiling the dictionary. Have students use illustration skills learned in art class or teach them how to do simple drawings before compiling the dictionary. (Drawings can be eliminated from the dictionary if not previously taught.)

2. Using a time line previously taught in social studies, have students identify the major events of this historical period (500 AD–1500 AD) that affected or were affected by economic/social structures.

3. Have each student make a semantic map that portrays topics such as feudalism (e.g., class of people, social rank, job responsibilities, class privileges, tools of various trades, family life, fashion). As a class, have students compile one big map from individual semantic maps.

4. Have students convert the class semantic map to an outline that explains the economic structure of the Middle Ages. Have students use outlining skills learned either in English or reading class (or teach the needed skills prior to this activity).

5. In groups of four, have students write their own text about the economic/social structures of the Middle Ages using the class outline, individual maps, and dictionaries. Students may use illustrations from dictionaries. Texts become part of the class library.

Objective Two To develop understandings of the similarities and differences of the Middle Ages and current society's economic/social structures.

Warm-up activity. Reexamine the information that was brainstormed from the warm-up activity of Objective One.

Focusing activity. Students create a class chart of the similarities and differences of the Middle Ages and their own society in terms of economic/social structure.

Expressing activity.

1. Have students verify or alter the time line created in Objective One. Students then create a time line of the major events of their lifetimes.

2. Have students compile a who's who of their society. Entries will describe the person and his or her contribution(s) to society. Use composing strategies taught in English class or teach students how to create a who's who entry.

3. Have students create poster and brochure files that compare the Middle Ages with their society (this activity may

be done individually or in groups). Students may create posters that emphasize the code of conduct in the Middle Ages (i.e., knighthood, the age of chivalry). Have students use skills of poster creating from art class. For brochures, areas of comparison might include food, clothing, government, or entertainment. Have students use comparison strategies taught in English or reading class.

4. Poster and brochure files are shared in pairs. Students provide feedback to one another about at least one feature they liked and why, and at least one that could be improved if it were to be done again and how.

Objective Three To predict the economic/social structure of a future society.

Warm-up activity. Using background experiences, students brainstorm how a future society might be. A science fiction story (taught previously in literature class) could be used as part of the stimulus. Ideas should be categorized as social or economic; ideas that fit neither category should be grouped separately.

Focusing activity. Students discuss the similarities and differences of the Middle Ages and their society and use those patterns to begin making predictions of future society. Students use their created texts and the poster and brochure files for the discussion.

Expressing activity.

1. Have students create a future society to present to another class. Information includes government structure, religion, education, monetary system, language, and entertainment. Using an exposition theme, students create sam-

ples of food, fashions, government, entertainment, and education. Scenery and plays can be created. When possible, use strategies, skills, and concepts developed in other content classes.

2. Have students design an invitation to the other class. Invite administrators and representatives of the local newspaper.

3. Through an exposition, students present their future society to the invited guests.

Summary of Second Sample Unit

The unit provides opportunities for students to develop their conceptual understanding about past, present, and future societies. Starting with students' understandings about their own society, develop interest in past and future ones. Use of language strategies helps students understand the interrelationships of language and world knowledge.

Third Sample Unit
Developing Understandings about Endangered Species through Subject Matter Integration

Overview This unit develops conceptual understandings about endangered species, using previously learned knowledge from English, reading, math, social studies, and art classes. Usefulness is stressed in that students try to influence politicians and government officials. Selected activities should help to create and sustain student interest.

Overall Goal To understand the balance of nature and those factors that upset it; to become familiar with plants and animals on the endangered list and preventive measures being taken to save them; to instill an appreciation of our environment and ways to ensure its future.

Objective One To increase awareness of the balance of nature and the problem of endangered species.

Warm-up activity. Using visuals (filmstrips, photographs), assess students' knowledge and understanding of endangered animals and plants and the balance of nature. Each student should create a semantic map of brainstormed ideas on these topics, using semantic map skills learned previously in reading or English class.

Focusing activity. Have students gain knowledge of the balance of nature and endangered species by reading textbooks or trade books. Students should take notes on the information they find, using notetaking skills learned in English or reading class. Alert students to the importance of cause and effect while reading about endangered species and the balance of nature, using strategies learned in English or reading class.

Expressing activity.

1. Have students discuss their notes in groups of four. One student is the facilitator and keeps everyone involved in the discussion, a second student keeps a written record of the discussion, a third student keeps the group on task, and a fourth student checks accuracy of information. Have students use cooperative learning techniques previously learned, or teach them the techniques. Each student orally provides information for the group. The notes are then grouped by categories and filed for future use during the unit.

2. Have students brainstorm a list of endangered species. Have each student draw a visually sequenced flowchart of a pyramid for the food chain for the endangered species of their choice, using graphing skills learned in math or social studies class.

3. Have students create a poster, bumper sticker, or drama relating to an endangered species (class notes of earlier discussions are available), using the reading strategies of selecting relevant information, and the English and art strategies of composing. Display students' work throughout the unit.

Objective Two To extend knowledge of endangered species and increase awareness of preventive measures being taken to save them.

Warm-up activity. Have students generate information currently known about endangered species in terms of numbers, habitat, food, reproduction, and causes of extinction. Have students create questions where knowledge is lacking about specific endangered species.

Focusing activity. Have teams of four students collect information on an endangered species of their choice, using as a guide questions generated in the warm-up. Have students use library skills learned in English or reading class. Students may use class notes generated during Objective One activities in addition to classroom or school library materials.

Expressing activity.

1. Students share collected information in their small groups, using the guiding questions as a way to share information.

2. All groups then share information as a class chart is developed showing the endangered species across the top and the guiding questions on the side.

Objective Three To develop an appreciation of the needed balance in nature regarding endangered species and an understanding of ways to ensure that the balance of nature is retained.

Warm-up activity. Using the class chart from Objective Two, have students generate questions about empty sections that could be answered by a speaker from the U.S. Department of Natural Resources.

Focusing activity. Invite an environmentalist to speak in class or take a field trip to a nature center. Have the speaker respond to the questions generated by the class. Each student should be responsible for verifying that a question is answered. If the question is not answered, that student is responsible for asking a question at the end of the talk.

Expressing activity.

1. Have students fill in the empty spaces on the class chart from Objective Two activities. Using the completed chart, have groups of students write persuasive letters to state and national political leaders encouraging them to enforce and extend laws that protect the balance of nature in our environment. Ask the political leaders to respond in writing or orally.

2. In a class discussion, share information collected from political leaders. Based on the class discussion, select an endangered species and create information designed to persuade citizens to support legislation for pre-

serving that species. Information can be presented on television or radio or published in newspapers or brochures.

Summary of Third Sample Unit

This unit provides opportunities for students to develop conceptual understandings about endangered species. Language strategies and knowledge learned in other subject area classes are used throughout the unit. Influencing government decision making helps to create an understanding of the unit's usefulness and should promote and sustain interest.

Fourth Sample Unit
Developing Understandings about Mystery Stories through Language Knowledge Integration

Overview The unit develops conceptual understandings about mysteries while providing for opportunities to integrate literature knowledge, writing strategies, and creative drama. Because students are generally interested in mysteries, the unit emphasizes usefulness. Conscious use of language strategies helps students understand how language strategies aid learning.

Overall Goal To understand the elements of mystery writing, create mystery stories, and develop oral presentation strategies.

Objective One To develop understandings of the role of problem solving in mystery stories.

Warm-up activity. Start with a minute mystery such as the baseball puzzle where students are told: "A man was running for home. He met a masked man. He turned and ran back the way he came. What is gong on here?" Have students apply a problem-solving model to figure out the puzzle. It can be the model learned in math class (see the first sample unit of this chapter), a model learned from another class, or a model taught in reading class prior to this unit.

Focusing activity. Read aloud to students a short mystery story, stopping occasionally for students to make predictions. If students do not know how to make predictions, they should be taught prior to this unit. Explain how problem-solving models work in literature and how authors deliberately put in clues to help readers solve the mystery.

Expressing activity.

1. Read aloud a second short mystery story and have students make predictions, using the problem-solving model.

2. Have the students, in pairs, read and predict outcomes, using a problem-solving model with additional short mysteries.

Objective Two To develop understandings about mysteries as a form of literature.

Warm-up activity. Have students recall mystery stories previously read. Have them brainstorm how mysteries are similar/different from other types of stories.

Focusing activity. Present the elements of mystery stories to the class, highlighting how mysteries are similar to and different from other types of stories. Use stories familiar to the students.

Expressing activity. Have students read mystery stories in cooperative groups. Assign each member a role within the group (facilitator, monitor, researcher, recorder) and have the group decide the story elements.

Objective Three To write mystery stories using the story elements of mysteries as a guide.

Warm-up activity. Have students recall the elements of mystery stories. Create questions about those elements for a published mystery author who will discuss how to write mysteries.

Focusing activity. Have a mystery author present information about how to write mysteries, highlighting the elements.

Expressing activity.

1. Have students ask the guest author questions that were not answered in the presentation. Have students use interview skills that were taught prior to the author's presentation. (Interview skills can be taught in subject areas such as language arts and reading.)

2. Have students (individually, in pairs, or in small groups) write mystery stories incorporating the elements of mysteries. Have students use the process writing format of brainstorming, writing, revising, and editing. Teach this format prior to the written activity or review the format if it has been taught in another subject area.

3. Have students orally present student-created mysteries to their class or other classes. Have students choose background music from music class to be used during oral presentations. Have students create props to accompany the presentation, using skills from creative drama.

Summary of Fourth Sample Unit

This unit provides opportunities for students to develop their conceptual understandings and their abilities in writing mystery stories. Mysteries generally activate curiosity, which helps to develop and sustain interest.

Note If several teachers who share the same students work together, strategies, skills, and concepts taught in other subject areas can be integrated into these units, thereby reducing the amount of initial learning for students. If a teacher does not have colleagues who are interested in integrated units, the teacher must teach these strategies, skills, and concepts before the students are expected to use them.

Conclusion

Language strategies can be integrated across the curriculum. We were able to achieve this goal, but it took time, additional information, commitment, energy, and knowledge of how to integrate. This chapter documents our story and provides examples of the units we developed. We hope that middle school teachers who read this chapter can use our experience when integrating knowledge across the curriculum.

References

Busching, Beverly, & Schwartz, Judith. (1983). *Integrating the language arts in the elementary school*. Urbana, IL: National Council of Teachers of English.

Roehler, Laura. (1979). Questions and answers about language arts. *The integration of language arts, multicultural education, and creative drama*. East Lansing, MI: Michigan State University, College of Education.

Schmidt, William, Roehler, Laura, Caul, Jacqueline, Buchmann, Margret, Diamond, Barbara, Solomon, David, & Cianciolo, Patricia. (1985). The uses of curriculum integration in language arts instruction: A study of six classrooms. *Journal of Curriculum Studies, 17*(3), 305-320.

Implementing Content Area Reading with Limited Finances

Donna E. Alvermann

Victoria G. Ridgeway

THIS CHAPTER DE-
scribes how to incorporate
a content area reading program into an existing curriculum when
finances for implementing initial staff
development are limited.

The reading program described in this
chapter was modeled after one developed
in the Orange County, Florida, Public
Schools (see Monahan, this volume).
Both programs have strategic reading as
their theme. However, the Southside
Learning in Content program in Greenwood, South Carolina (described in this
chapter), differed from the parent program in several important ways. These
differences are the focus of this chapter.

Background

During the 1981-1982 school year,
only 38.4 percent of the Southside students who took the Basic Skills Assessment Test met South Carolina's standards
on the reading portion of
that test. This fact, coupled
with Victoria Ridgeway's
move to Greenwood, South Carolina,
provided the impetus for the Southside
Learning in Content program.

Prior to moving to South Carolina,
Vicki had been a resource teacher in the
Reading in Content Areas (RICA) program in Orange County, Florida. Her experience as a science teacher in the
Orange County program made her aware
of the need for content area teachers to
take an active role in helping students
learn from text. She also was aware of
the program's effectiveness. Within a 5-
year period, students' scores on Florida's
basic skills test had risen 30 percent, a
fact partially attributed to their having
learned strategic reading skills through
RICA.

Although the Southside faculty and
staff were committed to improving stu-

dents' performance on the South Carolina basic skills test, they had no working knowledge of what Vicki had experienced in Florida. A few had talked informally with her about the possibility of implementing a similar program at Southside, but no money was available from the district to fund a staff development program.

Getting Outside Support

Funding for the Southside Learning in Content program initially came from the Self Foundation. Vicki had read about this foundation and its interest in supporting worthwhile projects in the Greenwood community. To pursue the idea, Vicki wrote a 6-page proposal that described the need for a content area reading staff development program, which was eventually funded in the amount of $3,746.

Some insights that resulted from the search for outside funding are shown in the form of suggestions to prospective proposal writers.

Suggestions for Prospective Proposal Writers

1. Locating private funding for a project is easier than you might imagine. Someone, somewhere, has money to invest in your ideas. Read your local newspaper. Sources for funding include private foundations, local banks, industries, and businesses. Look for a funding source with an interest in education.

2. Once you have located a possible source, find out the process involved in submitting a proposal. A letter stating your intent to apply for funding is the first step. The identity of the person with direct responsibility for funding decisions and the timetable on which these decisions are made are important to the success of your request. When you write the letter of intent, be certain that you request any guidelines available from the funding source. A note of caution: The approval and support of your local school administration are absolutely essential.

3. A proposal is an appropriate way to communicate your ideas to the identified source. The proposal should answer some basic questions. Why do you want the funding? Identify your needs. How will your proposed project address those needs? Include the rationale and assumptions underlying your project. Is there evidence that a similar project has worked in other locations? What are your objectives and the proposed duration of your project? What student outcomes will indicate the success of your project? Be specific and realistic. Include changes in teacher behavior, if appropriate.

4. Describe your evaluation process. How will you know if you have accomplished your objectives? How often will you report to the funding source and in what form? Will you use pre- and post-tests, student surveys, teacher evaluation forms, or a combination of these?

5. Detail your proposed budget. How much money will you need? A brainstorming session with colleagues will generate a list of needs. If the design of your project includes a workshop, budget items to consider would include consultant fees, stipends for participants, training materials, testing materials,

funds for photocopying, and professional resources. It's a good idea to present your costs in three forms: per student, per teacher, and total costs.

6. Consider proposing a project that is continuous over several years. Rarely do you accomplish what you want in one academic year. A project for a 2- or 3-year period that is contingent on evaluations is preferable to a one-shot deal.

The Southside Proposal

The rationale underlying the proposal to fund the Southside Learning in Content program was based on what Herber (1978) called a "functional" approach to teaching reading. That is, essential skills (such as developing meaning for technical vocabulary and reasoning about the author's message) are introduced by the content area teacher as they are needed by students to understand their assignments. The assumption is that when students learn reading skills in conjunction with course content, they are more likely to apply those skills independently in new contexts than if they had learned the skills in isolation in a reading laboratory or in a general reading improvement program.

The proposal objectives were to improve students' reading scores on two standardized tests (the California Test of Basic Skills and the South Carolina Basic Skills Assessment Program test), to improve students' attitudes toward reading, and to obtain teachers' ratings of the effectiveness of the content area reading program.

The participating teachers were to be selected from a pool of volunteers. They were to be paid a stipend for their partic-

ipation in the initial 5-day workshop to be held during the summer. Each teacher was to receive three resource books to be used in the preparation of instructional materials during the workshop.

Specific competencies targeted for development included: indentifying key concepts in a lesson or unit; evaluating the match between students' abilities and textbook demands; selecting, teaching, and reinforcing key vocabulary; developing appropriate learning strategies for students' use; and increasing students' interest in reading both as a tool for learning and as a source of enrichment and pleasure.

The syllabus for the proposed Southside Learning in Content program was divided by topics: overview of content reading; assessment (students, materials, cloze procedure, informal reading inventories); preteaching activities (content analysis, key concepts); vocabulary (graphic organizers, Frayer model, semantic mapping); comprehension (three-level guides, organizational pattern guides, guide-o-ramas, questioning); and study strategies (SQ3R, PQRST, note-taking, reference skills).

The proposed budget, based on 15 participants, came to $3,746. Teachers made up $2,250 of the total budget ($30/day for the 5-day workshop). Each teacher received a copy of the following resource books: *Teaching Reading in Content Areas* (Herber, 1978), *Reading in the Content Areas: Improving Classroom Instruction* (Dishner, Bean, & Readence, 1981), and *Content Area Reading: An Integrated Approach* (Readence, Bean, & Baldwin, 1981). In addition, each teacher received selected content area monographs published by the International Reading Association. The total amount budgeted for individual teacher materials was $771. An additional $100 was budgeted for reference books. Consultant fees for Vicki ($125/day for the 5-day workshop) came to $625.

The proposal stipulated that two written reports would be filed during the year. The first, an interim report, would include an evaluation of the summer workshop, a budget update, and a description of the workshop follow-up and staff reinforcement activities. The exit report would include an evaluation of the Southside Learning in Content program, a final budget report, dissemination activities, and future plans.

Implementing the Program

The Southside Learning in Content program had two main components: the initial summer workshop and the continued inservice component, in which the entire faculty participated. Implementing the program included monitoring the proposal to make certain that progress was being made toward meeting the objectives.

Summer Workshop

The workshop was held over 5 consecutive days in August. A total of 13 teachers participated. Although math was the best represented content area, the group also included teachers from social studies, English, science, home economics, physical education, and health. There were 3 teachers from special services, which included teachers of the emotionally handicapped and the learning disabled.

In conducting the workshop, Vicki followed this pattern of training: first she gave the background and rationale for the strategy she was introducing, then she modeled the strategy, and finally she provided time for the participants to develop their own materials under her guidance. Content for the modeled strategies came from one or more of the three resource books and included the range of topics listed in the syllabus.

At the end of the 5-day workshop, each of the participants completed a 12-item rating sheet. A summary of the evaluation results follows. (Note that a rating of 5 is high and 1 is low.)

Results of Summer Workshop Evaluation

1. How valuable to you were the ideas and concepts presented in this workshop?

5	4	3	2	1
13	0	0	0	0

2. How effective was the presentation of the material?

5	4	3	2	1
13	0	0	0	0

3. Were the goals and/or objectives of this workshop clearly explained?

Yes	No
13	0

4. Was the content of the workshop clearly and logically organized?

Yes	No
13	0

5. Did you have the opportunity to provide input and ask questions?

Yes	No
13	0

6. Were the physical arrangements and atmosphere conducive to the workshop activities?

Yes	No
13	0

7. Was the time adequate to cover the workshop goals and objectives?

Yes	No
13	0

8. What did you find most helpful about the workshop? (Write out answers.)

Ideas and variety of activities presented (N = 5)

Everything covered usable in the classroom (N = 3)

Positive attitude about the workshop and its value on the part of the instructor and class (N=1)

Knowledge of what regular classroom teachers will do with resource students (N=1)

Organization of material (N=1)

Handouts (N=1)

Having time to work on and complete a unit of study (N=1)

Ability of instructor to adapt and meet needs of everyone (N=1)

Emphasis placed on vocabulary (N=1)

Strategies to use in our own classrooms (N=1)

9. What was the least useful to you? Everything was useful (N = 13)

10. If this workshop were offered again, what changes would you suggest? (Write out answers.)

Provide more time for workshop (N =4)

Conduct workshop earlier in summer (N=1)

Have all teachers attend (N=1)

11. Overall, how would you rate this workshop?

5	4	3	2	1
13	0	0	0	0

12. List other workshops in our district in which you would like to participate.

No responses

Inservice Component

The teachers who participated in the summer workshop met once a month after school to discuss the strategies they had used and to share their successes. All teachers reported positive responses from the students toward the new strategies.

In addition to organizing the follow-up meetings for the original 13 participants in the program, Vicki edited a monthly newsletter that was distributed to the entire faculty. The content of the newsletter varied. Sometimes faculty shared strategies that worked for them; other times, Vicki included ideas from IRA's newspaper, *Reading Today*, or from Orange County's program. During the first year of publication, each issue of the newsletter had a theme: vocabulary, graphic organizers, library skills, mapping/feature analysis, and review strategies. In the second year, each issue was devoted to one strategy, with several suggested variations on that strategy.

Monitoring the Progress

Progress was being made toward the objectives of improving students' ability to read and obtaining teachers' ratings of the effectiveness of the content area reading program. However, no progress had been made in improving students' attitudes toward reading. Consequently, the decision was made to administer the BJP Middle/Secondary Reading Attitudes Survey (Baldwin, Johnson, & Peer, 1980). This survey consisted of 20 items on a 5-point Likert scale. Sample items included statements such as:

- Library books are dull.
- Reading is a waste of time.
- Reading is one of my hobbies.
- I believe that I am a better reader than most other students in my grade.
- Reading is almost always boring.

Following the summer workshop, the budget was reviewed and changes were made based on the fact that only 13 teachers actually participated in the workshop (as opposed to the 15 projected participants). The revised budget that was sent to the Self Foundation contained two proposals regarding the disposition of the remaining funds in the material and stipend categories. One was to purchase additional materials from IRA, and the other was to pay the registration fees of the teachers who elected to attend IRA's annual convention.

Results of the Program

The results of the program are reported in three parts. The first part addresses the first two objectives—improving students' reading scores on standardized tests and improving their attitudes toward reading. The second part addresses the third objective—obtaining teachers' evaluations of the effectiveness of the content area reading program. The third part describes the dissemination of the ideas behind the program.

Student Indicators

Two standardized tests are administered during Southside's academic year—the California Test of Basic Skills (CTBS) and the South Carolina Basic Skills Assessment Program (BSAP) test. All students take Form U of the CTBS test. In addition, seventh and eighth graders take Level H, while ninth graders take Level J. Because of the difference in the level of difficulty between Levels H and J, it is invalid to compare the scores of all three grades. This difference in difficulty is evidenced by the observation that the percentage of correct answers decreased in all areas from one test to the next. However, the percentage above the 50th percentile actually increased in 7 of the 10 subtests.

The 1983-1984 eighth grade students took the same form and level of the CTBS in Fall 1983 and in Spring 1984. A comparison of the scores from both years shows an increase in all areas tested, ranging from a low of 7 percent in reference skills to a high of 11 percent in reading comprehension, math computation, and math concepts and application. An average increase of 9.6 percent was realized overall.

The South Carolina BSAP test is administered in alternate years; therefore, in grades 7-9 only eighth grade students take this test. In the 1981-1982 school year (the reference point for the Southside Learning in Content program), 38.4 percent of the students tested met the standard on the reading portion of the test. In comparison, 41.6 percent met the standard on the 1983-1984 BSAP, an increase of 3.2 percent. During 1981-1982, 29.3 percent of the students met the standard in mathematics; in 1983-1984, 37.1 percent met the standard, an increase of 7.8 percent.

Using these test results as criteria for evaluating the effectiveness of the Southside Learning in Content program, it is evident that the first objective was met. Students' reading scores were improved on the two standardized tests. Because factors other than the Southside Learning in Content program undoubtedly contributed to the gains in students' test scores, it is impossible to determine how large a role the program played. Regardless, the results are encouraging.

Another student indicator of the effectiveness of the program was the BJP Middle/Secondary Reading Attitude Survey administered in the fall and spring of the 1982-1983 school year. The results of this measure of the program's effectiveness were not encouraging.

As evidenced by this erosion in students' attitudes toward reading, the second objective was not met. Several factors may have contributed to the disappointing decline in attitudes. First, the design of the project did not address students' attitudes toward *all* reading. Perhaps Uninterrupted Sustained Silent Reading, or similar components as suggested by Alvermann and Muth (this volume), would have promoted improved attitudes toward reading. Second, the particular survey used to measure students' attitudes toward reading may have been insensitive to the intervention. In retrospect, a survey to determine attitudes toward content reading or toward academic work would have been more appropriate. Third, the second administration of the survey occurred in late May, a time when students' attitudes tend to be negative toward many aspects of school.

Faculty Indicators

Participating teachers were asked to evaluate the Southside Learning in Content program at the end of the academic year. The evaluation form consisted of 17 statements that dealt with the effectiveness of selected strategies and the program in general. The highest rating was 5, the lowest, 1. A perfect score of 85 points represented 100 percent effectiveness in all areas. The average rating was 93 percent. However, this figure must be qualified. Only 50 percent of the teachers returned their evaluation forms, possibly because the evaluation took

Summary of Attitude Survey by Grade

	Seventh Grade		Eighth Grade		Ninth Grade	
	Fall	Spring	Fall	Spring	Fall	Spring
Good Attitude	46%	35%	34%	24%	35%	21%
Fair Attitude	52%	61%	60%	69%	59%	75%
Poor Attitude	2%	4%	6%	7%	6%	4%
Total Responses	188	173	192	117	173	118

place during the final weeks of the school year. Had the forms been completed earlier, before the rush of final exams and postplanning, the return rate might have been better.

Nonetheless, the results of the final evaluation, coupled with the extremely positive evaluation of the summer workshop, suggested that the third objective was met. Teachers felt that the Southside Learning in Content program had had a positive effect on their students. This positive feeling toward the program also was manifested in the topics of conversations among teachers in the lunch room and the lounge. General complaining was replaced by discussions of teaching strategies and their positive impact.

Dissemination

Another indicator of the success of the Southside Learning in Content program was the unplanned dissemination that occurred. The program received regional and national attention. For example, in 1984, presentations were made at the meetings of the Association for Supervision and Curriculum Development in New York City, the International Reading Association in Atlanta, the University of Georgia Reading Conference, the Georgia Association of Educational Leaders on Jekyll Island, Georgia, and the College Reading Association in Washington, DC.

As a result of their presentations at two of the meetings, participating teachers were invited to conduct content reading workshops in Georgia. Letters of appreciation that were received further attest to the effectiveness of the Southside Learning in Content program.

Adaptations

In 1984, Vicki joined the staff at Cambridge Academy in Greenwood, South Carolina. While academic dean at Cambridge, she instituted the Cambridge Applied Thinking Skills (CATS) program, which is an adaptation of the Southside Learning in Content program.

Twice a week, students in grades 6, 7, and 8 participated in seminars designed to improve their ability to process information encountered in their classes. The program focus of CATS included higher order thinking skills, such as comprehending analogies and problem solving. Before semester exams, the seminars focused on developing effective study strategies.

During the 1987-1988 academic year, the study skills component of CATS was extended to the third, fourth, and fifth grade levels. Concept mapping and other methods of independent study were taught to students at these levels on an elective, after school basis. Vicki served as resource teacher for the faculty. On request, she went into classrooms and modeled study strategies for students and teachers.

Southside's principal, Raymond Perkins, collaborated with Vicki to provide inservice support for content area reading. One idea that was popular with teachers at Southside was the "commercial," a 10- to 15-minute time slot set aside by the principal during faculty meetings for modeling some of the strategies that appeared in the newsletter. The success of the commercial was attributed to the ease with which the strategies could be implemented. Strategies that took minimal teacher preparation time but were particularly successful include the Great American One Sentence Summary, semantic mapping, and semantic feature analysis.

Without special funding, interested teachers can exchange ideas through their own commercials. Inservice training during the year might focus on a theme (content reading) or on a narrower topic (vocabulary development). Schools that do not have the resources to publish a content area newsletter can take advantage of *The Exchange*, which is published by the Secondary Reading Special Interest Group of the International Reading Association. Information about membership in this special interest group may be obtained by consulting the *IRA Desktop Reference* or writing to International Reading Association, PO Box 8139, Newark, DE 19714-8139.

If special funding is not available, adaptations of the Southside program also may come from reading resource specialists. States or school districts that provide funding for these specialists have opportunities to provide ongoing inservice training. Reading resource specialists also are available to model strategies in content classrooms and to act as resource personnel for teachers who wish to develop new teaching strategies. In the absence of a resource specialist, teachers with a background in content

reading might be assigned a limited teaching load so they can be available for modeling strategies in the classroom.

Conclusion

In this chapter we have blended the what, why, and how to of staff development in content area reading. To the extent we were successful, middle school personnel and support staff may be challenged to create their own variations of the Southside Learning in Content program. Although we recognize the limitations of the program, we are hopeful that other teachers will see its value and carry forward its theme. The funding for the Southside program was invested in teachers, who in turn invested in their students. Such investments invariably bring good returns.

References

Baldwin, Scott, Johnson, Dale, & Peer, G.G. (1980). *Bookmatch*. Tulsa, OK: Educational Development Corporation.

Dishner, Ernest, Bean, Thomas, & Readence, John. (1981). *Reading in the content areas: Improving classroom instruction*. Dubuque, IA: Kendall/Hunt.

Herber, Harold. (1978). *Teaching reading in content areas* (2nd ed.). Englewood Cliffs, NJ: Prentice Hall.

Readence, John, Bean, Thomas, & Baldwin, Scott. (1981). *Content area reading: An integrated approach*. Dubuque, IA: Kendall/Hunt.

Improving Staff Development through Cooperation

Mark W. Conley

Karen Tripp-Opple

AT LEAST THREE PROBLEMS interfere with meaningful participation in middle school professional staff development opportunities. First, teachers can be made to feel less valuable or less effective because they are not using the most recent program. Not knowing the meaning behind "anticipatory set" or the "jigsaw technique," such teachers concentrate on building their own self-esteem. The effects of their participation in a development program may not last. Teachers may develop a new vocabulary but never learn how to combine their own strengths and thinking with the features of the staff development program.

A second problem concerns the frequent cry, "Why are you always trying something different?" Staff development programs are often associated with fads that come and go in short cycles. One middle school teacher described a three-

14

year cycle in these terms: "In the first year, we get excited; in the second year, we make things; in the third year, we throw things out and start again." Teachers are hesitant to participate in staff development programs because of the energy they must expend during these cycles for what they see as limited benefits.

A third problem is the perception that few threads or themes unite different staff development efforts. In many middle school buildings, five or six staff development programs operate simultaneously. Teachers and administrators may hold allegiance to one or several programs. Attempts at sharing across programs can be met with: "I don't have time for that. I'm into my own projects." Or: "My program gives the kids everything they need." These attitudes make it virtually impossible to integrate different staff development programs so that they mutually contribute to students' success in middle school.

What do these problems have in common? They are nurtured by staff development practices that promote competition instead of cooperation. An environment frequently exists in which programs compete with one another rather than dovetail in a way that promotes synthesis and growth.

This chapter addresses the struggle to encourage cooperation among middle school reading and writing programs by: (1) describing one successful example of staff development based on cooperation; (2) describing various types of staff development efforts; (3) examining what contributes to competition in staff development efforts; and (4) detailing the elements necessary for cooperative involvement in growth and change.

Staff Development through Cooperation

Effective staff development relies on common needs and shared goals. When school staffs adopt a focused plan of action based on their needs, professional development takes root. In schools where cooperative staff development has occurred, there is a progression from year to year in staff choices. Some schools develop comprehensive plans for school improvement that are tied to a building's mission statement. A cooperative approach to school improvement is consistent with research findings about how schools change (Little, 1982; Nemser, 1983).

To illustrate this process, consider our efforts in a suburban school district. At the request of the superintendent, all schools in the district were asked to design and implement a school improvement plan. Schools were encouraged to come up with a plan that recognized the missions of the district and of individual schools. In our school, the staff already had been involved in a study of curriculum. The need for helping students become more independent learners (particularly in outside school assignments) had been identified. One teacher had completed an action research project investigating the possibility of integrating study skills instruction into the social studies curriculum for one of the grades, with results shared at an after school staff meeting.

To create our improvement plan, teachers decided to expand their focus on study skills into all four middle school grades (6-9) and into all curriculum areas, thereby broadening the study of the curriculum and of ways students become more responsible learners. We grouped ourselves according to grade level or curriculum area to conduct our analysis. From this study, each grade level and curriculum area adopted certain study skills appropriate to the curriculum and to the needs of learners of various ages. In addition, some buildingwide goals were established, including teaching time management skills and awareness of due dates for assignments and for progress and grade reports. Every five weeks, the school conducted a locker cleanout and provided assistance in helping students learn to manage their space and materials.

In spring of the school year, we reviewed the progress of the study skills project and established new goals. We voted in favor of continuing what had been accomplished and made suggestions for further improvements. At this point, some teachers wanted to think about other types of programs that could enrich the study skills emphasis we had already adopted. Other teachers were still getting comfortable with the goals and activities established for the current year.

At the start of the second year of the program, we planned two different approaches in light of the different comfort levels and interests of teachers in the building. For teachers who were just getting comfortable with the existing program, some of the approaches to study skills used in the previous year were refined. Each curriculum area and grade level continued to reinforce study skills learned at the previous grade level and taught strategies specifically designated for the current grade. To help students with time management, evaluation calendars were posted in every classroom. Each month, teachers received a calendar from the principal with special dates marked. Every Monday, a calendar displaying events for the week was printed for each classroom.

Teachers who were already comfortable with the program and were ready for something new investigated the possibility of combining content reading strategies with the study skills strategies we were already using. We were pleasantly surprised to discover that content area reading strategies often promoted student independence, thereby furthering the goals of the established improvement plan. In the second year, a handful of teachers from the building participated in a series of workshops dealing with content reading instruction.

By the third year, some of our teachers had been transferred to high school and new teachers were added. The need became evident to reexamine the staff development plan. Teachers who had been in the building all along thought about ways to include study strategies in their classes. We decided not to abandon study strategies, time management, or content reading but to examine underlying themes shared by each program. We identified thinking skills and skills necessary for responsibility as the common threads. It was decided that the year would involve mutual sharing of the various areas of expertise teachers had acquired.

Sharing sessions revolved around thinking and skills, getting students organized, and showing them how to read different types of text. Peer coaching was suggested as a way to help colleagues observe one another and provide feedback, and was made possible by funds that paid for substitute teachers. We could see clearly how our improvement plan, our collegial sharing, and our instruction contributed to students' success.

One reason our program worked was the integration among staff development efforts. Like many school districts, ours initially had snapped to attention as a result of fads that had swept the nation. Now, our improvement plan resembles interlocking pieces of a puzzle. The plan allows for careful joining of chosen pieces at appropriate times so that the results help everyone see the "big picture," which, in turn, reflects the mission of the school (see Figure 1).

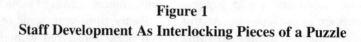

Figure 1
Staff Development As Interlocking Pieces of a Puzzle

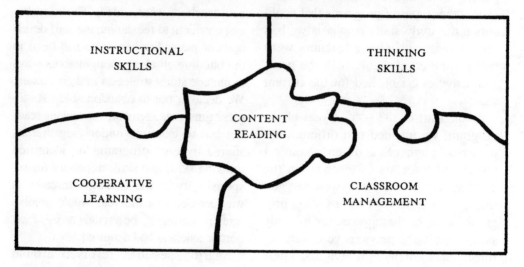

INSTRUCTIONAL
SKILLS

THINKING
SKILLS

CONTENT
READING

COOPERATIVE
LEARNING

CLASSROOM
MANAGEMENT

Types of Middle School Staff Development Programs

Sets of staff development programs commonly are found in middle schools across the nation. We review some of these programs before describing how competition can develop among them.

Literacy staff development often takes the form of content reading instruction, writing across the curriculum, or instruction in study skills. Programs in content reading stress reading-to-learn skills, or ways to learn subject matter through a better understanding of reading and reasoning (Herber & Nelson, 1983). Programs for writing across the curriculum emphasize how students learn to use writing as a vehicle for understanding their subject matter texts and their surrounding world (Tchudi et al., 1986). Programs emphasizing study skills often focus on the issue of teach-

ing students how to use their thinking. Marzano and Arredondo (1986), for instance, collected 22 tactics that teach students to analyze various problem situations.

Other staff development programs emphasize effective schooling. Two major components of the effective schooling movement are effective classroom management and teacher decision making. Early concepts of classroom management were narrowly focused on discipline. More recently the emphasis is on how teachers "produce high levels of student involvement in classroom activities, minimal amounts of student behaviors that interfere with the teacher's or other students' work, and efficient use of instructional time" (Emmer & Evertson, 1982, p. 342). Programs that ascribe to this broader view can be found under many titles, but they all share ways to teach students what is expected of them. A key feature of these programs is that they are proactive; that is, teachers actively teach students appropriate ways to learn and behave without waiting for a discipline problem to emerge (Cummings, 1983).

Two different types of programs reflect the broader perspective on classroom management. One incorporates concerns for active participation and equitable response patterns (Cummings, 1981). Programs with this emphasis make teachers mindful of who responds in class and how often. Raising sensitivities to sex, race, ethnic background, and perceived learning abilities causes teachers to actively reflect on the participation patterns found in their classrooms. A second type of program stresses coopera-

tive learning. Cooperative learning deals with the social needs of students by teaching them to interact productively in small groups (Johnson, Johnson, & Maruyama, 1983). A goal of cooperative learning is to increase student motivation and achievement by involving students in collaborative efforts The first type of program helps teachers raise questions about ways they offer opportunities for learning; the second opens possibilities for increasing involvement in the classroom.

Some programs emphasize instructional theory and the essential skills of instruction to help teachers with decision making. Hunter (1985) stresses frameworks for teacher decision making. Inherent in these programs are strategies

Figure 2
Staff Development As Scattered Pieces of a Puzzle

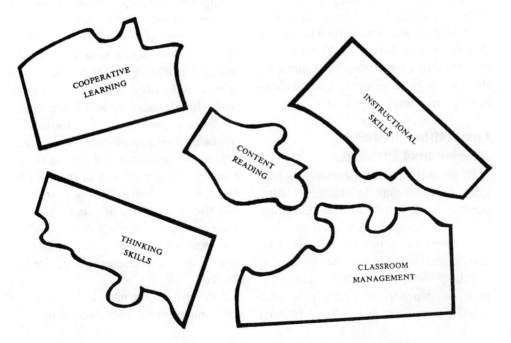

for identifying and selecting goals for instruction, teaching according to specified objectives, diagnosing problems, and monitoring students' progress. Within these frameworks, teachers often are given clearly prescribed ways to orchestrate the classroom for motivation, instruction, active participation, and effective management.

These are just a few of the staff development options open to teachers. Because of the needs addressed by these programs, one would expect to find teachers delighted with the help they can receive. Instead, teachers lament, "But I can't do one more thing." Some important questions are: Why are each of these programs viewed as one more thing? Why can't reading in a content area be viewed as an integral skill, supported by specific instructional techniques and by ways for managing and making decisions about the classroom? Why, in the same school, are reading and writing viewed as mutually exclusive, as if they were separate and noninterlocking pieces of a puzzle (see Figure 2). The next section tries to answer these questions by discussing how competition develops among programs.

Competition in Staff Development Programs

By definition, a staff development program is an attempt to change existing practice in a particular way. Consider this recent comparison of staff development programs in two schools, one successful and the other less than successful (Little, 1986). In the more successful program, teachers and principals were asked to participate as a group in training

and implementation.

In the less successful program, only the teachers were asked to participate. The content focus of both programs was a combination of principles from mastery learning and interactive teaching and classroom management. After 3 years, the more successful program could point to widespread implementation and adaptation of new practices, renewed professional commitment, and fundamental changes in school routine. In the other school, teachers continued to praise the program but rarely incorporated it into their daily instruction.

The successful program encouraged collective participation in training and implementation. Less successful programs often neglect the need for collegial interaction and cooperation as part of their delivery system and, consequently, develop a problem with competition.

Competition is fostered by using marketing rather than a reflective approach to staff development. Schlechty and Joslin (1986) use the factory as a metaphor for how some schools function within a marketing environment. In the school-as-factory, a hierarchy exists, with administrators viewed as managers, teachers as workers, and students as products. These relationships are characterized by dominance at the top of the hierarchy and submission at the bottom. Taken to an extreme, this view suggests that the most efficient school takes in students (raw material) of the highest quality and gets its direction for instruction from a predetermined, known source.

Any innovation introduced into this environment must contribute to the efficiency of the school-as-factory. In most cases, schools have limited resources, and not all teachers (workers) can participate. Principals have two options in determining participation in the program: (1) solicit volunteers, or (2) choose the best qualified teachers. Soliciting volunteers usually means drawing from the small group of teachers who seem to participate in every school program. An advantage of calling on these "staff development junkies," as they are sometimes called, is that they often become useful salespeople for marketing the program. Choosing the best qualified teachers means identifying individuals who demonstrate that they are most in touch with the school mission. An advantage of using this group is that they are most likely to use the innovation in ways that preserve the mission of the school.

Reform efforts in the school-as-factory take place with assembly line rigor and procedures for quality control. Under these conditions, competition emerges, along with the problems that interfere with meaningful change. Tight supervision to maintain performance and incentives to boost productivity (merit pay) are often features of staff development in these settings. As some teachers are recognized and rewarded for their participation, sometimes a gap emerges between those who can do IT (the latest program, a dazzling technique, or a trendy strategy) and those who cannot. Programs begun on a purely voluntary basis suddenly may become mandatory as the perception grows that the innovation is an "official" part of the school's mission. Teachers who began as volunteers may begin to drop out as they are analyzed

and compared through use of quality control measures designed to reduce adaptation and ensure faithfulness to both innovation and the school's mission.

This description of staff development is one of the main reasons that, in spite of hundreds of innovations over the years, the net result is little if any change in instructional practice (Cuban, 1984). Middle schools that function like a factory place a premium on maintaining the status quo. Ironically, staff development is not used as a way to create innovation and change but rather as a way to instill competitiveness and increase productivity according to existing practice. The most unfortunate byproduct of this type of competition is that it pits teacher against teacher, or teachers against administrators, for the sake of limited change.

Competition can emerge another way when many different staff development programs grow independently within the same school. In one school system, a content reading program began outside the district's existing (and officially supported) staff development programs in diagnostic reading and effective schooling (Whitford, 1987). The content reading program started in response to an expressed need of some middle school teachers in the district. Through assistance from the reading curriculum coordinator in the school, teachers began participating in regular workshops throughout the school year. These involved expenditures for substitutes, materials, and an outside consultant to conduct the workshops. The workshops became popular and requests grew for participation. As participation increased, both building and central office administrators noticed a surge in the staff development budget for a program they knew nothing about. The content reading program gradually faded because it was competing for resources devoted to programs that already had been approved on the basis of recognized needs.

A variation on the same theme is the multiple programs started in the same building with teachers volunteering for one or more of the programs. Competition appears in the form of scrambling for resources and soliciting the principal's support for some programs and not others. This type of competition is harmful since teachers confront one another to prove that a particular program is the best, rather than engaging in a discussion about the best ways to provide instruction for students.

Staff development efforts must avoid competition and focus more on cooperation. Instead of making teachers feel less valuable because they do not have the latest innovation, programs must build support for individual and personal change. Staff members who are always involved in innovation need as much support in this process as do those who ask, "Why are you always trying something different?" The perception of staff development as "always trying something different" points to a critical concern. Teachers and administrators are not seeing the plethora of programs as universal

Effective staff development translates into effective classroom practice.

and equitable in improving teaching and learning. More common is the perception that teachers have to pick one, and if it works, why try anything else?

Encouraging Cooperation

Encouraging cooperation both within and across programs requires two key ingredients: (1) an understanding of teachers as adult learners, and (2) a deliberate plan to reduce competition and foster cooperation.

As adult learners, teachers need to have choices. In offering new programs, administrators must provide alternatives so staff members can choose what they think will be most helpful in their situations. Volunteerism is fundamental to choice, but staff development also must be designed around those who do not wish to volunteer. Otherwise, a gap that produces competition and negative perceptions will emerge between volunteers and nonvolunteers.

Studies on staff development in content reading have found that teachers who volunteer enter with various kinds of knowledge about content reading that may or may not be consistent with the principles of the program (Conley, 1986, 1987). Teachers who do not volunteer may resist because of philosophical differences (Sparks & Sparks, 1984) or because they fail to see connections between the program and what they do in their classrooms (Ratekin et al., 1985). Philosophically, they may object to the principles of the new program, see techniques as too difficult, or just not want to deal with change. Within both groups, staff development must be designed to take into account the different types of

knowledge, beliefs, and experiences teachers bring with them.

Growth for the adult learner, particularly in staff development contexts, requires risk taking; that is, giving up older, more concrete notions of what works and going through the sometimes awkward process of change (Putnam, Roehler, & Duffy, 1987; Sprinthall & Sprinthall, 1983). This assumption creates yet another demand—that staff development begin with a teacher's experience and comfort level. However, to move teachers beyond what they currently know, they also must be exposed to experiences that take them outside their current role (Sprinthall & Sprinthall). The perennial struggle in staff development is to balance experiences that challenge current assumptions with those that recognize current levels of understanding or growth. Too much challenge gives rise to frustration, while too much affirmation can create further entrenchment in thinking and behaviors that need to be changed.

A staff development plan that encourages cooperation is one way to manage this dilemma. Teachers working together to identify needs and goals are better able to tackle difficult problems because cooperation provides collegial support, both intellectually and affectively (Lortie, 1975). A considerable body of research exists to document the effectiveness of cooperative learning for children (Slavin, 1980; Webb, 1982), yet our understanding of the benefits of cooperation for teachers is just emerging. In one recent study, it was found that collaborative planning allowed preservice teachers to comfortably focus on problems and generate many creative solutions as part of their planning for reading instruction (Niles & Lalik, 1987). While a similar study is yet to be conducted with practicing teachers at the middle school level, several researchers suggest that cooperative learning could be used during staff development as a way to help teachers expand their knowledge base about teaching (Little, 1982; Nemser, 1983).

What principles would a cooperative staff development program follow? First, the program should be sensitive to the needs and goals of all participants. To do this, cooperative relationships among participants need to be established before there is any talk about school change. In instruction about cooperative learning, students are taught that successful group work relies on the recognition that individual success comes about only through the success of the group. The same principle could apply in a staff development setting. While teachers may differ in perspective on various programs, they should strive to agree on what needs and goals are unique to their building or district. Sometimes, opportunities for this type of discussion arise in devising school or district mission statements. At other times, opportunities emerge from self-study, including action research and curriculum review.

Cooperation about common problems and goals tends to increase participants' commitment. Early sessions devoted to needs assessment should develop into a plan of action, including long and short term goals. At regularly scheduled staff development sessions, participants can start to genuinely discuss instruction, not gripe about it. The tone should be one of solution-oriented problem solving devoted to improving everyone's effectiveness. It is during these sessions that cooperation among programs becomes possible. Listening to colleagues describe what and how they are teaching and how students are achieving motivates teachers to try similar activities. Hearing how Sue uses active participation methods to promote prediction skills will give Tom an idea for using prediction and reaction in preparing students for a biology lab. As he mulls it over and does some thinking aloud, Judy describes a problem with students' response to a similar activity and offers a suggestion to help avoid the same error.

Several important insights can be established from this cooperative reflection. One is that while the needs and goals of a school appear to be fixed and finite at the time they are written, they actually continue to evolve. Changes in the school context—whether in students, textbooks, instruction, or staff—make it necessary to think about the process of school improvement as being continuous. A second insight is that there are many ways to address identified needs and goals. A teacher emphasizing one approach to the curriculum may be addressing school goals as effectively as another teacher with an entirely different approach. Cooperation needs to focus on respect for and integration of various ways to improve instruction within a school.

Another principle necessary for establishing a cooperative approach is that participants need to collaborate in discussing and implementing new programs. Once cooperation has been established about basic issues like shared needs and goals, teachers may be more willing to involve themselves in new programs. With cooperation built into the format, participants are allowed sufficient opportunity to discuss the nuts and bolts of making specific changes in their classrooms and to share how the changes are working for them. When this happens, teachers may be more receptive to many different ways of experimenting and learning (Sparks & Sparks, 1984).

While trying something new, teachers must perceive their administrators as supportive and encouraging. Administrators demonstrate support when they encourage faculty to participate, publicly express enthusiasm and praise for the participants, and arrange for meeting rooms, materials and equipment, and released time for participation.

A powerful way for administrators to show support for teachers is by teaching alongside them. In one content reading program where this is happening, teachers are pairing with one another and administrators are pairing with teachers to to try out and reflect on new strategies (Conley et al., 1987). The risk is for administrators to go back into the classroom after performing a supervisory role for many years. Because of the collaborative nature of the project, however, administrators learn to accept the risk for the benefits they receive in acquiring a more balanced perspective of the school and greater credibility in supporting change.

Peer observation and coaching also can be strong vehicles for learning and adapting new skills (Joyce & Showers, 1982). Assuming trust has been devel-oped among participants in previous sessions, this strategy allows for nonevaluative observations among colleagues. Peer coaching provides followup, which is imperative in promoting change. When a teacher feels safe and comfortable having the colleague observe and provide feedback, significant gains can be realized. When new techniques do not work on the first or second try, practitioners often give up, complaining that "this new brainstorm doesn't work either." When a colleague observes, the practitioner is able to evaluate the experience objectively at a later time. The practitioner also may ask the observer for some verbal feedback, allowing the two to begin a supportive interaction, reflecting on the experience from both the teacher's point of view and the students' perspective. It is rare for teachers to watch one another teach, but when given the opportunity, teachers say they feel professional, satisfied, and challenged.

New skills must be consciously practiced and monitored if long term change is to occur. Research on staff development indicates two basic ingredients for success: a supportive context or environment and a well thought out set of activities that ensure classroom application of the skills or knowledge taught in the inservice program (Sparks & Sparks, 1984). The chances of success may increase dramatically if the focus of these activities is on cooperative goal setting and implementation of new programs.

Conclusion

Staff development based on competition often reflects a "quick fix" approach to school change. Competition arises from buying into any one of a number of programs available for middle schools, committing oneself to that program to the exclusion of all others, and failing to see how an individual program fits into the overall school mission. In an environment of competition, teachers and administrators quickly become polarized, either as they dedicate themselves to individual programs or as they attack the self-esteem of those who do not (or cannot) participate. There is a "Here we go again!" attitude that defeats both meaningful and long term change.

Our experience in our staff development program suggests that teachers and administrators can be empowered to grow from wherever they are. Schools can come to grips with the idea that staff development is not about a single program in the middle school but about linking programs to identifiable needs and goals and helping adult learners grow and learn so their students grow and learn. Middle school reading stands a better chance for long term success if programs are developed in an environment that emphasizes cooperation based on these principles.

References

Conley, Mark. (1987). *The role of staff development in the growth of expertise in content reading instruction*. Paper presented at the annual meeting of the National Reading Conference, St. Petersburg, FL.

Conley, Mark. (1986). Teacher's conceptions, decisions, and changes during initial classroom lessons containing content reading strategies. In Jerome Niles & Rosary Lalik (Eds.), *Solving problems in literacy: Learners, teachers, and researchers* (pp. 120-126). Rochester, NY: National Reading Conference.

Conley, Mark, Mester, Fran, Mester, William, & Rappaport, Shirley (1987). *The Bay/Aronac/Iosco demonstration center for content reading*. Bay City, MI: Bay/Aronac/Iosco ISD.

Cuban, Lawrence. (1984). *How teachers taught*. New York: Longman.

Cummings, Carol. (1983). *Managing to teach*. Edmonds, WA: Teaching, Inc.

Cummings, Carol. (1981). *Teaching makes a difference*. Edmonds, WA: Teaching, Inc.

Emmer, Edmund, & Evertson, Carolyn. (1982). Synthesis of research on classroom management. *Educational Leadership*, *39*, 342-347.

Herber, Harold, & Nelson, Joan. (1983). *Final report for the network of secondary school demonstration centers for teaching reading in content areas*. Syracuse, NY: Network of Secondary School Demonstration Centers for Teaching Reading in Content Areas.

Hunter, Madeline. (1985). What's wrong with Madeline Hunter? *Educational Leadership*, *42*, 57-60.

Johnson, David, Johnson, Roger, & Maruyama, Geoffrey. (1983). Interdependence and interpersonal attraction among heterogeneous and homogeneous individuals: A theoretical formulation and meta-analysis of the research. *Review of Educational Research*, *53*, 5-54.

Joyce, Bruce, & Showers, Beverly. (1982). The coaching of teaching. *Educational Leadership*, *40*, 4-10.

Little, Judith. (1982). Norms of collegiality and experimentation: Workplace conditions for school success. *American Educational Research Journal*, *19*, 325-340.

Little, Judith. (1986). Seductive images and organizational realities in professional development. In Ann Lieberman (Ed.), *Rethinking school improvement: Research, craft, and concept* (pp. 26-44). New York: Teachers College Press.

Lortie, Daniel. (1975). *Schoolteacher: A sociological study*. Chicago, IL: University of Chicago Press.

Manzano, Robert, & Arredondo, Daisy. (1986). A framework for teaching thinking. *Educational Leadership*, *43*, 20-27.

Nemser, Sharon. (1983). Learning to teach. In Lee Shulman & Gary Sykes (Eds.), *Handbook of teaching and policy* (pp. 150-170). New York: Longman.

Niles, Jerome, & Lalik, Rosary. (1987). Learning to teach comprehension: A collaborative approach. In John Readence & R. Scott

Baldwin (Eds.), *Research in literacy: Merging perspectives* (pp. 153-160). Rochester, NY: National Reading Conference.

Putnam, Joyce, Roehler, Laura, & Duffy, Gerald. (1987). *The staff development model of the Teacher Explanation Project* (Occasional Paper No. 108). East Lansing, MI: Michigan State University, Institute for Research on Teaching.

Ratekin, Ned, Simpson, Michele, Alvermann, Donna, & Dishner, Ernest. (1985). Why content teachers resist reading instruction. *Journal of Reading*, 28, 432-437.

Schlechty, Phillip, & Joslin, Anne. (1986). Images of schools. In Ann Lieberman (Ed.), *Rethinking school improvement: Research craft, and concept* (pp. 147-161). New York: Teachers College Press.

Slavin, Robert, (1980). Cooperative learning. *Review of Educational Research, 50*, 315-342.

Sparks, Dennis, & Sparks, Georgia. (1984). *Effective teaching for higher achievement*. Alexandria, VA: Association for Supervision and Curriculum Development.

Sprinthall, Norman, & Sprinthall, Lois. (1983). The teacher as an adult learner: A cognitive-developmental view. In Gary Griffin (Ed.), *Staff development* (pp. 13-35). Chicago, IL: University of Chicago Press.

Tchudi, Stephen, Tchudi, Susan, Huerta, Margie, & Yates, Joanne. (1986). *Teaching writing in the content areas*. Washington, DC: National Education Association.

Webb, Noreen. (1982). Student interaction and learning in small groups. *Review of Educational Research, 52*, 421-445.

Whitford, Betty. (1987). Effects of organizational context on program implementation. In Walter Pink & George Noblit (Eds.), *Schooling in social context: Qualitative studies* (pp. 120-152). Norwood, NJ: Ablex.

PART FOUR

Reading in the New Decade

PRELUDE

The following is a "crystal ball" chapter. On the basis of the cumulative information provided in Chapters 1-14, it attempts to forecast where middle school literacy programs are headed. In doing so, it serves the dual purpose of summarizing the book and predicting the future.

Where to from Here?

Patricia L. Anders
Gerald G. Duffy

ALTHOUGH WRITTEN by a variety of individuals possessing a variety of views, the foregoing chapters communicate a unified theme about middle school reading. In a general sense, this theme emphasizes the simultaneous challenge and joy associated with developing literacy at this crucial educational level. Clearly, middle school reading demands the best we have.

In a more specific sense, however, the book reflects the impact of research on middle school reading. In the first edition of this book (1974), there was scarcely a mention of research, largely because in those days educational research had not progressed to the point where findings could be directly applied in practice. In contrast, this edition incorporates three specific lines of research: (1) research on the integrated nature of language and literacy, with reading viewed as a component within that holistic view rather than as a separate entity; (2) research on the curriculum, instruction, and assessment of reading within a broad literacy perspective that influences how we think about what to teach, how to teach, and how to assess; and (3) research on the realities of classroom life, constraints on instructional practice, and ways in which researchers, teacher educators, and school practitioners can work collaboratively to improve literacy instruction.

This research perspective does not mean that the problems of reading and literacy development are at an end. As Moore and Stefanich (Chapter 1) and Allington (Chapter 3) point out, our problems in achieving the envisioned potential for middle schools are far from solved. Overall, however, the outlook is optimistic. Fifteen years ago middle school reading and literacy instruction were viewed primarily as crafts guided by untested suggestions made by well-intentioned teacher educators. Current thinking about developing literacy is guided by theory and research tested in school settings. As a result, the middle school movement generally, and literacy programs specifically, possess a more coherent and substantive direction.

This chapter builds on the foregoing chapters, assessing what needs to be done in the future to meet the middle school potential for reading and literacy development. Five areas are developed: the future of the middle school concept, the needs of students and how to meet those needs, the evolution of middle school reading in the years ahead, instructional issues practitioners need to resolve in the future, and our expectations for changes in assessment.

Major Trends and Issues

The Middle School Concept

The middle school is a unique educational institution designed to meet unique needs, as discussed in the first four chapters of this book. However, for a variety of reasons, we have not yet achieved the potential originally envisioned for these schools. So what does the future hold for the development of literacy and reading at the middle school level?

The recent movement toward making curricular, instructional, and programmatic decisions on the basis of research bodes well for the future of the middle school. Historically, demographics, budgets, and inappropriately trained teachers and administrators were driving

forces behind key decisions. These forces will continue to influence the evolution of the middle school concept, but they will be less influential because they are balanced by the power of research evidence. The chapters in this book point to three types of rational evidence, or research and theory, that will affect the future of the middle school.

First are psychological theories of development, specifically early adolescent development. These theories inform educators about the educational climate most conducive to the growth and development of 10- to 13-year-olds. The work of researchers discussed in Chapter 2 recognizes the social and interactive nature of development and provides educators with knowledge that can be used to provide a nurturing environment for the early adolescent.

Parallel with the construction of models of early adolescent development is the notion of interactive theories of reading and writing, which have received wide support from the authors of this volume (see the chapters in Part 2). Viewing reading and writing as reciprocal processes involving an author and a reader who are creating and interpreting meaning for genuine communication purposes has significant implications for early adolescent development. Likewise, the notions of metacognition (see Chapter 6) complement and enhance our understanding of reading and writing. As these models gain acceptance, educators increasingly will recognize the power of reading and writing for understanding and controlling both oneself and one's world. The result will be a middle school designed to provide students with a wide

Computer use is likely to continue to grow in importance as an integral part of the school curriculum.

selection of reading and writing opportunities. Thus, reading and writing will be viewed as processes used to help students learn content and to help adolescents cope with this complex and difficult stage of development.

Concurrently, interactive models of instruction have implications for teaching (see Chapter 8). Instruction is particularly important when it puts a premium on activating prior knowledge, asks students to share that knowledge, helps students set purposes for reading, and encourages the processes of selection, prediction, confirmation, and integration. Such methods share assumptions put forth by both child development experts and reading and writing researchers. Efforts reported in Parts 2 and 3 support instruction that helps students become strategic monitors of their comprehension, composition, and learning in content area materials while also helping students become independent in negotiating the meaning of text (what Conley, Chapter 8, calls "active instruction").

Thus, *interaction* is likely to be the cornerstone word of middle school literacy development in the new decade. Models of development, of processes of literacy, and of instruction are complementary and mutually supportive. The theoretically based research findings from each will strengthen the middle school concept and help middle schools achieve their potential.

Meeting Middle School Needs

Fundamental to meeting middle school needs is recognizing that *change* undergirds the nature of both the student and the school. Adults who understand and accept change are more likely to generate and maintain an environment suited to middle school students.

There are several barriers to educators' understanding and acceptance of change as a necessary condition of adolescent development (see Chapters 10 and 14). Critical to establishing an environment that encourages such acceptance is the administrator's attitude toward change. If teachers are to encourage and support student change, they must be comfortable in risking change themselves. This risk-taking orientation will occur only in an environment fostered by an administrator who is not afraid of change. Thus, there is a clear and immediate need for appropriately trained administrators.

A closely related need is training for teachers. Although certification does not guarantee good teaching, a middle school certificate makes a public statement that being a middle school teacher requires special knowledge, skills, and attitudes. As of this writing, several certification agencies in the United States are developing middle school certification requirements. As a result, colleges of education are adjusting their curricula to respond to the new certification requirements.

While changes in preservice training are imminent, staff development also is needed. For instance, teachers need help developing up-to-date interdisciplinary curricula and age-appropriate projects and activities (see Part 3).

As more attention is given to the middle school concept, increased resources will be provided. A school that closely adheres to what is known about early adolescents is a busy and potentially expensive place. Flexibility and accessible resources are needed.

A final need is the development of multidisciplinary, integrated curriculum models that use reading and writing as vehicles for engaging the curriculum. One appropriate example is Atwell's (1987) notion of inviting students to sit around her dining room table to discover the world through literature. The specific content to be learned is not as important as the process of engaging that content.

The Reading Curriculum

Since the first edition of this book, views about what to teach in middle school reading have undergone vast change. In the language of Valencia, McGinley, and Pearson (Chapter 9), we have moved from a focus on the infrastructure of skills to holistic processes and functions. What changes can we expect in the future?

We can expect to see the continuation of three movements (all of which are foreshadowed in various chapters in this book): (1) emphasis on integration, (2) emphasis on building conceptual understandings about the utility of literate activity, and (3) emphasis on cognitive and metacognitive dimensions.

Integration. An emphasis on the integration of language pervades this book. This trend will continue. Specifically, two kinds of integration will influence how we think about teaching reading in the middle school.

First, we can expect more integration across the language arts. Rather than viewing reading as a subject to be taught by itself, reading increasingly will be integrated with the other language modes of listening, speaking, and writing (see Chapter 12). The emphasis will not be on reading as a receptive activity but on reading as one of several communication modes. In this regard, a particularly heavy emphasis will be placed on integrating reading and writing. For instance, teachers will not teach reading as much as they will teach written communication, they will not teach reading strategies as much as they will teach how strategies have reciprocal functions in reading and writing, and they will not teach comprehension in isolation from composition.

Second, there will be more integration across subjects. As pointed out by Peters (Chapter 5) and by Roehler and colleagues (Chapter 12), the emphasis will be on integration within and across the various content areas in the curriculum. Such integration will become more important for two reasons. The first has to do with motivation. Literacy and reading make little sense when taught in isolation from meaningful content. As a decontextualized set of activities, they offer little to motivate students. In contrast, when reading is presented within the context of the pursuit of stimulating and inspiring content, students have a compelling reason to learn to be literate (see Chapter 9). The second reason for content area integration has to do with application. Reading is not a static skill applied uniformly to all situations. To the contrary, expert readers do different things when faced with different textual situations. For students to learn the flexibility required for expert reading, they must be given opportunities to apply reading in a variety of contexts. The best way to do this is to integrate reading with the various disciplines in the curriculum.

Conceptual understandings. In the past, the utility of reading and literacy has been taken for granted. It was assumed that everyone could see how important reading is and would exert effort to learn to read.

It is now clear that this assumption is not necessarily correct. It is more accurate to say that many students build understandings about the utility of reading on the basis of the reading they do in school. If that reading is boring and trivial, they tend to conclude that all reading is boring and trivial; if that reading is exciting and useful, they tend to conclude that all reading is exciting and useful. Consequently, students' lifelong concepts of the function of reading are shaped by the reading they do in school.

The implication for teachers is clear. They must teach students not only *how* to read in the traditional sense of teaching them skills and strategies, they must also teach students *why* to read. Teachers cannot simply tell students why reading is important. They must *show* them, primarily by engaging them in meaningful reading. Students learn the function of

Encouraging students to become readers is one key goal of the middle school program.

reading by being involved in literate activities that emphasize the utility and joy of reading. A major curricular emphasis in the future must be the development of accurate concepts about the functions of reading (see Chapters 7 and 9).

Cognitive and metacognitive goals. Skills were a major curricular emphasis in the past. A skills emphasis was characterized by both automaticity and isolation. It was assumed that if students memorized skills in isolation from content they would become expert readers.

Hence, curricular emphasis in the past was on drill-and-practice of skill fragments.

However, as Herrmann (Chapter 6) notes, recent research has caused us to move away from that emphasis. Language is now viewed as a cognitive process, and language users are seen to be thoughtful and strategic. Consequently, the emphasis is not on proceduralized rules but on flexible cognition; not on memory but on understanding; and not on drill-and-practice but on adaptive application. This is a major change. Rather than approaching reading as a finite set of skills to be taught in isolation, educators view reading as an indefinite number of strategic processes, applied in diverse ways according to the demands of the text when beginning to read, during reading, and after reading. Not only will this trend continue but, as Peters (Chapter 5) suggests, it will become the framework for middle school literacy programs.

We can expect to see two important developments in the area of cognitive and metacognitive dimensions of the reading and literacy curriculum. First, greater emphasis will be placed on readers' metacognitive awareness of what they are doing when they are reading. The strategic flexibility required to be an expert reader, particularly when faced with difficult text, cannot be achieved without an awareness of when to be strategic, how to initiate strategic processing, and how to adapt what is known about strategies to the specific demands of the text. Consequently, curricular emphasis in reading will help students develop awareness of what they are doing when they successfully comprehend text. When students encounter new and difficult text, they can access what they know and apply it in the new situation.

Second, the cognitive and metacognitive dimensions of the middle school reading curriculum will increasingly emphasize a balance between process and content. As Peters (Chapter 5) notes, much of the reading debate in past years has placed process and content in diametrically opposed positions. Advocates of process have argued that students need

to learn the processes by which expert readers read because these processes are the means of comprehension. Advocates of content have argued that domain-specific knowledge is the only important aspect of reading since comprehension of the content message is the essence of language communication. Research on cognition and metacognition, however, illustrates that such either/or positions are shortsighted, and that a balanced view is more realistic. Duffy and Roehler (1989) have labeled this balanced view "process-into-content" in order to highlight that cognitive processes are useful only to the extent that they are applied to content. This move away from extreme positions and toward a balanced curricular emphasis on teaching cognitive processes in the context of their application to specific content will continue in the future.

Summary. There seems to be little doubt about the future of the middle school reading curriculum. The trends toward integration, conceptual understandings, and cognition reported in this volume will continue to gain momentum in the years ahead. Reading in the middle school will continue to assume dimensions that are holistic, meaningful, and cognitive.

This is not to suggest that this future will be achieved easily. The clarity of the research that supports such movement and the intuitive sensibleness of these directions notwithstanding, traditional practices and the constraints posed by such realities as existing policy, public expectations, and difficult working conditions indicate that curricular change will be gradual. Despite this, we can expect the changes noted to find their way into the middle school reading curriculum. Staff development efforts based on cooperation (Conley & Tripp-Opple, Chapter 14) will be particularly helpful in this regard.

Instruction in Reading

Until recently, instruction has been viewed as a matter of engaging students in tasks and ensuring that they remain on task. A premium has been placed on effective classroom management, and instructional activities have focused heavily on student recitation in either oral or written situations. However, two developments indicate that instruction will change considerably: the role of students in the instructional process and the kinds of teacher actions that make a difference in student achievement.

The student's role in instruction. Traditionally, students have been viewed as recipients of instruction. Teachers provided information; students absorbed information. Cognitive psychology and instructional research has shattered this view. Rather than being passive recipients of instruction, students now are seen to be mediators of instruction. When students participate in instructional activities, they restructure the meaning of the experience in terms of their own background knowledge. Consequently, what students understand during instruction often is considerably different from what teachers intend.

Student mediation of instruction puts a new and more difficult light on the teacher's instructional role (Roehler & Duffy, 1989). Rather than being responsible merely for disseminating accurate infor-

mation about curricular content, teachers must determine how students restructure that information and in recursive, spontaneous ways provide additional information students can use to continue restructuring their understandings. Hence, teachers must be in metacognitive control of their own professional knowledge. Rather than following the dictates of a teacher's guide or prescriptions in a kit, they must be decision makers who continually assess what students are coming to understand and adaptively construct appropriate instructional experiences to move students closer to the desired curricular understanding.

Appropriate teacher actions. Within the framework of the student as a mediator, teacher actions take on new meaning. For instance, while planning always has been considered an important teacher action, the student's mediational role means that the plan is a blueprint, not a script. As soon as students begin restructuring their understandings, the lesson takes unanticipated turns and the plan must be adapted.

Similarly, explanation long has been considered an important part of instruction, but it has been viewed as a static activity that occurs at the beginning of lessons. This is a limited view. While teachers frequently explain at the beginning of lessons, the student's role as a mediator means that teachers also must be prepared to explain throughout the lesson. That is, when students restructure the teacher's first explanation in ways that result in misconceptions, the teacher must spontaneously generate elaborations and reexplanations designed to move students closer to the desired outcome. Once again, the emphasis is on the teacher's creativity in the midst of instruction.

Summary. Research on the student's mediational role in instruction makes teacher decision making mandatory. Given the idiosyncratic ways students restructure, no program, kit, or textbook can be prepared ahead of time to anticipate the infinite number of directions in which instructional dialogues will go. The only way instruction can be kept moving toward desired curricular ends is by putting teachers in a position where they can make necessary decisions. Hence, middle school instruction in the future will place more emphasis on teacher independence and self-regulated control of instruction. There will be less emphasis on simply engaging students in tasks by using management procedures and prescriptive or semiprescriptive scripts in teacher's manuals.

As was the case with curricular trends, the shift in instructional emphasis will not occur overnight. The movement will be evolutionary, involving gradual changes in policy, staff development, and teacher evaluation. However, over this new decade, we can expect a steady and gradual movement toward more teacher autonomy regarding instruction.

Assessment and Accountability

Issues of assessment and accountability heavily influence middle school reading instruction. Student assessment in reading (as noted by Valencia, McGinley, & Pearson, Chapter 9) influences what is taught in reading; teacher assessment for purposes of accountability influences how

teachers perceive their role. In the next decade, we can expect changes in both kinds of assessment.

Changes in student reading assessment. Student assessment in the past rightly reflected the theories driving instruction. It was a tight package: both instruction and assessment were based on available learning theories. It is clear that current assessment practices do not reflect what we now know about reading, writing, or learning processes. As discussed by Valencia, McGinley, and Pearson (Chapter 9), several agencies and institutions are responding to the need for new and better ways of assessment. These new tests are not the final answer to the assessment question, but they are steps in the right direction.

Ultimately, the best assessment is assessment that informs the user; thus, "running records" of students' work—kept over time and reviewed with the teacher, student, and parent—are likely to be used more often in middle schools. The recent popularity of holistic scoring and writing folders also is consistent with an interactive model of learning and instruction.

Overall, it seems clear that assessment in the middle school will move away from traditional testing and toward evaluation that informs teachers, parents, and students of development as it progresses.

Changes in teacher assessment. Teacher assessment in the recent past has been based primarily on a competency-based model. In this model, specific teacher behaviors are identified and placed on a form that principals and other supervisory personnel use to rate teacher performance during classroom observations. This model proved restrictive because teachers who demonstrated each of the specified behaviors tended to receive high ratings regardless of their effect on student growth. Teachers' responsiveness to students' emerging understandings, their ability to spontaneously create appropriate instructional interactions, and their skill in making defensible decisions in the midst of instruction were minimized or not measured at all.

This situation is likely to change in the future. Rather than being based on rigid, noncontextual competencies to be observed by supervisors, teacher assessment (and teacher accountability) is more likely to be based on evidence teachers provide as a part of their own professional work. The Teacher Assessment Project at Stanford University (Shulman, 1987) is a case in point. In this project, prototypes for new approaches to teacher assessment are being developed and field tested. Primary among these methods are teacher-developed portfolios with which teachers document their professionalism in terms of student growth and pedagogical independence. This new technique differs from current techniques in many ways, but the most important difference is the priority given to teachers' control of the evaluation process and articulation of their own professionalism. It is evidence once again of teachers being placed in positions where they regulate their own destiny. This movement can be expected to continue, resulting in teachers becoming more professionally independent.

Summary. Assessment, then, is moving away from rigid, inflexible models and toward models that account for the more qualitative aspects of teaching and learning. This trend will be reflected in our evaluations of student literacy progress and in our evaluations of teacher performance.

Conclusion

The message of this book is one of optimism and excitement. Significant progress has been made in the 16 years since the first edition of *Reading in the Middle School* was published. This progress is particularly noticeable in the increased rigor of the research being applied both to broad literacy issues and to the problems of developing literacy in the middle school. This rigor is resulting in greater knowledge. And from knowledge comes improvement in quality.

Yet the battle is not over. The middle school concept itself is still far from achieving its potential, and the role and function of literacy instruction is still being developed. Consequently, while the message is basically an optimistic one, much hard work remains. Hopefully, this book will stimulate and guide that work.

References

Atwell, Nancie. (1987). *In the middle: Writing, reading, and learning with adolescents*. Portsmouth, NH: Boynton/Cook.

Duffy, Gerald, & Roehler, Laura. (1989). Why strategy instruction is so difficult and what we need to do about it. In Christine McCormick, Gloria Miller, & Michael Pressley (Eds.), *Cognitive strategy research: From basic research to educational applications*. New York: Springer-Verlag.

Roehler, Laura, & Duffy, Gerald. (1989). The content area teacher's instructional role: A cognitive mediational view. In Diane Lapp, James Flood, & Nancy Farnan (Eds.), *Content area reading and learning*. Englewood Cliffs, NJ: Prentice Hall.

Shulman, Lee S. (1987). Assessment for teaching: An initiative for the profession. *Phi Delta Kappan, 68*, 38-44.